HATE UNLEASHED

HATE UNLEASHED

America's Cataclysmic Change

EDWARD DUNBAR

BLOOMSBURY ACADEMIC
NEW YORK • LONDON • OXFORD • NEW DELHI • SYDNEY

BLOOMSBURY ACADEMIC
Bloomsbury Publishing Inc
1385 Broadway, New York, NY 10018, USA
50 Bedford Square, London, WC1B 3DP, UK
29 Earlsfort Terrace, Dublin 2, Ireland

BLOOMSBURY, BLOOMSBURY ACADEMIC and the Diana logo
are trademarks of Bloomsbury Publishing Plc

First published in the United States of America by ABC-CLIO 2018
Paperback edition published by Bloomsbury Academic 2024

Cover photo: Fire background. (lassedesignen/Shutterstock)
Jacket design by Silverander Communications

Bloomsbury Publishing Inc does not have any control over, or responsibility for,
any third-party websites referred to or in this book. All internet addresses given
in this book were correct at the time of going to press. The author and publisher
regret any inconvenience caused if addresses have changed or sites have
ceased to exist, but can accept no responsibility for any such changes.

Library of Congress Cataloging-in-Publication Data
Names: Dunbar, Edward, author.
Title: Hate unleashed : America's cataclysmic change / Edward Dunbar.
Description: Santa Barbara, California : Praeger, 2018. |
Includes bibliographical references and index.
Identifiers: LCCN 2017032812 (print) | LCCN 2017043348 (ebook) |
ISBN 9781440858154 (eBook) | ISBN 9781440858147 (hardcopy : alk. paper)
Subjects: LCSH: Social conflict—United States—History—21st century. |
Hate—United States—History—21st century. | Violence—United
States—History—21st century. | Authoritarianism—United
States—History—21st century. | United States—Politics and
government—2017- | United States—Social conditions—21st century.
Classification: LCC HN90.S62 (ebook) |
LCC HN90.S62 D86 2018 (print) | DDC 303.60973—dc23
LC record available at https://lccn.loc.gov/2017032812

ISBN: HB: 978-1-4408-5814-7
PB: 979-8-7651-3592-1
ePDF: 978-1-4408-5815-4
eBook: 979-8-2160-9471-5

To find out more about our authors and books visit www.bloomsbury.com
and sign up for our newsletters.

Contents

Preface

I had been running out this line in the first few days after November 8, 2016, when Donald Trump became the president-elect of the United States: "Be close to those you are close to, and become active in some cause you care deeply about." To the writers, film professionals, and artists I knew, I said, "Consider how your art can engage the problems you are seeing." It was at this point in time that I got an e-mail from my editor at Praeger, Debbie Carvalko, who said in essence, "Do you want to write on this issue, how and why hate crimes increased during and even more so after the election?"

It became my "put up or shut up" moment.

This book is an effort to look at the link between social change as fueled by intergroup animus and our changing attitudes about government, civility, and public safety. The first section of the book considers the psychological dynamics that shifted our government from a liberal democratic tradition toward an autocracy. This is followed by a discussion of the psychological processes of hate violence and bias. I then explain the interpersonal processes of influence, conflict, and coping with a culture of intolerance.

Superficially, this project may sound like an effort to excoriate the Trump administration. I would argue this is essentially wrong. Rather, what I am trying to speak to is the challenge of the loss of a political system that, while not wholly satisfactory to most voters, was a model of governance and politics that has been largely unchanged during the past century. It is with the potential loss of this system of governance via the championing of intolerance—a decidedly old-fashioned word itself—that this project actually is concerned. It aims to look critically at not *who* won but *what* was lost.

As one colleague of mine said, "You are going to try and make something out of nothing." I think at some level people might consider that statement quite right. However, I hope the reader will understand that this is not a book about being a sore loser in a political election. Rather, it is about the process of cultural upheaval and how people value (or disregard) the question of how they wish to be governed. It also considers that what our recent regime change speaks to is a very old and universal issue, one of how individuals value their sense of freedom and, when this sense of freedom is suddenly compromised, how they endure and seek to survive under conditions of autocratic threat and the whims of powerful and indifferent political leaders.

I would like to thank the team at Praeger for their assistance in getting this to press, Debbie Carvalko for asking me to take this on, and my wife, Megan Sullaway, for her support of me in my monomaniacal state as I worked to complete this project. I would also like to give a special thank you to Giovanni for soliciting survey participants and strategizing. Finally, many thanks to Victor, Michelle, Sigi, Penrod, and Molly for their help with the work that was needed to get this done.

CHAPTER 1

Shock and Awe of Cultural Cataclysms

I was sitting in Mr. Harold Sternovsky's trigonometry class when we heard the announcement, "President Kennedy has died." I'll never forget that moment. Mr. Sternovsky left the front of the class and went back to his desk. He sat down and put his head in his hands and began to cry. The bell sounded, and many kids left the classroom, but some of us went back up to our teacher's desk to ask him what was going on. Mr. Sternovsky rolled up the sleeve of his long-sleeved shirt and showed us the numbers that had been tattooed on his arm during his time in a German concentration camp. He had survived the war and had come to the United States to build a new life. His words were piercing as he said, "I never thought anything like this could happen in this country."

—The Rev. Larry Wildemuth, recalling the day
President Kennedy was assassinated (*Mercury News*, 2013)

It was a massacre. Dozens of people were shot right in front of me. Pools of blood filled the floor. Cries of grown men who held their girlfriends' dead bodies pierced the small music venue. . . . As I lay down in the blood of strangers and waiting for my bullet to end my mere 22 years, I envisioned every face that I have ever loved and whispered I love you. Over and over again, reflecting on the highlights of my life, wishing that those I love knew just how much, wishing that they knew that no matter what happened to me, to keep believing in the good in people.

—Isobel Bowdery, survivor of the Paris theater attack
on November 13, 2015 (Blasberg, 2015)

Two or three of us were sitting in the dining room Sunday morning having a late breakfast and talking over coffee. Suddenly we heard planes roaring overhead and we said, "The 'fly boys' are really busy at Ford Island this morning." The island was directly across the channel from the hospital. We didn't think too much about it since the reserves were often there for weekend training. We no sooner got those words out when we started to hear noises that were foreign to us. I leaped out of my chair and dashed to the nearest window in the corridor. Right then, there was a plane flying directly over the top of our quarters, a one-story structure. The rising sun under the wing of the plane denoted the enemy. Had I known the pilot, one could almost see his features around his goggles. He was obviously saving his ammunition for the ships. Just down the row, all the ships were sitting there—the [battleships] California (BB-44), the Arizona (BB-39), the Oklahoma (BB-37), and others. My heart was racing, the telephone was ringing, the chief nurse, Gertrude Arnest, was saying, "Girls, get into your uniforms at once, this is the real thing!"

—Lt. Ruth Erickson, nurse and survivor of Pearl Harbor attack
(Historian, Bureau of Medicine and Surgery)

The feeling was overwhelming, only to be topped a few minutes later by the towers starting to crumble and fall.

—Rebecca O. Bagley, survivor of 9/11 terrorist attack
(Bagley, 2011)

And I recall that crisp, sunny day when the world changed. I had an appointment with my doctor and remember scuffling through crunchy, red and orange autumn leaves in Hyde Park, N.Y., top reach his office. I walked into the waiting room to find everyone—the doctor, his nurse, his receptionist, and the other patients huddled around the reception desk. Some were sobbing. Their eyes were glued to the small plastic Zenith radio.

—Pauline Chand, recalling the day President Kennedy
was assassinated (*Mercury News*, 2013)

How do you tell the world that a great man, a black man, has been shot by a white man for wanting to be a free man?

—Deborah Preble, recalling the day Dr. Martin Luther
King Jr. was assassinated (Rothman, 2015)

My feelings during the bombing of Pearl Harbor were encased in shock and bewilderment. I was amazed that the Japanese would do such a thing. I was not angered to the extent that my thinking was affected, but I would have been willing to shoot them all to stop the attack.

—Dale Gano, survivor of Pearl Harbor attack
(Gano and Gano, 1996)

I was in Mrs. Paine's 3rd grade class in the tiny gold rush town of Nevada City, California. We had just come in from recess, where I remember I had passed the time jumping rope, swinging, and sucking sweet nectar out of the honeysuckle plants that grew along the chain link fence surrounding the playground. Such simple pleasures those were. There was an ominous silence as we entered the classroom, not the usual noisy aftermath of recess. Our teacher, Mrs. Paine, was visibly upset—so much so that she could not speak. So she quietly turned to the chalkboard and wrote in her best cursive, "President Kennedy has died." I cannot remember how we spent our time the rest of that day, but I suspect we carried on with our lessons. It was most certainly, however, the end of innocence for all of us even though we were only 8 years old. We knew something had changed.

—Cheryl Perez, recalling the news of President
Kennedy's assassination (*Mercury News*, 2013)

Cultural Cataclysms

History is marked by the occurrence of sudden and often unexpected events that fundamentally change society. Every culture has experienced dramatic events that have redefined its social stasis—that is, the relationship of the state and its agents with its citizenry. In the long view of history, these events become narratives that legitimize the social norms and beliefs of a society. Events that are particularly traumatic, while personally destabilizing, serve to create a collective narrative that defines a group and its age.

For Americans, the most compelling shared memories of the past century concerned collective threat and rapid social change. In a 1999 Gallup poll (Newport, Moore, & Saad, 1999), Americans nominated World War II as the most significant event of the 20th century (71% saying this was "most important"). This was followed by events such as the

Nazi-led Holocaust (65% as "most important"), the dropping of the atomic bomb on Japan (66% as "most important"), the right to vote for women in 1920 (66% "most important"), and passage of the Civil Rights Act of 1964 (58% "most important").

What the historical events described above have in common is the (often) sudden and dramatic shift of the societal stasis. What I will refer to as the cultural cataclysm of the 2016 election (or "11/8" to refer to the date of the election) will be considered in terms of the habitual introjection of intolerance into our political discourse and the normalizing of intergroup conflict as a means of solving social problems. This process of social change will be examined in terms of the psychology of out-group animus and hate violence, which have suddenly come to compromise the liberal democratic model of governance that had existed during the past half century. This psychological autopsy will examine how tolerance was lost and—importantly—consider how individuals who aspire to a multicultural society will endure during this period of ambiguity, chaos, and hatred.

The liberal democratic tradition presumes the willing and active engagement of the populace in choosing how they wish to be governed. Under such a model, access to diverse political information is provided by a media that is seen as credible; additionally, government institutions responsible for justice and voter engagement are seen as trustworthy. When the political system is seen as fair and equitable, individuals are motivated to engage in electing leadership through voting. This model of voter engagement has been referred to as the principle of rational choice—or simply choice theory—in which the individual is able to weigh options in terms of personal needs and values (Tversky & Kahneman, 1991). Choice theory views political decision making as essentially rationalist in the linking of action and decision making. The individuals' decisions are based on deliberation of political alternatives and determining the utility of their political choice. Classically, choice theory reveals that how we wish to be governed is presumptively constant for the individual and the community over time (Habermas, 2000).

An early exponent of the choice model was found in the work of Downs (1957) in his *Economic Theory of Democracy*. He argued that political choice often relied on microeconomic concerns, frequently as a consequence of voters' incomplete knowledge of (other) competing positions of candidates in the democratic process. He saw this decision-making process as responding to an economic–political continuum from communist/state-planned economies to a completely deregulated/right-shift marketplace choice.

The influence of choice theory is substantial but not without its critics. Emily Hauptmann (1996) has argued that political choice is not reducible to consumer decision making alone. She has raised concerns that inherently point to the social and psychological aspects of how individuals support models of governance. Her assertion is that political decisions occur in a social context on the one hand and efforts at exerting choice are frustrated by institutions and powerful others on the other. Her critique introduces some of the issues that we will address, namely that not only do individuals ultimately make political decisions based on emotion-based arguments but that the social contexts in which choice occurs are constrained by political practices that increasingly resist freedom of political decision making.

The argument put forward here is that the 2016 U.S. presidential election—as well as political events such as the Brexit vote in the United Kingdom—breaks sharply from the tradition of rational choice and exerts on liberal democratic societies a cataclysmic impact, one that holds significant consequences for the functioning of a multicultural society. The "what" and "how" of cultural cataclysm are distinguished from normal (choice for) change in political direction in terms of three factors: (1) the enmeshment of political choice with intergroup conflict, (2) the habitual introjection of hate speech and vitriol into the rhetoric of the political contest, and (3) the framing of the political outcome as a winner–loser scenario in terms of economic and societal power. These three signifiers—making political choice a function of intergroup conflict, the chronic use of hate speech in political discourse, and the punishment of the political loser groups—are frequently manifested via the presence of a figurehead leader who legitimizes the use of hate as a defining political tool. Additionally, the presumption of threat or economic deprivation for the in-group, the abandonment of a common ground for political debate, and the creation of a triggering crisis that becomes part of the collective narrative of the populace are part of the sudden social upheaval. The cultural cataclysm of 2016 constitutes a dramatic and sudden degradation of the state, its institutions, and its communities. A shorthand that I will employ to refer to the 2016 election is the "culture wars" argument, first described by sociologist James Davison Hunter in his 1991 book *Culture Wars: The Struggle to Define America*. Hunter describes the conflict over the nature of American culture as being fought between conservative religious groups and their politically progressive counterparts. This theoretical perspective was transformed into a political tool by the commentator Patrick Buchanan in his 1992 speech at the Republican National Convention: "There is a religious war going on in our country for the soul of America. It is a cultural war, as critical to the kind of nation we will one day be as was the Cold War itself" (Buchanan, 1992).

In comparison to tragedies such as earthquakes or tsunamis, which, while devastating, are not done by people, to people, cultural cataclysms are human-driven events. These events frequently impart a redistribution of power between social groups and appoint a new class of winners who serve as the dominant social group in the new societal stasis. This cultural change is frequently driven by movements based on authoritarian, ultranationalistic, and xenophobic (AUX) social philosophies that stand in contrast to the liberal democratic principles of choice, secularism, freedom of expression, and multiculturalism.

2016 in Context: Global Challenges to Democracy and Multiculturalism

The practice of liberal democratic governance has sought to mitigate the risk of global warfare, and, as with other global initiatives such as the United Nations, has been a dominant form of international relations since the end of World War II. Determining the status of global democracies and human rights has involved numerous nongovernmental agencies focusing attention on the status of nation states as a means of keeping the peace and promoting the rights of the individual. The examination of democratic practices around the world has been conducted by the organization Freedom House for over the past half century. Their annual report relies on analysis of indicators of civil rights, freedom of expression, and rights of the person. This methodology, evaluates 10 political rights and 15 civil liberties indicators on a nation-by-nation basis. In the annual report for 2016, Freedom House noted that there has been a 10-year decline in global freedom. The report notes that "the world was battered by crises that fueled xenophobic sentiment in democratic countries, undermined the economies of states dependent on the sale of natural resources, and led authoritarian regimes to crack down harder on dissent" (*Freedom in the World*, 2016). In this report, it is also noted that more countries showed a decline (72) than gains (42) in terms of democratic practices/civil liberties and that the most frequent deterioration of democratic practices was related to a decline in freedom of expression and the enforcement of the rule of law. What this suggests is that the 2016 U.S. election, while experienced as an aberration of the electoral process, may reflect a movement away from democracy toward less-inclusive forms of governance—including oligarchies and autocracies—globally.

Liberal democratic practices—which have recently proven vulnerable to AUX-type movements—have supported diffusion of power away from a nation state to a more globally focused and culturally diverse society. Examples include the formation of the European Union and the promulgation of international trade agreements. This move toward globalization has occurred against a global backdrop that has seen a rise in awareness concerning international terrorism. Human rights policies that support a culturally inclusive and relativistic social philosophy have emphasized the civil rights and protection of minority out-groups—members of society who are often the targets of hate violence. Hate crime laws represent one manifestation of this political model. As I have commented previously, "A guiding assumption concerning hate crime initiatives is that these laws are a product of democratic political systems. These initiatives are particularly relevant in societies experiencing significant in-migration and where women have evidenced increasing levels of income equity" (Dunbar, 2016, 2).

An important manifestation of liberal democratic thought that stands in distinction to an AUX ideology is the civil society movement (CSM). The CSM has served as a global social philosophy that has advocated for multiculturalism and political diffusion—one that is independent of the sitting government (Kumar, 1993). The CSM is consistent with the enactment and enforcement of antibias and hate crime initiatives and may serve as a nexus of advocacy for civil rights that is superordinate to the political leadership of the state. As Mouffe (1993) has emphasized, the civil society movement constitutes a nonviolent form of dissent—one that emphasizes democratic participation, cultural diversity, and free speech. The CSM is inherently then in opposition to nationalism of any ilk—particularly authoritarianism. For a civil society to flourish, the practice of dissent, freedom of speech, and independence of the press are essential. It, therefore, is not surprising that the nationalistic and civil society movements inherently find themselves on a collision course.

Collective "Shock and Awe" of Cataclysmic Cultural Disruption

Sudden social and political upheaval inevitably impacts both the collective and the individual. Mental health problems of acute stress and trauma are often found in the literature in the aftermath of cultural cataclysms. Of course, individual responses to traumatic events have been well documented in accounts of warfare for quite a while. Post-traumatic stress symptoms include physiological arousal, intrusive cognitions, and efforts at avoidance (Horowitz, Wilner, & Alvarez, 1979; Sluzki, 1993).

Individuals who manifest severe psychological trauma frequently meet the criteria for post-traumatic stress disorder (PTSD). This diagnosis is frequently assigned to victims of sexual assault (Foa, Molnar, & Cashman, 1995), combat veterans (Grieger et al., 2006; Lapierre, Schwegler, & LaBauve, 2007), and with intrusive ideation (Foa, Rothbaum, Riggs, & Murdock, 1991) and numbing phenomena (Schnurr et al., 2007) with victims of violent crimes. Additionally, many individuals experience secondary problems such as substance abuse (Epstein, Saunders, Kilpatrick, & Resnick, 1998). The flashbulb memories of historical events—the first reactions to the MLK and JFK assassinations, the Pearl Harbor attack of 1941, or being the victim of a terrorist attack in Paris, all capture the shock, confusion, fear, and poignancy of sudden traumatic change. These traumatic memories of events from decades ago continue to define the individuals and remind them of the frailty of their worlds.

Collective trauma constitutes an assault on a group. Within the group there is a shared recognition of the event and its impact on members of the target community. A well-documented (politically based) traumatic event is the impact of the 9/11 terrorist attacks on the general population. The Centers for Disease Control and Prevention (CDC) reports on the Behavioral Risk Factor Surveillance System (BRFSS) telephonic interviews with 3,512 respondents in the Tristate New York City area that was conducted from October 11 to December 31, 2001. Interview results found high levels of psychological symptoms in the respondents. Findings indicated that 48% of respondents reported anger episodes, 37% reported worrying after the attacks, nearly 15% reported sleep problems, and 7% reported feeling helpless. Of the respondents, 3% indicated an increase in alcohol consumption, and 21% reported an increase in smoking (Centers for Disease Control and Prevention, 2002).

Sudden and traumatic events frequently disarm political discourse—and hence criticism—of the new emergent cultural realities. The shock and disorientation makes true critical discourse unavailable when the world changes. Collective trauma may also have ramifications across extended periods of time. In some cases, the collective injury may become codified in group stories or traditions. In some instances, the beliefs and behaviors of the impacted individuals may be transferred to other group members who are temporally or locatively removed from the traumatic incident itself. A contemporary example is the intergenerational effects of families of survivors interned in death camps during the Holocaust (Niederland, 1961). The survivor trauma transmission of much of this literature has also been considered in terms of characteristic familial survivor types of acute victimization, numbing/catatonia, fighters, and healthy families of "those who made it" (Danieli, 1981).

Examples of collective trauma under conditions of political oppression in stable political systems are also found in the centuries-old experiences of black Americans under conditions of slavery, segregation, and the Jim Crow years in the United States. These transmitted experiences of collective trauma may be found in reactions to the political shift of 11/8 in the United States. The transmitted beliefs of collective trauma may reflect the learned helplessness of the individual, feelings of shock, or disorientation. The worldview of the group members frequently includes fear of future (random and intermittent) victimization—such as experiences of microaggressions or de facto sanctions against the exercising of civil liberties. In these situations, the expression of concerns and arguments for retribution are muted—or expressed with recognition of the consequences to be leveled against those who speak up. The collective group experience is therefore internalized and largely eliminated from the larger social consciousness.

Survey Reactions to the 2016 U.S. Presidential Election

In the week following the election of Donald Trump, I posted an online survey for colleagues and associates—initially this included university- and health care–affiliated professionals and their social cohorts and subsequently colleagues of colleagues. The survey gathered demographic information, voting decisions, attitudes about social risk in the aftermath of the election, and measurement of acute stress symptoms on the Acute Stress Disorder Scale (ASDS) (Bryant, Moulds, & Guthrie, 2000). In addition, open-ended narrative questions were included to examine respondent's first thoughts and feelings about the election and their personal associations to similar life events.

Respondents to the survey who voted for candidates other than Secretary Hillary Clinton—e.g., Trump, Gary Johnson, and Jill Stein—were aggregated into a group reflecting voters who rejected her liberal democracy platform. With these respondents, the expressed concerns were notably lower both in the weeks after the election and in the first month of the Trump presidency.

The analyses of the survey will be discussed in terms of two waves of data collection. Wave One consists of responses to the survey in the first six weeks after the election. In total 357 respondents were included in this initial sample. Fifty-six percent of the respondents were over the age of 50; 27% were under the age of 30. Seventy-seven percent of the respondents were women; 12% identified as LGBT and 9% bisexual.

Wave Two consists of respondents who completed the online measure starting the first week after the inauguration of January 20, 2016. Wave

Two data consisted of a parallel online survey; responses were collected during the first 30 days of the Trump presidency. The Wave Two sample consisted of 1,155 respondents. Approximately 30% of the respondents were over the age of 50 and with about 30% were under the age of 30. Sixty-four percent of the respondents were women.

First Reactions to Election Results

In Wave One, responses to the election elicited a range of emotions related to the experience of collective trauma—shock, anxiety, confusion, fear, a sense of unreality, and dread. This classic negative introjection had to do with dread of personal vulnerability and fear for friends and family who might suffer uniquely under a more oppressive regime. The most frequent emotional responses described by the losing voters included shock (15.8%), sadness (14.4%), and a series of complex feeling states (38.7%). The anti-Clinton voters responded in some cases with feelings of relief but also feelings of sadness and shock. In this sense, then, opposing the liberal democratic tradition did not make these respondents immune to the cataclysmic nature of the election outcome. These findings are tabulated in Table 1.1.

An example of the responses reported by people is provided by this individual:

> I felt as if the progressive country I was proud to be a part of had suddenly taken a million steps back. I couldn't believe how many people were racist, sexist, and homophobic. I was shocked to see how easily it was for the Republican Party to manipulate so many people into believing that what they stood for was going to make America "great" again. How did this county elect a man who continuously harassed people, openly disrespected people, especially women and the disabled? It disgusts me that the country chooses to ignore all these terrible facts and thought that this man would be fit to lead the most powerful country in the world. What kind of example does that set for children? It made me realize how ignorant we are as a country. We truly need to invest more in the education system so this doesn't continue to happen in the future. My heart broke on Election Day imagining all the hate and suffering that would come within the next 4 years.

When Clinton supporters were asked about their emotional reactions to the election after the inauguration, they remained significantly

Table 1.1   First Reactions to 11/8 Election Outcome: For Clinton Supporters

	Wave One November 14, 2016–December 31, 2016 (*n* = 292)	Wave Two January 29, 2017–February 16, 2017 (*n* = 978)
Emotions:		
Shock	15.8%	21.3%
Anger	1%	4.1%
Fear	9.6%	4.9%
Sadness	14.4%	18%
Happiness	0%	15.1%
Multiple emotions	38.7%	31.3%
No emotions	13.3%	6.6%
Content:		
Issues of bias	7.4%	9.8%
Terrorism	0.7%	0%
Environmental risk	0.3%	0%
Economic risk	0.3%	0%
Loss of faith	3.1%	6.6%
Political process:		
Positive expectations	0.3%	1.6%
No response	88.2%	80.39%

unchanged. In the first month after the inauguration, Clinton voters recalled their feelings at the time of the election as reflecting shock (21.3%), sadness (18%), and complex/varied emotions (31.3%). Reactions of shock, dysphoria, and emotional confusion are all part of the acute stress response that we will discuss further below.

Personal Associations to Election Results

A follow-up question asked respondents to associate what prior life event the election was associated with (e.g., when had the individual felt like this before). Personal associations of the election supporters of Secretary Clinton were varied. The predominant issue was one of

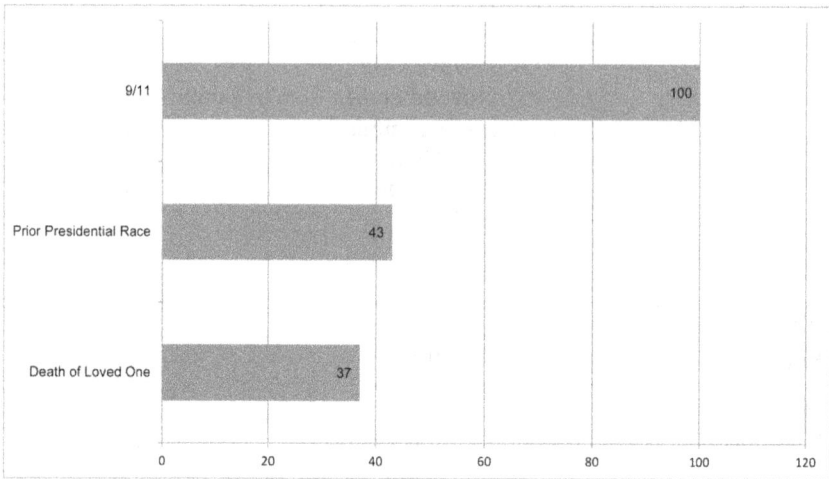

Figure 1.1   Personal Associations of 11/8 to Prior Events ($n = 357$)

associations to terrorism. The terror response was almost always related to 9/11. This was reported by over one-third (34.6%) of the Clinton voters. Other common themes were recall of prior elections for 13.9% of Clinton supporters and 19% of non-Clinton voters, and death of a family member for 22.9% of Clinton voters. The most frequent associations are reported in Figure 1.1.

Survey results directly after the election revealed that the range of traumatic associations was mediated by respondent gender and age. For women who voted for Clinton, a frequent association to the Trump victory was similar to being harassed or sexually violated. For respondents under the age of 25 the association with 9/11 was very infrequently (3%) reported, as, for many in this age range, this was not part of their personal experience. As one mid-20s person said, "I can think of it like 9/11, but all I really know is when 9/11 happened, I knew we were at war, but I was not sure with whom? In some ways it is the same with Trump, I know he hates us, exactly who is it he hates and why? I am not sure." In Table 1.2, the reported associations to 11/8 are summarized for Clinton and non-Clinton supporters.

In the first weeks after the election, many of the voters who did not support Clinton (e.g., one in three) did not associate the election with a prior life experience. This was more than three times lower than the voters who did support Clinton. Another subset of Wave One respondents stated the 11/8 election was unlike anything they had experienced before in terms of being so problematic and ominous, with roughly 6%

Table 1.2   Comparing 11/8 Election Results to Prior Life Events: Postelection and Postinauguration Voters for Clinton and Other Candidates

	Wave One November 14, 2016– December 31, 2016		Wave Two January 29, 2017– February 16, 2017	
	Clinton (*n* = 292)	Others (*n* = 61)	Clinton (*n* = 978)	Others (*n* = 157)
9/11 terror attack	34.6%	4.9%	13.9%	7.6%
Prior elections	13%	19.7%	3.3%	1.9%
Personal loss/grieving	22.9%	6.6%	4.6%	1.3%
Worst thing ever	6.2%	3.3%	23.9%	17.8%
No association	10.2%	36.2%	23.9%	6.9%
Hate victimization	1.4%	1.6%	2.2%	1.3%
Genocide	1%	0%	0.8%	0.4%
Political assassinations	4.8%	3.3%	0.8%	0.6%
Relief	0%	2.8%	0%	0.6%
Other	2.7%	3.3%	1.5%	17.6%

of Clinton and 3% of non-Clinton voters stating the election was worse than anything they had previously encountered. Many respondents in Wave One thought about the election "all the time" (41.7%) in the first weeks after 11/8; another 45% thought about it "more than once a day." Some of these respondents recalled prior political reversals that were in turn linked to concerns for the future.

The impact of the election also connected with individuals who were the descendants of families that had previously suffered under political trauma. One person described how she had had a recurrent dream after the election, which had first been experienced by her half a century before:

As a child I had had this dream of stepping over rubble and walking between burned-out buildings. . . . One of my grandparents had told me about the Nazi invasion of Russia and what they had seen there. From what they had been through they chose to emigrate after the war ended and came to the West, they had no home there, which is how I feel now about being here.

Vulnerability to Acute Stress Symptoms

In the Wave One survey, symptoms of acute stress on the ASDS were examined in relationship to voter choice and behaviors characteristic of acute distress. It was found that Clinton supporters reported much higher acute stress symptoms than voters who opposed her candidacy.[1] Additionally, consistent with the collective trauma hypothesis, the acute stress symptoms were correlated with avoidance behaviors—that is, strategies to avoid contact with persons who held opposing political views—used after the election.[2] The symptoms of acute stress disorder were also significantly higher for respondents in their 30s; these individuals also reported more frequent thoughts about the election—with more than half of these people saying they thought about the election at least once a day—which was also correlated with the ASDS scores for acute stress.[3]

The acute stress symptoms on the ASDS were also significantly more powerful for women than men, who also engaged in more avoidance tactics to deal with interpersonal problems in the first six weeks after the election. Women were almost twice as likely as men (31% versus 18%) to associate 11/8 with 9/11. Women were also less likely than men (63% versus 75%) to indicate they had arguments with other people about the election; women also tried to avoid individuals because of issues related to 11/8 and "unfriended" people due to political fallout more frequently than did men.

For all respondents the scores for acute stress were correlated with concern for future community risk to hate violence and terrorism.[4] The clinical and mental health issues of how individuals may adjust under these at-risk settings will be more thoroughly examined in the following sections of this book, particularly in Chapters 4 and 5.

Expressed Concerns for Family and Friends

The survey included a series of items asking the respondent about concerns they had for friends and family. For Clinton voters, the majority of the respondents by a wide margin expressed concerns of economic, health care, and mental health problems for friends and family. In the first weeks after the election, roughly 75% of Clinton supporters were concerned about friends and family being vulnerable to economic problems with similar levels of concern for cohorts in terms of medical and mental health concerns. For voters who did not support Clinton, the concerns were not as strongly endorsed, being an area of concern for one-half to one-quarter of the respondents vis-à-vis Clinton supporters.

Table 1.3   Comparing Postelection and Postinauguration Survey Concerns—Clinton Voters vs. All Other Voters

	Clinton Voters	All Other Voters
Risk to friends/family		
Postelection[a]		
Economic risk	79.1%	31.3%
Medical care risk	77.1%	19.7%
Mental health risk	80.8%	42.6%
	$n = 292$	$n = 61$
Postinauguration[b]		
Economic risk	73.5%	
Medical care risk	74.2%	
	$n = 978$	$n = 157$

[a] = November 14, 2016–December 31, 2016
[b] = January 29, 2017–February 16, 2017

In Table 1.3, the frequencies for Wave One (postelection) and Wave Two (postinauguration) concerns are summarized for these three areas of concern for friends and family.

The survey responses in the first month of the new administration found an escalation of concern about economic security and health care. Generally, there was a moderate increase in concerns for friends and family in the postinauguration sample, though the level of expressed concern remained far below that of the Clinton voters.

Online Survey Results—One-Month Postinauguration

In the subsequent online survey, the experiences of interpersonal conflict concerning 11/8 were examined in the first month after the Trump inauguration. Findings revealed that the association between 11/8 and 9/11 remained largely unchanged from the survey responses gathered right after the election.[5] Associations with 9/11 were most frequently endorsed by persons in our online survey aged 30 to 60; associations to 9/11 were lower for people under 30 or over 60. The reported symptoms of acute stress reported in the first few weeks after the January 2017 inauguration were associated with a higher level of awareness of 11/8, including thinking about it "all the time"; ASDS symptoms were modestly correlated to recall of 9/11 and were highest for persons under 30.[6] As in Wave One, the postinauguration scores for acute stress on the ASDS were again significantly higher for women than for men.[7]

Cultural Cataclysm and In-Group–Out-Group Power Relationships

We need to step back, conceptually, and consider that any shift in political and cultural regimes happens in a context of preexisting power relationships between the dominant cultural in-group(s) and the social out-group(s). A consequence of the disruption of the social stasis is the realignment of power relationships between dominant and minority groups.

These intergroup power relationships, *when viewed from the perspective of the dominant group*, can be represented along a continuum. This approach can provide a means of considering anticipated shifts in in-group attitudes and prescribed behaviors toward social out-groups. Such a framework can provide a means of analysis of sudden political change and its consequential cultural shift.

A detailed method of examining social change is found in the work of Schwartz (2015) in his study of cultural values and social change. He describes one of the underlying cultural value continuums as: egalitarianism–hierarchy. For Schwartz, in his research, cultural norms can be isolated along this spectrum from the endorsement of individual behaviors that "induce people to recognize one another as moral equals who share basic interests as human beings." People are socialized to internalize a commitment to cooperate and to feel concern for everyone's welfare. They are expected to act for the benefit of others as a matter of choice (key values: equality, social justice, responsibility, and honesty). Hierarchy, by comparison, requires that "people are socialized to take the hierarchical distribution of roles for granted, to comply with the obligations and rules attached to their roles, to show deference to superiors and expect deference from subordinates." This dimension of culture is particularly important in understanding the prescribed social norms in terms of civil rights and intergroup relationships and will be applied to the issue of culture change and hate behavior.

As described below, this model allows for us to consider how intolerance and xenophobic ideology serves to sanction hate violence as a function of autocratic and totalitarian models of governance. These are summarized in Table 1.4.

Table 1.4   Cultural–Political Status: Dominant Group Power Relationship with Out-Group(s)

Multicultural Model—Equity between Groups

Relationship to out-group(s): Participation

Role of the populace: Diverse identity politics philosophies

Examples: Educational curriculum on culture and society—Teaching history

Liberal Democratic Model—Cultural Relativism

Relationship to out-group(s): Toleration

Role of the populace: Incorporation of identity politics within traditional democratic process

Oligarchies and Theocracies—Faux Democracy and Control

Relationship to out-group(s): Domination

Role of the populace: State-controlled parties; minimal citizen involvement

Authoritarianism Autocracy—Nondemocratic Nationalism

Relationship to out-group(s): Elimination

Role of the populace: Obedience to one-party/one-leader governance

Totalitarian Xenophobia—Genocidal Fascism

Relationship to out-group(s): Extermination

Role of the populace: Subjugation to one-leader governance

In-Group and Out-Group Equity—*Guiding Principle Is to Investigate Intergroup Relationships*

As a model of social functioning, systems of between-group equity reflect many of the principles of multiculturalism, in which multiple cultural groups with distinct traditions and behaviors participate in all of the important functions of commerce, worship, and governance. Sanctioned individual behaviors include openness to experience of others, egalitarianism, and a capacity for inquiry and learning about diverse cultural worldviews.

The prescribed need for the individuals in this society is to develop the capacity for inquiry and learning about a contrary cultural worldview or belief and the ability to investigate in-group–out-group differences. Sanctioned collective norms are signified by intergroup communication and understanding. The enhancement of intergroup relationships and normalizing multiple identities draw on the underpinnings of multiculturalism and civil society. The Allport contact hypothesis serves as a model of engagement to bridge differences. The educational curriculum addresses the relationship of culture and society; the teaching of history is valued. Social influence is practiced by stakeholders of diverse social groups. Political power is diffuse.

Cultural Relativism—*Guiding Principle of Tolerance*

Sanctioned individual behaviors include adherence to policies that seek to reduce or eliminate social inequities, with the goal to tolerate difference. Collective norms emphasize adherence to a democratic model of governance, and community decision making is a guiding principle. The theoretical underpinnings of tolerance (Walzer, 1997), egalitarianism (Schwartz, 2015), and managing intergroup distress/anxiety through self-regulation (Stephan, Stephan, & Gudykunst, 1999) serve to enhance coexistence and effective cross-cultural/cross group contact experiences (Pettigrew & Tropp, 2006). Individual norms value equity and regulation of need for social dominance. The collective need emphasizes intergroup communication and understanding. This is manifested in the capacity for participation in a democratic social system.

Dominant Group Control of the Societal Stasis—*Guiding Principle of Dominance*

In predominantly monocultural societies the operant social standard is that of a dominant social and cultural standard that reflects the history, needs, and norms of the dominant in-group. Sanctioned individual behaviors emphasize the privilege of the individual to avoid contact with out-group persons and the assumption of entitlement to material and experiential rewards that are denied to out-group persons. Interpersonal interactions reinforce the presumption of dominant group entitlement as legitimate and organic to the realities of the society. Values of individualism, delay of gratification, patriotism, and nostalgia—what will be referred to in Chapter 2 as cultural anchors—are reinforced for both the members of the dominant group and members of social/minority out-groups. Social norms are fluid in terms of egalitarianism and hierarchy, shifting as a function of the favorableness of the contact experience.

Socioeconomic and power inequities are seen as "cost of membership" for out-groups. This includes the de facto segregation of out-group persons. A legitimizing myth is the separate but equal rationalization of the dominant-out-group power differential. Systematic restriction in the size and/or scope of government, as a philosophy, has also been considered as a form of institutional racism. As Gainous (2011) has discussed, restriction on the structures, policies, and practices of government can serve to maintain social inequities—the "New New Racism Thesis"—experienced by minority and out-group persons. This veiled form of racism reflects a combination of conservative economic principles and the notion of individualism—arguing that bootstrap-efforts for success are preferred to dismantling systematic forms of discrimination (Kinder & Sanders, 1996). A highly relevant theoretical model to this form of in-group–out-group governance is found in social dominance orientation (SDO) (Sidanius & Pratto, 1993, 1999). Social dominance is characterized by an overarching attitude concerning intergroup relations with a concern that such relationships be hierarchical rather than egalitarian. Social dominance also inherently reveals a desire of the individual for their social group to be in a place of superiority and control over other social groups (Pratto, Sidanius, Stallworth, & Malle, 1994).

The social benchmarks include formal and informal segregation and "Jim Crow" policies, the ghettoization of ethnic minorities, the separate but equal argument of *Plessy v. Ferguson*, privatization of government services, and valuing small government for problems of public education, culture, and public safety.

Hegemony of Dominant In-Group—*Guiding Principle of Elimination of Out-Groups*

Hierarchical societies with a dominant cultural group frequently evidence faux or transitional democratic forms of governance. Social attitudes of the inherent cultural or biological inferiority (Kinder & Sanders, 1996) of out-group persons is assumed. Collective norms include establishing and adherence to in-group hegemony, engagement in unbalanced contact experiences, adherence to in-group hierarchy, practice of de facto social segregation, and the maintenance of in-group–out-group inequity. The state typically functions as an autocracy or oligarchy to support the ruling elite via a dominant political party and/or strongman figure. Systematic control and suppression of alternative political ideologies is maintained. The suppression of race-conscious policies or other initiatives to explicitly benefit out-groups such as affirmative action, educational assistance, or civil rights is practiced by agents of the state. Out-group persons are inherently seen as marginalized at best, or threatening at worst, by the dominant group to maintain the societal stasis. The psychological underpinnings are represented by classical authoritarianism of the Adorno and the Berkeley school (Adorno, Frenkel-Brunswik, Levinson, & Sanford, 1950).

A range of social and state-controlled practices are found in the control and elimination of out-groups. These include voter suppression in faux democracies—for example, as seen in the United States in states that have actively sought to introduce discriminatory forms of voter-identification practices. More violent forms of out-group dominance include state-run death squads, as found with the Colombian warfare of the past quarter century (Davies, Blanco, & Miron, 2016) or the "dirty war" or Processo in Argentina in the kidnapping and murder of citizens and state control of print media in the late 1970s. Other examples of a domination of a racial out-group are found in the U.S. government internment camps of Japanese Americans during World War II or the ongoing practice of Chinese in-migration to Tibet to obliterate the indigenous culture by massive expatriation.

Authoritarian forms of government not surprisingly manipulate political discourse in social media. The former Soviet states illustrate how authoritarian regimes systematically reduce the presence of an independent press and Internet use that is in opposition to the state. As Sarah Kendzior has discussed in her research in Azerbaijan and elsewhere, systematic forms of suppression of social criticism have proven more effective than outright censorship. What she and her colleagues have examined is what she termed "networked authoritarianism."

In her research on Azerbaijan, an oil-rich state dominated politically by one family for the past quarter of a century, a range of policies to stifle social media use have preempted opposition to the regime (Guliyev, 2009). The role of an authoritarian form of governance, based upon patrimonial lines in Azerbaijan, is evidenced via propagandistic state media, suppression of NGO groups in the country, and harassment of dissident journalists. A consequence of this form of government has led to the discouragement of political engagement by citizens or groups independent of the state and has enforced a top-down system of social change.

In their study of Azerbaijani use of social media, Pearce, Freelon, and Kendzior (2014) found that the frequency of Internet use was associated with civic but not political engagement. Results of a predictive logistic regression study found that the Internet was associated with public civic engagement but not with political government engagement. Their argument is that authoritarian regimes, such as Azerbaijan's, view the Internet as it does nongovernmental agencies: it is unacceptable because it functions independently of the state. Pearce and Kendzior (2012) have also found via content analysis of three years of Azerbaijani media how the government successfully dissuaded frequent Internet users from supporting political protest and in-country users of social media from using the Internet for political discourse.

Kendzior (2011) also has commented on how the Uzbek regime has similarly worked to suppress the use of social media for political discourse and criticism of the state, arguing the regime has sought to foster a political culture of cynicism and distrust in the citizenry concerning social media (a "fake news" approach to independent discourse). She has also commented on how the state has promoted fear of terrorism as a legitimizing strategy to control civil rights. The terror group Akromiya, Kendzior argues, was largely supported if not created by the state, serving as a proxy threat to reign in public discourse and political opposition; this is not unlike the trumped-up terrorism of Argentina's regime that legitimized the *processo* from a generation earlier.

Totalitarian Xenophobia—*Guiding Principle of Out-Group Extermination*

In a totalitarian system sanctioned individual behaviors include obedience to actions involving persecution of out-groups; this may include agentic behaviors in state-prescribed forms of discrimination, aggression, and violence perpetrated against social out-groups. The final solution to out-group relationships is the removal of the out-group(s) from the society. Systematic forms of extermination are, of course, found most ominously in the Holocaust but also importantly in the killing fields in Cambodia and the ethnic cleansing in Africa and Eastern Europe over the last decades of the 20th century. The collective need of the dominant culture is found in authoritarianism, social dominance, and the pursuit of "purity" of the social or racial heritage of the society. Intergroup contact, when it occurs, is unbalanced. Social interaction works from a strongly hierarchy-based relationship to the state and in turn to social out-groups. These power relationships are summarized in Table 1.5.

Theoretical underpinnings in the psychological literature include Allport's hierarchy of prejudice, in which out-group extermination is characterized as the highest level of prejudice. Additionally, the work

Table 1.5 Cultural–Political Status: Power Relationships and Operant Political Systems

Dominant-Minority Group Relationship	Political System
Investigation of out-group(s)	Multicultural democracies
Toleration of out-group(s)	Liberal democracies
Domination of out-group(s)	Faux democracies, transitional democracies, oligarchies, and monarchies
Elimination of out-group(s)	Authoritarian autocracies and transitional oligarchies
Extermination of out-group(s)	Totalitarianism

on SDO again is explanatory of the dominant hegemony model. There are behavioral and organizational differences in this extreme form of bias. Specifically in some cases the work of extermination is under the purview of the state—such as the Stalinist purges of the 1930s or the genocide in Bosnia in 1990. As with the political homicides in Chile under the Pinochet regime in the 1970s and 1980s, these state initiatives are often conducted under the pretense of political crisis, be it civil war or suppression of domestic terrorists. These include the death camps of National Socialists in Germany and Central Europe in the 1930s and 1940s, intersectional murders in Uganda under Idi Amin, and the lynching of blacks over decades in the United States.

There are also covert forms of genocide conducted by the state. The 40-year-long Tuskegee Syphilis Study conducted covertly on black men is one such example. Carried out by the U.S. Public Health Service, this study followed 600 untreated black men—the majority of whom were diagnosed with syphilis—for over 40 years. Most of the subjects were uneducated sharecroppers living in Macon County, Alabama, who were incentivized to remain in the study for nearly 30 years after a viable treatment for syphilis had been found. The program only terminated when national media reported on it in 1972 (Tuskegee University).

Another contemporary form of state-sponsored genocide is found in the assassinations of journalists in Russia. According to the Committee to Protect Journalists, since 1992, 56 journalists have been killed in Russia (Committee to Protect Journalists, n.d.) with approximately one-half of the killings occurring since Vladimir Putin became the de facto czar of his country. Some of these deaths—such as that in 2006 of Anna

Politkovskaya—appeared to be directly related to journalistic work that was critical of the standing government, in her case concerning human rights abuses in Chechnya.

In some cases in recent history, individual actors who have engaged in forms of genocide have been tolerated if not encouraged by the state.

The very complex issue of political change will be considered in terms of two issues: how changes in the form of governance impact the attitudes of social inclusion and how "cataclysmic" social change psychologically impacts the individual. Models of political change often are considered in terms of macroeconomic shifts; in democracies these regime changes occur typically in conjunction with changes in the presidency rather than congressional elections (Blomberg, 2000). These regime-switching models have been employed to examine economic cycling—e.g., expansion and recession or "bull" and "bear" markets as well as political changes (Hamilton, 2005 Hamilton & Lin, 1996). Political change that is accomplished by revolution or the subversive overthrow of a standing government is by comparison seen as a pathological form of change.

The process of social inclusion (e.g., racial integration, the rights of women, or in the U.S. DOMA), interestingly, is marked in our recent past by both presidential elections and nonelectoral events. The former is most clearly represented by the election of President Barack Obama and the candidacy of Secretary Clinton in this century, the latter by nonelectoral events such as the civil rights movement of the 1950s and 1960s and the Supreme Court ruling of *Brown v. Board of Education of Topeka* in 1954 or Jackie Robinson's breaking the color barrier in major league baseball in 1947. These later events of changes to social inclusion were not only unrelated to a presidential election but were not decided by popular vote. The transformation of norms and laws concerning racial integration and inclusion were also incremental—if also in some cases violent. This prodemocratic shift is similar to the notion of paradigmatic revolutions in scientific discovery (Kuhn, 1962) in which a growing body of evidence comes to supplant a dominant assumption that has proven inadequate. This crisis of incongruity of a dominant assumption with observed contrary evidence results in a reconsideration or loosening of the tenets of dogma, allowing for more adaptive and parsimonious models (or practices) to emerge. This application of the scientific method, while not complete, is consistent with the choice model of democracy. With sufficient access to information, the argument goes, members of a social group can choose viable options that appear logical and beneficial.

The limitations to choice theory and the notion of scientific paradigms are clear in that scientific proof and political truth are not perfectly equitable. Political arguments and change are importantly driven by efforts to amass power and privilege for both powerful elites and social groups. Additionally, not all incremental change of social power results in the inclusion of social out-groups. The problem of anti-Semitism and its consequential tragedy of the Holocaust can be traced back to numerous cultural events that precede the rise to power of the national socialists. For example, more than a dozen years before the Nazi regime took power, Hitler presented his 25-point program for the domination and segregation of Jews through the restriction of their political civil rights and by recognition of Aryans as being the only viable comrade in an emergent Germany.

Preceding the national socialists, the Dreyfus affair—a political trial of a Jewish French military officer charged (ironically) of espionage with Germany—continued in the courts and French/European press from 1894 to 1906. During this time rabid anti-Semitic news accounts and innuendo became a source of social discussion and led to activation of stereotypes of a Jewish fifth column in the European community. During this period, violence against Jews (the hate crimes of their age) occurred throughout France (Makow, 2017). In defense of Dreyfus, the author Emile Zola published "*J'Accuse*," an attack on the French military and state for its engagement in a protracted case of anti-Semitism. His influential article in turn led to his prosecution in 1898 for libel—in which he exposed the plaintiff to public hatred, contempt, ridicule, or disgrace (Zablotsky, 2012); Zola was sentenced to a year in jail and fined 3,000 francs. The Dreyfus affair is not simply sifting through the history of dead white men. This case lays out many of the themes we are now dealing with—the fake news of the case both led to hate violence and created a sustained dialogue of religious and ethnic intolerance—and it also provides a warning of what can happen when political speech is treated as grounds for legal action against critics of the ruling government. Ominously, this case, which was influential throughout Europe, serves as a precursor to the systematic anti-Semitic genocide of a generation later.

Conceptually, then, we can look at the problem of intolerance and social change in terms of both the fluidity of dominant and minority group power relationships—the process of inclusion and exclusion in the cultural mainstream—and the shift in the form of governance along a continuum from a democratic multicultural model of governance to that of a totalitarian system of rule. The shift of social group inclusion can in principle move from progressive (liberal democracy) to regressive (autocracy), and the attendant problems of discrimination, and hate violence, can therefore be considered as a consequence of this shift, regardless of whether it is discordant with the rule of law.

A more recent illustration of the gradual shift in social inclusion of out-groups is provided by the transformation of South Africa from a segregated society—a vestige of European imperialism in Africa—to a multiracial/multicultural democracy.

A further and more ominous illustration of a decline of social inclusion that led to an extreme form of intolerance is found in the history of Budapest during the 20th century. At the turn of the century in 1900 the city was a cultural center for Magyar culture and a multilingual and multicultural community for Jews, Christians, and people from regions of the Balkans and Middle East (Lukacs, 1994). With a strong national culture and support for intellectual and artistic activities, the city and its region was an exemplar of cosmopolitan progressivism, under the leadership of Károly Kamermayer (1829–1897), its long-standing mayor, and his successor József Márkus (1852–1915). This liberal nationalism, however, gave way to a particularly potent form of anti-Semitism that has only minimally been suppressed to this day. After World War I and the collapse of the Hapsburg Empire, the region saw a brief effort at a Communist takeover in 1919, which was replaced by ultranationalist Magyar and anti-Semitic political factions. This increasing xenophobia led to the establishment in the mid-1930s of the Arrow Cross Party, an explicitly Fascist ultranationalist organization. The city and its society provide an example of how Western cultural progressivism may rapidly fall apart under the constraints of an ultranationalist ideology. This core ultranationalism is represented today by the contemporary far-right party Jobbik, which has strong anti-Semitic leanings, and by the influential politician Viktor Orbán, who has frequently rallied his supporters during the past decade with his criticism for the political left "foreigners" and "foreign cosmopolitans." To frame this in our model, Budapest moved from a cosmopolitan center of social dominance under the Hapsburgs to that of a multicultural city under the stewardship of Kamermayer and Márkus and, with the fall of the Hapsburgs, to a social dominant culture and then to a totalitarian culture—which gave way to foreign totalitarian control by the Soviets after World War II. The contemporary faux democracy is at risk of moving into an antiforeigner and anti-Semitic autocracy, or worse.

Summary

Cataclysmic cultural change constitutes a sudden social psychological shift in the relationship of the individual to the state. The dramatic shift impacts the institutions, norms, and civil liberties of the members of the nation-state. The consequences of this cultural change are unevenly experienced by the members of the nation, with a winner–loser ethos being central to the new social stasis. The traumatic impact of change on members of diverse social groups is defining of both the narrative and the collective injury suffered by the cataclysmic social upheaval. This collective trauma may marginalize social groups and stifle political dissent as a consequence of the shock and awe of the suddenness of the regime change.

Our survey research conducted immediately after the election of November 2016 revealed the notable psychological impact on the voters for the losing candidate, Secretary Clinton. Results also illustrated the emotional link of the election for many individuals to the 9/11 World Trade Center terror attack and to the loss of a loved one.

In terms of social power, the change in status is defined along identities of race, gender, religion, sexual orientation, and nationality. The creation of a new social stasis reflects the imposition of sanctions against marginalized out-groups. Additionally, out-groups are further penalized for being in the "losing camp" in terms of restriction of civil rights and, importantly, increasingly becoming the targets of microaggressions and ultimately forms of hate violence. This aggression toward out-groups is conducted via governmental sanctions (such as laws against immigration or women's reproductive rights) as well as actors of the state (such as federal police) and empowered vigilante members of the "winner camp." Finally, the new social stasis results in significant shifts in the representation of social problems in the media and the capacity of minority voices to exercise dissent.

CHAPTER 2

Selling Biased Ideology, or How to Elect an Autocrat

The U.S. presidential election revealed that the conventional wisdom about voter perceptions and their subsequent behavior was fundamentally wrong. Hillary Clinton was consistently seen as the clear front-runner in the mainstream polling leading up to the November 8, 2016, election in terms of both national and state-based projections. Well-thought-through statistical models were consistently supportive of her election. While she won the national plurality by over 2.5 million votes, her performance in the Electoral College proved way off the statistical mark. So, at a time of big data and scientifically massaged opinion surveying, this high-profile election delivered a surprising outcome, which resulted in a fundamental reset of the societal stasis of the United States.

We will consider how characteristics of bias, and the *social psychological correlates associated with bias,* influenced voters to enter into this period of social instability. Two particularly powerful motivators, mortality salience and cultural anchoring, influenced the voter decision making that led to the precarious situation in which we, at this writing, find ourselves. These two psychological factors in the run-up to November 8 emphasized the threat to the nation state and activated voters' collective vulnerability. Other rallying points in overturning the political status quo included linking immigration with crime and making Islamic faith synonymous with terrorism. The failure of the state to address economic fears of the constituency was tied to the practice of liberal democracy, intellectual elites, and women asserting their reproductive rights. These themes were presented as explanatory of a cultural vulnerability that led to the risky right shift of the electorate. We consider these factors more fully below.

Fear Activation: Mortality Salience and Terror Threat

How do we feel when we think about our death? A body of research indicates that heightening an individual's awareness of his or her own mortality influences how they view the needs and experiences of other people. We live in an age in which information of all kinds—the Dow Jones industrial average, the terror alert level, the short-term interest rate, the national jobs numbers—serve to inform us, supposedly to tell us how we are doing. So how does information about our mortality prime our concern and awareness to risk? Additionally, how does heightened self-awareness of mortality impact the attitudes we hold about the world around us? The study of "mortality salience" and what is also called terror management theory (TMT) have provided insight into *what type* of information impacts us and *how* it impacts our attitudes toward others.

Mortality salience involves heightened awareness of our death. Our response to this existential threat results in a value- and attitude-based identification with traditions that may suggest life after death (Jonas & Fischer, 2006) or that allows us to live in terms of our group or nationality across generations. Mortality awareness is also related to how persons respond to perceived threat. For example, Pyszczynski and colleagues (2006) reported that politically conservative persons, primed by mortality salience, led to increased support for military intervention in a Middle East political crisis. Pyszczynski, Greenberg, and Solomon (2003) also observed in the experimental manipulation of mortality awareness a shift toward more punitive judgments of defendants in mock-trial simulations. Their research underscores how awareness of one's own demise can result in a less empathic and more punishing approach in dealing with the problems of (weak) others.

Research has also shown that awareness of terror threat is moderated at a collective level by identification with our in-groups—as evidenced by embracing values and behaviors of the in-group. This response, to find meaning in the face of mortality, is consistent with the proposition of Becker (1973) that human activity constitutes a means by which to avoid awareness of one's own death. As Harmon-Jones and others (1997) have reported, the individuals' mortality fears are reduced by thoughts and experiences that enhance positive self-esteem. As they note, greater personal self-appraisal is associated with a reduction in perception of group vulnerability. This issue of self-esteem and economic threat will be considered below.

When people perceive threat, they show a greater desire for a social order that is imposed by leaders who espouse authority and control. As research has demonstrated, mortality salience raises in-group identification. Li and colleagues (2015) found that priming individual mortality awareness enhances in-group favoritism. Greenberg and his colleagues (1990) had already established that hostility toward out-group persons increased when there was a perceived threat to the individuals' in-group or the *in-group's values and prejudices*. Along these same lines, the study of *actual terror threat* has been found to result in higher tolerance of policies against ethnic minorities. As Canetti-Nisim, Halperin, Sharvit, and Hobfoll (2009) have observed in Israel, exposure to terror activity reduces individuals valuing out-group persons. In their longitudinal research, they found that perceived threat from Palestinian citizens was related to terror experiences as well as to personal levels of distress, which predicted policies excluding Palestinian citizens in Israel. As was already suggested in Chapter 1, cataclysmic cultural change occurs when the voter activity is transformed from a process of political choice to aligning with cultural norms in a context of conflict. This framing of a political choice as participation in a cultural war is consistent with TMT.

In looking at the November 8 contest, we can see how this cultural war argument—of choosing between cultural worldviews—framed the election in terms of religious faith. For white Evangelical Christians, there was significant opposition to legalized abortion at the time of the election, with 69% stating in a 2016 Pew Research survey that abortion should be illegal in all or most cases (Fingerhut, 2016). Many Evangelical voters noted that they chose Donald Trump as a function of his pledge to place jurists on the U.S. Supreme Court who would restrict a woman's reproductive health. In the 2016 election, Trump received roughly 80% of the Evangelical vote, according to *Washington Post* exit polls; this is the highest reported Evangelical support for a Republican presidential candidate since 2004 (Pulliam Baily, 2016). For these voters, this single-issue approach to the election reflects a response to mortality: faith leads to decisions that keep culture stable and predictable over time. For Evangelical voters, the cultural war was won, even if the figurehead is incongruent with many of the core values that these voters hold dear.

A powerful motivator found in polling results concerned economic threat. Again, consistent with TMT, the perceived vulnerability of many voters played a role in the election of Trump. Although this is consistent with the mortality threat right-shift phenomenon, it is incomplete if consideration of the cultural embeddedness of privilege is not also considered in the rejection of a model of governance that had endured throughout the life span of the electorate. We will consider how deeper cultural forces influenced voter behavior in this regard.

Activating Deep Cultural Traditions

The psychological study of culture can help us recognize the underlying motivational factors that can shape political attitudes. Liu, Sibley, and Huang (2013) have identified how deeper core cultural symbols influence social attitudes. As was found in the U.S. survey research on critical historical events (see Chapter 1), Liu and his colleagues found in Southeast Asian countries a high level of consensus as to what constituted major national events of the culture (Huang, Liu, & Chang, 2004). For Liu et al. (2013), this connection to a deeper cultural reference point is called *anchoring*. The anchoring of culture-specific symbols and events to a political message can both activate social identity—that is, identification with a specific social group—and influence attitudes about political issues. As Liu et al. note, "History is an important symbolic resource in mobilizing support for public policies regarding intergroup relations, because temporal continuity is central to claims of legitimacy for peoples" (2013, 2). These anchoring phenomena constitute basic propositions of what is good or bad for the in-group. They identify with and remind the members of the in-group of the values and norms to which each social group ascribes. Historical events, therefore, occurring in specific cultures, both shape member attitudes and solidify their in-group identity.

The process of cultural anchoring is critical in the current movement away from a liberal democratic tradition, one that has loosened the constraints on cultural inclusion and toward a nationalistic—and potentially autocratic—political system. What will be discussed below is how specific cultural themes and psychological strategies were utilized to motivate the populace to dismantle the liberal democratic system in the 2016 election. The anchoring phenomena of relevance to November 8 include the privilege of male whiteness and the historical tradition of the subjugation of racial and ethnic minorities.

As I have noted previously (Dunbar, Blanco, & Crèvecouer-MacPhail, 2017), the shared beliefs of many persons in the United States are not that far removed from hate crime offenders and the emerging alt-right ultranationalist movement. "Often the hate crime perpetrators reflect the social biases of substantial numbers of the dominant culture. The ascription to anti-immigration, anti-taxation, pro–gun ownership, and hostility to sexual minorities—which arguably reflect the worldview of many U.S.-based domestic terrorists—are commonly endorsed by many Americans in national opinion surveys" (Marsden, 2012, www .pewresearch.org). As we observed in the 2016 election, this anchoring to nationalist, in-group privilege served as a vehicle for support of reactionary political platforms and the unleashing of a heightened level of intergroup animus. So the potential to link (i.e., anchor) a political campaign to a core belief system of xenophobia is viable, even if fraught with the risk of mobilizing individuals to engage in intolerant and hostile behaviors with out-group persons.

A critical anchoring tactic of the Trump campaign was the striving for a culturally homogeneous past. For many white people, and particularly white men, the anchoring was to a time of racial and linguistic dominance. U.S. Census data shows that the percentage of residents identified as white in 1900 was 87.9%, with 89.5% of the population classified as white in 1950, and in 2000 75.1% residents were non-Hispanic white; the most recent census in 2010 identified 72.4% of the population as white.

White men, specifically, are overrepresented in positions of political leadership; while they make up 31% of the U.S. population, they hold 65% of all elected public offices (Henderson, 2014). White privilege is not just for the wealthy, at least from an economic standpoint. For example, countrywide data shows that whites are less likely to live in poverty than the national average (U.S. Census, 2004). Additionally, in a review of male racial differences in income levels, Hamilton, Austin, and Darity (2011) found that for all white men over the age of 25, the median hourly wage for full-time employees was $20.84, whereas for black men the median hourly wage was $14.90.

For the first 364 years in which Europeans colonized North America, slavery was legal. From 1501 to 1865, slavery was sanctioned in North American society (Draper, n.d.). For the first 89 years of the United States, slavery was found in many of the states. As of this writing, by comparison, for 151 years the country has existed as a political and cultural institution in which involuntary servitude has been abolished, though the experiences of the Chinese immigrant "Coolie" workers, coal miners, and sharecroppers may raise questions as to the veracity of this claim.

In terms of the 11/8 campaign, the mobilization of this embedded xenophobia in the United States was a function of emphasizing repeatedly the risk to the collective, inclusive of the threat of terror and violence, and one that was best responded to by harking back to a time when the culture was "great" and implicitly more culturally homogeneous. So a (terror) threat that connotes harm to the collective is effectively addressed by raising the group identity, via cultural anchoring, to a place of privilege and dominance over social out-groups. We will now review some of the specific talking points that amplified our sense of vulnerability.

Culturally Anchored Themes of Terror Threat

A powerful and unifying theme of the 2016 election was the depiction of immigrants and visible ethnic minorities as forces invading the homeland. In activating an array of out-group stereotypes, this campaign issue was singularly divisive among voters and the media alike. As Trump stated as part of his announcement of running for president on June 16, 2015, "When Mexico sends its people, they're not sending their best. They're not sending you. They're not sending you. They're sending people that have lots of problems, and they're bringing those problems with us. They're bringing drugs. They're bringing crime. They're rapists" (*Washington Post*, 2015).

In some cases, the fear invoked was accompanied by specific consequences. So when Trump asserted Mexican immigrants were criminals and rapists, he proposed building a wall along the border between the two countries and established with his audience that the Mexican government would "pay for it!" His statements indicating Islamists were inherently terror risks led to his proposal of banning entry of all members of the faith into the United States; subsequently the idea of an Islamic "registry" was proposed as a way of monitoring individuals within the United States. In one case, Trump linked the issue of Latin heritage to de facto bias against Euro-whites, specifically himself, when he asserted he could not receive a fair trial if a lawsuit in which he was involved was adjudicated by a judge with a Hispanic surname.

The recent invocation of hostility toward immigrants reflects a longstanding ambivalence concerning persons relocating to the United States. This ambivalence has been evidenced in ethnic violence since the founding of the republic, informal discrimination of non-U.S.-born persons, and systemic forms of restriction of in-migration. Examples of the latter are found in the Immigration Act of 1917, the Johnson-Reed Immigration Act of 1924, the National Origins Act, and Asian Exclusion Act, which established quotas on immigrants—at the time, often from eastern European and Mediterranean countries. These laws also banned Arab and most Asian immigration (Hayes, 2001). The Johnson-Reed Act, based on the 1790 and 1870 Naturalization Acts, established that only Caucasian persons were eligible for naturalization. This legislation stayed in place with only modest modifications for the following 40 years.

Anti-immigrant attitudes were reflected in the infamous criminal trial and execution in the 1920s of Sacco and Vanzetti. These two men, who were born in Italy and had immigrated to the United States, adhered to an anarchist political philosophy. Their trial, which included many elements suggesting their innocence of charges of having murdered a paymaster during a robbery, drew international attention and underscored the hostility toward immigrants of the post–World War I United States. Thematically, this case shares a good deal in common with our current concerns about Islamic terrorists in that Sacco and Vanzetti were both members of an Italian anarchist network—the Galleanist group—which advocated violence against the government. Along with other less-celebrated cases, the Sacco and Vanzetti trial illustrates the linking of political violence and immigration in U.S. history. As a country of immigrants, our hostility to foreign-born persons includes a perceived threat to cultural norms, to economic security, and to public safety due to ideological violence.

Role of Perceived Economic Deprivation

The U.S. presidential election served as—or was seen as serving—an effort of the marginalized members of society to upset the established means of governance of the state. Pundits now view these voter behaviors as evidence of their desire for fundamental political and economic reform. Specific grievances, worries, and resentments were found in the themes of oppression of the core culture of the country, impacted by perceived immigration threat. The economic failures of the traditional members of the society—characteristically white, male, and less educated—were linked to the perceived discrimination against them by the welfare state, the jury-rigging of and complex bad practices of institutions such as Wall Street, and the behemoth financial institutions that taxpayers bailed out after the 2008 economic crisis.

This "protest vote" came to incorporate animosity toward perceived corporate greed, political dishonesty, and, significantly, a broad array of out-group scapegoats. The linkage of economic vulnerability and bias against out-groups includes not only a sense of competition but also resentment. Krefetz (1982) argues, for example, that anti-Semitic stereotypes involve envy and jealousy of Jewish affluence, rather than religious animus. The psychographics of these voters, who were frequently middle-aged and older white men who were unemployed or underemployed and frequently less educated, suggests a group of individuals who experienced relatively low status in their society. Psychological research would depict many of these men as encountering life adjustment and self-esteem problems, which illustrates the impact of unemployment on adult well-being in terms of self-denigration and low self-esteem (Goldsmith, Veum, & Darity 1977). Developmental research has shown that self-esteem typically increases through adulthood and begins to decline around age 60 (Orth, Trzesniewski, & Robins, 2010). Indeed, as a block of voters, these individuals seemed to be quite contrary to candidate Trump, who epitomized a nouveau riche lifestyle of glamor, deal making, womanizing, and publicity seeking. This bloc of voters, experiencing low self-esteem and suffering from the stress of economic threat and occupational failure, might have viewed Trump as an exemplar figure whom they wished to emulate.

Similar narratives of economic deprivation in prior epochs have been linked to hate violence and cultural cataclysms that shifted democracies to the autocrats. One infamous example of the former is found in the study of the epidemic of lynching of blacks in the late 19th and 20th centuries. This is further discussed in Chapter 3.

A frequently cited illustration of the linkage between economic threat, cataclysmic cultural change, and xenophobia is found in Weimar Germany after World War I. Runaway inflation of the German currency in the mid-1920s led to widespread social unrest and political agitation from both right-wing and leftist groups. The hyperinflation of 1922 and 1923 was one of the most destabilizing experiences of the German government in the aftermath of losing World War I (Widdig, 2001). The severe inflationary problems experienced by the German populace led to fundamental distrust of the Weimar Republic. Widdig observes how this decade-long economic crisis was experienced throughout popular culture as a traumatic ending of the society that had existed before World War I of 1914. This economic trauma sensitized individuals to consider more radical political solutions across the political spectrum. With numerous political parties to represent siloed constituencies, the most influential of the radical antirepublican parties were the Communists and the National Socialists (Nazis). The state remained in power only through the maintenance of precarious unity governments. Many of the political parties that came to influence social discourse questioned the legitimacy of the state and sought scapegoat out-groups, including the Jews, capitalists, Communists, and international governing bodies like the League of Nations. In the later stages of rule after 1930, the Brüning government implemented an austerity program in response to the world economic crisis that resulted in further monetary destabilization and, importantly, mass unemployment. The desperation of the age led many voters to support the agenda of the National Socialists, who garnered 36% of the vote in the second round of the election for the presidency. Within months of the election the National Socialists were positioned in the government, and after the February 1932 Reichstag Fire, many civil liberties were restricted under the Reichstag Fire Decree. After many years of economic deprivation, the swift shift in political rule allowed for the replacement of a democratic system with that of a totalitarian state—one which never received the support of the majority of the German citizenry.

The examples of economic deprivation found in the rise of National Socialism in Germany and the lynch violence in communities of poverty in the United States illustrates the vulnerability of the citizenry to engage in social protest via the commission of hate violence. At the same time, the majority of poor whites in the South did not perpetrate antiblack violence and the National Socialists never garnered even 40% of the popular vote in Germany. So if economic deprivation is a risk factor for the perpetration of violence toward out-groups in liberal democracies, it only is so for a handful of individuals. In autocratic governments, this enactment of violence may be taken up by agents of the state (e.g., the police).

It is also worth considering that more authoritarian and politically conservative individuals may respond more harshly under conditions of economic threat. Rickert (1998) noted that experimentally, economically threatened authoritarians, when compared with noneconomically threatened authoritarians or low-scoring authoritarian subjects were significantly more likely to support restriction of government assistance to marginalized social groups and to oppose state support for a woman's right to secure an abortion.

Examining the Rhetoric of Cataclysmic Change

How a political message is communicated may be more important than *what* it says. Since Aristotle's fourth century BC treatise on rhetoric, the practice of persuasion has been considered in terms of not only its technical but its performative qualities. In his framework, the ethos of persuasion included sincerity, knowledge, empathy, charisma, and power. Psychological science has considered these qualities in leaders specifically in regard to the influencing of listener/follower attitudes. The psychological study of charismatic leaders has been examined in terms of their influence in changing workplace behaviors, social attitudes, group norms, and political attitudes (Fiol, Harris, & House, 1999). Charismatic leadership theory (Weber, 1946) proposes that highly charismatic leaders effect change by presenting the follower with a discernible vision that motivates the follower toward obedience and attitude change.

Highly charismatic leaders appeal to the followers' emotions and sense of connection to the leader (House, Spangler, & Woyke, 1991).

Charismatic persuasion (Conger & Kanungo, 1998) and the stylistic strategies of the leader are important in terms of how they influence their followers. Specifically, the charismatic leader seeks to create a commitment of the follower to both the ideology and the leader themselves (Musser, 1987). Some of the elements of charismatic leadership include articulation of a belief or vision, the creation of the impression of an empathic bond with their followers, and a level of risk tolerance that challenges social or institutional conventions. Leadership *tone* may even be more important to political persuasion than perceived threat. In a study seeking to assess the role of threat exposure to facilitate a "conservative shift" for 2004 and 2008 candidates George W. Bush and John McCain (Sterling, Jost, & Shrout, 2016), it was found that perceptions of the candidates' charismatic leadership traits were more influential than exposure to death primes.

Leader-driven hate-based persuasion often invokes stereotype activation targeting a specific out-group. Additionally, as seen in the election of 2016, the cultural anchoring of bias, signified through the use of hate speech, amplified the themes of social inequity to establish in the follower the perceived threat posed by social out-groups. The practice of hate-based persuasion includes legitimizing in-group privilege, reminding the follower of experiences of intergroup conflict, using the priming power of inequities between the in-group and out-group, and establishing a means of redress for intergroup problems. For Trump, the use of ethnic stereotypes and hate rhetoric blew through conventional "code" of opposition to multiculturalism; the immediacy of his rhetoric relied on his explicit hostility toward cultural out-groups. In their analysis of Trump's stump speeches, the *New York Times* (Healy & Haberman, 2015) noted "the most striking hallmark was Mr. Trump's constant repetition of divisive phrases, harsh words and violent imagery that American presidents rarely use."

The rhetoric of intolerance employed by candidate Trump invoked this "cultural wars" argument. This was reflected in the themes of an immigrant invasion, of immigrants being a fifth column for terrorists, and of a ruling cultural elite who were indifferent to this degradation of society by "the other"—religious, ethnic, linguistic, and cultural out-groups. This was juxtaposed with the vision to reestablish a great tradition of nationalist hegemony. The vitriol of the Trump speeches created an emotional bond with his followers. The themes of threat activated adverse out-group stereotypes and validated the emotional needs of resentment and revenge of his followers. The sense of vulnerability that he activated in his followers was intimately tied to security and economic concerns related to immigration, even though research shows that immigration attitudes are minimally correlated with the individual's actual economic condition (Hainmueller & Hopkins, 2014).

Connecting with the Common Man

Donald Trump, a graduate of the Wharton School of Business, adopted a public speaking style that sounded more like a truck driver from New Jersey than a child of privilege. This creation of concern for the follower is one of the core dimensions found in the literature on charismatic leadership. For Trump, this included running as "the outsider candidate," as the nonpolitician in the primaries, and as an adversary to a lifelong politician like Secretary Clinton.

In commenting on the image of Trump, Michael D'Antonio, who wrote a biography on the candidate, discussed some of what can be considered the deeper reference points that his image invokes. He noted, "You know what I think is really odd about this is that this sort of makes him the classic '60s, early-'70s baby-boomer, anti-establishment ruffian. Everybody talks about how it was, this cliché version of the anti-war hippie person that represents the '60s, but I think this narcissistic, anti-establishment tenor of his personality and what he's doing now makes him the inheritor of all of that chaos. He just never outgrew it" (Kruse, 2017). When we look at the rhetoric and arguments put forward by candidate Trump, it becomes clear how his transformation from a person of privilege into the voice of the common man is accomplished through the simplicity of his message and the harkening back to a bias-based perspective on the problems of the nation being due to social out-groups. This xenophobia is particularly tied to a sense of a world we have lost, in which cultural out-groups have despoiled the country.

The Vision of Nostalgia

In the U.S. presidential campaign, Trump drove home his mantra of "Make America Great Again." As we have discussed, this referring back to a better time is consistent with a Eurocentric view of when the country was better. This looking back to a better time also harmonizes (as we shall discuss) with the emergent alt-right valuing of white dominance.

This appeal to the past derives its power from its ambiguity. The most consistent aspect of the argument has involved prescribing means of excluding and deporting ethnic and cultural out-groups. The appeal from a hate-based worldview is therefore viable for what it proposes to do to the denigrated other, but it is unclear how this will improve the economic welfare of the supposedly economically marginalized white populace (even though, again, data suggest whites do better financially than other economic groups aside from Asian-Pacific persons). As with many of his proposals, Trump has abstained from providing a detailed platform and has instead provided an agenda driven by emotional devices. Trump did not promote specific policies but rather provided culturally anchored arguments that play on the xenophobia of his followers. This approach in his campaign—relying on emotional appeals at the expense of policy details—may have resonated more effectively with voters with lower education levels particularly those concerned about their economic privation.

Consistent with the literature on charismatic leadership, Trump connected with what was often referred to as his base. In the run-up to the election many pundits expressed concern for his candidacy that this voting constituency was too narrow. Perhaps one of the lessons from his surprising victory is the depth and breadth in the general population's concern about economic threat—and our culturally anchored latent xenophobia. The cultural wars formula of immigrant invasion, vulnerability to terrorism, nationalist resentment, and taking back "our society" was consistently interwoven with old-fashioned hate speech. The discourse was unvarnished and bereft of code. This is a reversal of the use of language that was obliquely biased. Rather the rallying arguments were explicitly biased. As has been found, anger, more than anxiety or enthusiasm, will motivate voters to act (Valentino, Brader, Groenendyk, & Hutchings, 2011). The harsh political invective of Trump constituted "fighting words," for both his target (e.g., Latinos), for whom they inflicted a reminder of their outsider status, and for his followers, via his incitement of their anger and xenophobia.

Trump's stated vision and discourse was generally pitched at a very simple level. As the Web site Politico's reporter Jack Shafer found in his text analysis of the Trump speeches, "Run through the Flesch-Kincaid grade-level test, his text of responses score at the 4th-grade reading level. For Trump, that's actually pretty advanced. *All the other candidates rated higher* (italics added), with Ted Cruz earning 9th-grade status. Ben Carson, Mike Huckabee, and Scott Walker scored at the 8th-grade level. John Kasich, the next-lowest after Trump, got a 5th-grade score." In connecting with his followers, Trump has modeled their comprehension of intergroup and social problems at a very immediate and elementary level. What may be persuasive is also fundamentally incomplete.

In a variety of studies, it appears Secretary Clinton's speeches came in at a modestly higher grade level than did Trump's. One review indicated that Clinton's speeches fell between the fifth- and seventh-grade level ("The World's Smartest," n.d.). This modest discrepancy between Trump and Clinton suggests his speech could appear more direct than her somewhat more rhetorically complex language. Given that estimates indicate roughly a quarter of Americans read at or below a fifth-grade level (Statistic Brain, 2016), this may have been an advantage to Trump.

In addition, importantly, out-group prejudice has been linked to lower levels of intelligence, finding, for example, that lower verbal intelligence was related to more negative attitudes toward blacks (Wodtke, 2016) and, specifically, groups seen as unconventional (Brandt & Crawford, 2016). This association is hardly new; Adorno and his colleagues suggested that authoritarians evidenced a paucity of cognitive complexity (Adorno et al. 1950). A recent large-scale study found that poor abstract-reasoning skills, anti-LGBT attitudes, and lower childhood intelligence predicted higher levels of racism in adulthood (Hodson & Busseri, 2012). So, although the simplification of speech was not dramatically different between Trump and Clinton, the impact may have been significant for up to a quarter of the population and more particularly persons who are receptive to blaming out-groups for their social and economic problems. Trump's simple speech may have had more of a stimulating effect on individuals prone to bias. His use of language to persuade, in terms of content, complexity, and emotionality, was more closely matched to voters vulnerable to stereotype activation.

Attacking the Standing Government and Its Institutions

Questioning the standing government and the leadership of President Obama was a central theme throughout Trump's campaign. Explicitly, Trump spoke to the ideal of a preferred national past that needed to be resurrected. Implicitly, he anchored his message to (historically) racial dominance.

The cataclysmic change of 11/8 resulted in the rejection of the liberal democratic tradition; this denigration of the democratic model of governance underscores the shift to a potentially autocratic system. For Trump, in the run-up to 11/8, this denouncement incorporated U.S. international relations, the process of voter participation, and the role of the media. The use of alt-right conspiracy theories out of whole cloth was linked to criticism of the election process itself being rigged (pre-November 8 voting) and of the vote tally being compromised by illegal voting (post-November 8 voting) and to charges of the Obama administration being complicit in efforts to blame hacking of data sources on Russia. His comments and actions toward the media were frequently provocative. His criticism of Arianna Huffington, the owner of the Huffington Post online newsfeed was "@ariannahuff is unattractive both inside and out. I fully understand why her former husband left her for a man—he made a good decision" (Strochlic, 2015). Similarly, Trump criticized as corrupt evidence of economic stability; he lambasted the "fake" stock market rally fueled by the Fed's policies. He charged over and over again that "Obama is manipulating the jobs numbers." And the U.S. economy was in "terrible shape" (Richter, 2016).

For Trump, charges of corruption in the standing government became an important message that he channeled to his constituency. His reference to "draining the swamp" is perhaps unintentionally Biblical, as with Jesus in his casting out of the money changers from the temple. So candidate Trump, a presumed billionaire, assumes the faux-populist perspective of banning lobbyists from his government, as in driving them out of the institution, which politics as usual has made into a den of thieves. Likewise, he employed a form of clinical projection in accusing his adversary Clinton's charitable foundation of being illegal when his own foundation was reported to have used funds for purchasing personal paintings of himself. His observation of fighting the established order was a critical rhetorical device to bond himself to the alienated electorate "I am running against the Washington insiders, just like I did in the Republican Primaries," as he once tweeted during the presidential election.

"Oh, it looks good" is an example of the use of objectifying rhetoric. For Trump, this most famously applies to his many comments about women. However, racism inherently objectifies and deindividuates the (racial) other. At best, the other person is a member of a group—and not seen as a unique individual—at worst they are viewed as a thing. People have rights, objects don't. In addition, we find in the rhetoric of Trump how an array of social out-groups was seen as objects. As his rival Clinton noted during their second debate, Trump has objectified an array of groups: women, immigrants, Mexicans, Muslims, and people with disabilities. As Liu et al. (2013) noted, the use of objectifying rhetoric can anchor an attitude in a cultural context, making such attitudes impervious to change.

In his many speeches, Trump portrayed out-groups as threatening and undesirable. Objectification of individuals—or social groups—represents to the listener, in a concrete fashion, concepts which are otherwise abstract, unfamiliar, or alien. Objectifying other people simplifies experiences of intergroup contact and eliminates the capacity for empathy. It further allows for the depiction of the out-group individual in terms of visual characteristics, which may be judged in terms of their favorability. As Trump commented about a woman he was admiring, "Oh, it looks good."

This objectification is not to be taken as just another comment about being intolerant. Rather, objectification serves as a gateway to punishment and violence. As many experienced criminal investigators know, seeing the victim as a thing and not a person facilitates aggression. Studies show that men's capacity to objectify women by their appearance is linked to their tolerance of sexual violence and harboring negative attitudes toward women who have been the victims of sex crimes (Rudman & Mescher, 2012). As Rudman and Mescher stated in their research on objectification and sexual violence, "Automatically objectifying women by associating them with objects, tools, and things was also positively correlated with men's rape proclivity. In concert, the research demonstrates that men who implicitly dehumanize women (as either animals or objects) are also likely to sexually victimize them."

People as such take precedence over objects. An implication of the rhetoric of Trump is his use of authoritative power to promote aggression against an objectified out-group—Trump's "it." As some of the classical studies of Milgram (1963) have shown, followers will largely submit to commands of authorities to inflict harm on strangers. Two of the implications of Milgram's work are the manipulation of the follower to be obedient to the leader and the creation of an agentic state—in which the follower feels they become the agent for an authority's requests. Again, the theme of establishing a need for obedience is a core element in the authoritarian leader and the authoritarian system.

The use of authoritative influence is critical in linking rhetoric with ideology. Trump has employed a classical form of persuasion—the argumentum ad baculum—or arguing with the implication of threat and fear (Walton, 2000) to those who disagree with him (and where compliance often results in accepting a fallacious conclusion). "The ad baculum derives its strength from an appeal to human timidity or fear and is a fallacy when the appeal is not logically related to the claim being made" (Philosophy 103, n.d.). In other words, the emotion resulting from threat, rather than logical persuasion, is employed to gain acceptance of the purported conclusion of the argument. This method of argumentation is again consistent with the authoritarianism, with the explicit threat of failure to comply being linked to subsequent punishment. One of the more striking examples of this is Trump's statement that he was elected in a landslide, which has often been disputed (Kessler, 2016), and that he would have won the popular vote except for millions of fraudulent illegal voters having supported Clinton—to which the news site Politico commented, "Donald Trump on Sunday used his platform as president-elect to peddle a fringe conspiracy theory to justify his loss of the popular vote, claiming without evidence that millions of people voted illegally Nov. 8" (Restuccia, 2016).

Another example of his merging threat and authoritative power into his discourse occurred during the second presidential debate. Seemingly spontaneously, Trump expressed his intentions to prosecute his opponent, Secretary Clinton, after his election as president. As he stated, "If I win, I am going to instruct my Attorney General to have a special prosecutor to look into your situation. . . . There's never been so many lies, so much deception. We're going to have a special prosecutor." He subsequently tweeted on October 9, "If I win—I am going to instruct my AG to get a special prosecutor to look into your situation because there's never been anything like your lies" (Fernholz, 2016).

Of note were the subsequent calls of "Lock her up!" from his audience, which were heard at his rallies after this debate. Similarly, Trump has linked the idea of his personal power and threat when he noted that he would force U.S. military personnel to engage in interrogation techniques more severe than waterboarding and retaliatory executions of terrorist's families—both of which are war crimes under international law. As he stated at the March 3, 2016, primary debate, "They won't refuse. They're not going to refuse me," he said. "If I say do it, they're going to do it" (Morton, 2016).

It is equally striking how frequently Trump effectively employed an argumentum ad hominem in talking about his political opponents; that is, his critiques were of the opponents as individuals—and not of substantive differences over policies. He did this to redirect an attack on the character of the individual. Candidate Trump used this form of argument in comments about the character of his political rivals and the appearance of his female adversaries. For example, he said of Carly Fiorina, "Look at that face! Would anyone vote for that? Can you imagine that, the face of our next president?" (Zimmerman, 2015), of Ted Cruz, "Ted Cruz is sick . . . there's something wrong with this guy" ("Trump: Cruz," 2016), Jeb Bush "poor, pathetic, low-energy guy" ("Trump: Bush," 2016), and Secretary Clinton's appearance, "I'm standing at my podium and she walks in front of me, right, . . . She walks in front of me, you know? And when she walked in front of me—believe me, I wasn't impressed" (Earle, 2016).

Core Elements of Hate-Based Political Rhetoric

So how are biased attitudes promoted in the political arena—specifically in a society that permits free speech under the First Amendment of the U.S. Constitution? We have reviewed some of the key themes in the recent presidential election and will now distill them to provide a simple form of analysis of bias-based persuasion. The activation of biased beliefs involves the following: (1) defining membership, (2) anchoring the argument to cultural signs, (3) defining the out-group, (4) characterizing the power relationship between the in-group and out-group, and (5) establishing a remedy to intergroup problems. These elements are summarized in Table 2.1 below. For the recipient/follower of the message, the consequence is the alignment of their personal experiences with the in-group–out-group power relationship. The follower's emotional and cognitive response is shaped to allow for behaviors to be guided by group-prescribed norms. Individual needs and responsibilities are shifted to that of the needs of the in-group, as defined by the core argument. The application of this model can be illustrated in terms of some of his critical policy points: immigration and terrorism.

In applying this model to the speeches and social media declarations of Trump prior to his election, we can examine his argument for his being

Table 2.1   Rhetorical Elements of Hate Persuasion

Membership:
> Who are we?
> How do we know who we are?

Anchor:
> What is our shared history?
> What symbols recall our heritage?

Who are/is the other:
> What transgressions are there?
> What harm have they caused?

Power relationships:
> Are we dominant?
> Equivalent
> Dominated

Solutions:
> How do we resolve this imbalance/transgression?

president vis-à-vis the issue of immigration. In his announcement of his intention to run for the presidency, Trump almost at once defines his base as an in-group by saying we are "not like them"—his characterization of immigrants included such threatening terms of rapists, terrorists, ISIS members, and "strongmen." The representation of the power relationship of the standing government vis-à-vis immigrants was one of impotence ("we don't know who they are") and bureaucratic indifference.

In terms of his solutions to this problem, Trump argued for the management of out-group relationships via exclusion, control, and elimination—characteristics of authoritarianism and ultranationalism. Specific prescriptions he proposed included "building a wall," carrying out mass deportations, and creating a more aggressive border policy in general. This is summarized in Table 2.2.

"Something really dangerous is going on" constitutes the core theme of Trump's narrative on terrorism. A theme repeated over and over is the link of Islam to terrorism. Images of the 9/11 terror attack (anchoring the issue to U.S. history) linked to a culturally alien ("not like us") religion becomes a basis of the narrative. The problem further is that the ruling government does not know what is happening, or worse is complicit in the terror threat. In commenting on his campaign speeches of late 2015, the *New York Times* noted, "On Thursday evening, his message was equally ominous, as he suggested a link between the shootings in San Bernardino, California, and President Obama's failure to say 'radical Islamic terrorism.' 'There is something going on with him that we don't know about,' Mr. Trump said of the president" (Healy & Haberman, 2015).

Table 2.2 Rhetorical Elements of Hate Persuasion: Immigrants

Membership:	You (we) are not them, system is weak ("Politicians aren't going to find them because they have no clue.")
Anchor:	Protect "us"—native-born, get us jobs
Who is the other:	Rapists, criminals, strongmen, terrorists
Power relationships:	Government is weak, borders are porous, we know nothing of who enters the country
Solutions:	Build a wall, carry out mass deportations, have a policy of exclusion; control them, eliminate them, expel them

Table 2.3 Rhetorical Elements of Hate Persuasion: Muslims

Membership:	You (we) are not them, system is weak ("Politicians aren't going to find them because they have no clue.")
Anchor:	Protect "us" —native-born, get us jobs
Who is the other:	Rapists, criminals, strongmen, terrorists
Power relationships:	Government is weak, borders are porous, we know nothing of who enters the country
Solutions:	Carry out mass deportations, have a policy of exclusion; monitor and control them with a Muslim registry

Trump famously reported witnessing after 9/11 thousands of Muslims in New Jersey celebrating the terror attacks, once more activating stereotypes that fail to make sense when checked against the historical record. The solution to the problem is classic authoritarianism, namely to eliminate the presence of persons from the Middle East by banning immigration to the United States and to document via a registry Muslims living in the country. In Table 2.3 the core elements of his prepresidency rhetoric are summarized.

The Role of Rapid Social Media Messaging and Trump

An important (current) form of social media is Twitter. As a form of communication, it provides a rapid means of self-expression and self-promotion. This has proven to be the most frequent method of communication for Trump. The range of issues and individuals he has crossed swords with is substantial, as is his use of the medium. Journalists Kevin Quealy and Jasmine Lee set out to analyze the content and patterns of Trump's Twitter communiqués. Reviewing his Twitter activity for over 14,000 tweets revealed the range of opponents he took on. These included the other Republican presidential hopefuls as well as Clinton. In addition, however, he has engaged in criticism of entertainers, media pundits, and the National Football League. As they commented in their review, "Mr. Trump likes to identify a couple of chief enemies and attack them until they are no longer threatening enough to interest him."

The contemporary social media provides an extremely condensed means of communication, be it postings on Facebook or Trump's tweets. This shaping of content to hot terms and keywords makes political commentary all but iconographic. What is important to consider, both as a commentary about candidate Trump and the issue of political rhetoric, is the absence of a stand-alone position that can be referred to. To put it simply, his not having a clear policy paper or fact sheet on his positions requires us to turn to his speeches and tweets as his policy position. What this also leads us to realize is how his shifting attitudes challenge his followers and critics alike to remain fluid in their own judgments about his positions, as they become inconsistent themselves.

Linking Alt-Right and Populist Ideologies

Trump, as a minor celebrity and business figure for the past three decades, was not initially associated with any specific political ideology. As his presidential campaign progressed, his alignment to extremist white groups became more discernible, merging the alt-right, traditional neo-Nazi, and Nazi themes into some of the online media materials his campaign produced. For example, his July 14, 2016, Twitter image of the American flag included a photograph of Nazi soldiers (Tharoor, 2015). On July 2, 2016, Trump's Twitter account tweeted an attack on Hillary Clinton that used anti-Semitic imagery with the commentary "Crooked Hillary—Makes History!" (Sottek, 2016). The image of the six-pointed Jewish star had previously been found on 8chan's/pol/ ("politically incorrect") board, an alt-right Web site.

As of this writing, the alt-right movement consists of a range of subgroups who are independent of the traditional conservative movement and frequently affiliated with white supremacy ideology. The term was initially employed by white supremacist Richard Spencer in 2010. Alt-right advocates predictably oppose civil right groups for minorities, immigration policies, and multiculturalism in schools and universities. Minimally, most alt-right advocates support restriction of immigration and a nationalistic foreign policy, which is isolationist. More critically, however, the alt-right subgroups frequently support a prowhite belief in governance and cultural dominance of the country. What has proven politically expedient for the Trump campaign has been, however, the amorphous composition of the alt-right itself. Some social critics would also stop short of considering the alt-right a formal movement with a core ideology that its members adhere to. This less-than-definite sense of who and what the alt-right represents—beyond being an alternative conservative political orientation—allows for political discourse to invoke the alt-right perspective when it is convenient and to ignore it when it is of less value. For an ideologically ambiguous candidate such as Trump, the alt-right moniker was particularly valuable as a means of rallying enthusiasm without being saddled with a formal doctrine or manifesto.

The alt-right and nonconforming stance of candidate Trump was also found in his range of prominent political supporters who came out for him prior to the election. This included alt-right extremists such as Don Black and David Duke and totalitarian leaders such as Vladimir Putin and Kim Jong-un. The commonality of these disparate individuals is their antidemocratic and ultranationalist political orientation. Some of these individuals were reported in Table 2.4 below.

The linking of two independent—and in many cases discrepant—political philosophies, the emerging alt-right fascism and the historical populism movements was both perplexing and effective. Historically, populism has referred to a range of popular social movements evidencing both conservative and progressive ideologies. Most frequently, the term has been applied to people's movements that are in opposition to ruling elites of the society. Issues of civil rights, of independence, and self-determination are frequent populist themes (McMath, 1993). Populists strive to overcome the dominance of elites and the state in seeking out opportunities for prosperity, self-expression, and representation in government affairs. In this way, populism shares some of the same responsibility for advocacy from outside the ruling government as does the civil society movement. In the United States, prior to our current political situation, populism has been associated with early 20th-century socialist movements based in the Great Plains states and the Midwest (Kazin, 1995; Wood, 2002). Perhaps the most widely recognized populist

Table 2.4   Political Figures Who Endorsed Donald Trump

Kim Jong-un, North Korean dictator, June 2, 2016

Rebel Brigade Knights of the Ku Klux Klan, May 2, 2016

Shafiq Rahman, Imam of Omar Mateen, the Orlando, Florida, nightclub assailant, June 16, 2016

Vladimir Putin, April 30, 2016

Don Black, founder of Stormfront, white nationalist Web site, December 14, 2015

Chinese Communist Party, April 18, 2016

Vojislav Seselj, Serbian war criminal, January 5, 2016

David Duke, former Grand Wizard of the KKK, February 26, 2016

Ilias Panagiotaros, Greek neo-Nazi leader, April 8, 2016

politician in U.S. history is Robert "Fighting Bob" La Follette, a progressive politician from Wisconsin who ran for the U.S. presidency in his "Progressive Party" in 1924. La Follette was against the larger corporate powers of his day but was also what would now be considered an isolationist—consistent in part, then with some of the current notions of early 21st-century populists on the right.

A more recent analysis of the term *populism* suggests it has come to represent fairly diverse political ideologies rather than a unitary idea. Schamis (2006), in applying the idea of populism and social democracy to Latin America feels that these terms "are not very useful today." Historically, the term populism has been applied to groups who may reject the classification itself (Canovan, 1981). So, in 2016 we find a political moniker frequently associated with left-of-center politics being assigned to a billionaire presidential candidate who admires totalitarian leaders such as Russia's Vladimir Putin. Importantly, the news media employed this reference point to Trump repeatedly, perhaps reflecting a lack of historical perspective or indifference to ideological accuracy.

The Hard Facts: Consequences of Normalizing Hate

We have reviewed the critical themes of a political campaign that has substantially focused on problems of race, immigration, poverty, and gender. These aspects of diversity have been linked by candidate Trump and other conservative presidential aspirants to social problems of unemployment, economic privation, and issues of reproductive rights. The solutions to these problems have been presented in a largely unidirectional fashion, in which diversity *is* the problem, and the solution is largely based on managing intergroup relationships via control and exclusion. In the bias-based rhetoric these problems of the country are associated with culture at a time when society has become increasingly multicultural, in which our economy has become highly dependent on international trade, and in which the world around us has also seen a growing level of interdependence.

So what are the consequences for us in this shift of social discourse from cultural relativism to overt intolerance? It would seem that for one thing, the idea of assigning blame for our material woes is substantially tied to the actions of the social out-groups—persons "not like us." It also is evident, as our leadership speaks in generalities of the problems of people who are different, that we too can become uncritical in our thoughts, attitudes, and behaviors. To put it simply, the rhetoric of intolerance has created a "permission-giving to hate" in our new societal stasis. This is what liberal democracy advocates lament. Persons on the end of the political spectrum that lost in the recent election are concerned about this new harsh speech about culture and nationality. There is a lot to be concerned about in terms of this lowering of the bar of cultural civility.

There is something else occurring, though, the classical conditioning of the populace via repeated exposure to intolerance as a normative social attitude. Getting used to hate as a social norm reflects the demise of a once healthy debate between tolerance of diversity and embracing diversity. In the liberal democratic tradition, this issue of social decorum had essentially served as a test as to what constituted being a better citizen in a multicultural community. So, the liberal democratic—or civil society—debate can center on whether we need to incorporate cultural values and behaviors from others into our own identity or do we practice the awareness of relativism, of valuing what we do not aspire to, which is what Walzer (1997) saw as a higher level of true intercultural acceptance? So, in a civil society, experiencing diversity asks the individual to reconceptualize who he or she is vis-à-vis the experiences of others and it also challenges us to be adaptive in our exposure to the lives of others whose beliefs, cultures, and values are unlike our own.

So what does this new societal stasis ask of us? Frankly, conformity to the norms of the winner of the cultural war. For some of us as Euro-whites and men, this is to retreat into who we are conventionally supposed to be—to paraphrase a quote of the comic Lenny Bruce—"Be a man, sell out." For many of us, however, this asks us to ascribe to a cultural standard that has little use for us, or literally, no place at the table for us. This points toward a giving over of power to the winning social norms that are intolerant of our heritages, beliefs, and elective affinities. So the risk here is of habituation to the norms of the new intolerance, of becoming obedient to the new intolerant norms of the winning side.

The foregoing proposition of simply being compliant is reductionistic on several fronts; in regard to intergroup violence, this is most critical in the presumption that we are all logic-driven, conforming, and compliant individuals. What does this new norming look like—under conditions of societal cataclysm—for the dissocial or impulse disturbed persons among us? For some of us, habituation to hate speech serves as a gateway to hate behavior. To speak about this from a mental health perspective, for impulse disordered persons and antisocial individuals generally, intolerance rapidly moves from ideas to actions. In what follows we will look at how bias speech and ideology mobilizes some individuals to act violently.

Finally, what are some of the real challenges for people "fighting" hate crimes in a culture that is normalizing hate speech? Not unimportantly, this will create a greater divide between social conservatives and left-of-center liberals, state and federal agencies, and public and private institutions than we have seen to date.

Summary

Many nation states in the West that have been governed under a liberal democratic tradition have recently shifted their political center to a nationalist and autocratic model. This transition has been accomplished via the mobilization of the voters to respond to deeply anchored cultural attitudes of in-group bias and fears of "the other." Activating old-fashioned xenophobia has proven to be politically expedient in the United States in the election of an isolationist and potentially autocratic government. In the election, the pervasive employment of out-group hostility and sexism created a stark challenge for voters in the linking of culture and governance as a singular choice. The linking of anti-immigrant attitudes to motivate support for Trump, coupled with opposition to a female alternative in Clinton played into the culture wars rhetoric. Individuals experiencing economic privation and a sense of falling behind as well as more stable communities of white populations at or near poverty levels appeared to be most vulnerable to the invocation of nostalgia, as signified in the campaign promise to "Make American Great Again." What this backward-looking rhetoric has activated are themes of male dominance, white privilege, and the desire to isolate or expel cultural out-groups.

Unfortunately, this invocation of bias has activated deep cultural divides, which have manifested in violence against institutions, public figures, and the general public alike. Having looked at the core themes and the rhetorical devices of persuasion, we will now look at some of the characteristics that make a follower a believer of the new societal stasis of intolerance and hatred.

CHAPTER 3

We Aren't in Kansas Anymore:
The Followers of Regime Change

I knew something historic was happening. I don't always have that feeling with things that later become historic. . . . There was a feeling of quiet determination in that church that night. . . . It was kind of like the feeling the night before you think you might be in battle—quiet acceptance and a kind of eagerness for it to start.

—Don Pfarrer, recalling being at the March on Washington and the "I Had a Dream" speech of Dr. Martin Luther King Jr. (Jones, 2013)

It was just 8:40 when a thundering wave of cheers announced the entrance of the presidium, with Lenin . . . loved and revered as perhaps few leaders in history have been. A strange popular leader—a leader purely by virtue of intellect; colorless, humorless, uncompromising and detached, without picturesque idiosyncrasies—but with the power of explaining profound ideas in simple terms, of analyzing a concrete situation. And combined with shrewdness, the greatest intellectual audacity.

—John Reed, 1919

Storms of applause and praise for the Führer fill the stadium. . . . A command interrupts the jubilation. The columns are lined up perfectly, the Presentation March sounds out, accompanied by the rhythmic beating of the drums. . . . Again and again the Presentation March plays. The Führer admires the wonderful discipline of the faithful youth of his only youth movement. The flags rise once more as young throats sing the songs of the nation as if in prayer.

The Führer stands in his car for a drive through the stadium and only after Adolf Hitler is long gone to the shouts of Heil fade.

—account of the Hitler Youth Day at the 1936
Nuremberg Rally (Bytwerk, 1998)

The horrible thing about the Two Minutes Hate was not that one was obliged to act a part, but that it was impossible to avoid joining in. Within thirty seconds any pretense was always unnecessary. A hideous ecstasy of fear and vindictiveness, a desire to kill, to torture, to smash faces in with a sledge hammer, seemed to flow through the whole group of people like an electric current, turning one even against one's will into a grimacing, screaming lunatic. And yet the rage that one felt was an abstract, undirected emotion which could be switched from one object to another like the flame of a blowlamp.

—George Orwell, *1984*

I was a little shocked at the faces, when Hitler finally appeared on the balcony for a moment. They reminded me of the crazed expressions I once saw in the back country of Louisiana on the faces of some Holy Rollers . . . they looked up at him as if he were a Messiah, their faces transformed into something positively inhuman.

—Peter Shirer, diary entry on the 1935 Nuremberg
Rally (*The Triumph of Hitler*, 2001)

These accounts, of which one is, of course, pure fiction, reflect the thoughts of persons caught up in a political event remembered by not only those who attended but the world community. The language reflects the sense of membership, energy, and awareness of something occurring of significance that will shape the feelings and attentions of those who were present. We have considered the psychological rhetoric of the influencer/leader already, what follows is an accounting of the dynamics of the influenced/follower. The focus, of course. will be on the 2016 U.S. presidential election, an event that in and of itself may not compare to the Russian revolution or the Nazi rallies, to Orwell's imagined group hate, or to the experiences of the members of the March on Washington, D.C., on August 23, 1963.

There are a range of psychologically laden issues impacting how individuals viewed the 2016 election, several of which directly are related to the study of intergroup conflict. We consider, largely in sequence, problems of economic privation, regional traditions of bias, deeper cultural traditions—anchors—of hate violence, which have all revealed their role in the shift in the United States after 11/8. Additionally, three specific forces that are based in decimation will be examined in terms of political choice and 11/8, namely, the suppression of out-group bias—the Bradley effect—the role of explicit and implicit sexism, which we will argue moved many ambivalent voters away from the conventional candidate, Secretary Hillary Clinton, and toward the ideologically provocative Donald Trump, and importantly the evolving role of real and imaginary social media content in framing arguments concerning culture and perceived threat.

The 2016 U.S. presidential election was decided by a narrow margin in three critical "swing states." As noted in the Cook Political Report, "Effectively 77,759 votes in three states (Wisconsin/Pennsylvania/Michigan) determined the Presidency (for) Republican presidential nominee Donald Trump" (Cook Political, 2016). So again, although Clinton had over 2% more of the popular vote, she lost the Electoral College and the presidency, by losing in regions often supportive of a Democratic candidate. This narrow but dramatic shift of the voting public will be considered for years to come. What we will consider in the initial period following the election are some of the psychological factors that impacted voter behavior: educational stratification, economic concerns, regional, urban–rural differences, and explicit and implicit out-group bias related to race and gender. How the issue of out-group bias and sexism were assessed in polling studies and how these issues were addressed in the media are crucial to understanding the dynamics that led to this cultural sea change.

Psychology of the Follower: Economic Deprivation

A good deal of what was argued for in the run-up to 11/8 was how to "make American great again." This implicitly spoke to the fears and concerns of millions of Americans. What we need to consider is the psychological impact that this theme of economic privation had on voters of diverse political ideologies. What we will look at is the role economic issues had on the voting public and then consider a second and important issue of how hate violence is related to economic problems found in our communities.

Many commentators since the election have asserted that a significant number of voters felt that their ongoing economic vulnerability was likely going to continue under Clinton and turned to Trump as a potential solution, even if there was reason to wonder about his ability, as a political novice, to deliver on his rhetoric of an economic rebirth in vulnerable industries such as manufacturing and coal production, concerns that ran deep in the swing states that voted for Trump and gave him the presidency.

Quattrone and Tversky (1988) have considered under what conditions individuals will avoid risk and conversely tolerate higher levels of risk. In most instances risk is linked to material reward in terms of the potential for subsequent financial gain. In what has been termed "prospect theory," it is observed that under status quo conditions of perceived gain, risk is avoided to maintain a (seemingly) stable reinforcement condition. However, under conditions of decline or perception of economic loss, individuals are open to risk when there is a perceived opportunity of reward.

As applied to choice theory, incumbent candidates are preferred when the opportunity for continued reward remains viable, as the individual does not want to risk a loss of what they currently experience. However, under conditions of loss, individuals are willing to pursue risk as a means of avoiding (further) loss. The work of Quattrone and Tversky suggest that this risk perception process is more explanatory when the decision-making process is contingent on the individual perceiving themselves as being in either a secure or an insecure condition. This contingency aspect of prospect theory can therefore explain outcomes better than the rational choice argument.

As applied to the 2016 election, voters' frustration with their economic situation would then reduce their level of risk avoidance. It would follow that if voters perceived Clinton as continuing the policies of the prior administration—in which she had held a senior leadership role—then the sense of personal benefit would dictate if a change to a high-risk candidate, such as Trump, was worthwhile. As Christopher Heintz comments, "With Trump and Brexit voters, we face people who, perceiving that they have lost something, are willing to take high risks. Economic frustrations cause risk seeking preferences, which contribute to motivating votes for Trump and Brexit" (Heintz, 2016). What is additionally important in this process of choice was how economic privation was married with xenophobic attitudes. Concerns of how immigrants were portrayed as taking away jobs and foreign governments were seen as jury-rigging trade agreements, so the argument goes, while the U.S. power elite was seen as a passive observer.

So what does the data suggest? A 2004, U.S. Census report indicated that the median income for white non-Hispanic families was $46,697, for Asian-Pacific families $57,518, for Hispanics $34,241, and for blacks

$30,212 (U.S. Census, 2005). Ten years later, 2014 U.S. Census data reported family median income for white non-Hispanics as $60,246, for Asian-Pacific families as $74,297, for Hispanics as $42,491, and for blacks as $35,398 (U.S. Census, 2015). The approximate income increase over this 10-year period (2004 to 2014) for whites and Asian-Pacifics is 29%, for Hispanics 24%, and for blacks only 17%. So nationally, on the average, whites have not fallen behind income-wise versus other ethnic/racial groups and have actually done significantly better than Hispanic and black families. So, while there are very significant regional and age issues that can be further explored in the income data, the idea of a dramatic economic decline nationally for most whites leading up to the 2016 election is not borne out.

In spite of the absence of a nationwide income drop for whites, Trump polled very well with them. For white voters, 58% supported him with only 37% voting for Clinton; for whites with less than a college education 67% voted for Trump—72% of men and 62% of women. For all voters, individuals who earned under $50,000 a year (36% of the electorate) voted 52% for Clinton and 41% for Trump (Henley, 2016). The sense of economic duress found in many Trump voters was at odds with government jobs data. In a *Washington Post* study conducted two weeks before the election, a large number of supporters of Trump overestimated the unemployment rate threefold; the majority selected the highest answer offered—"15 percent or higher" (Aytaç, Rau, & Stokes, 2016).

In examining the issue of economic well-being at a state level, several clear relationships were found between income and voting for candidate Trump. In a state-by-state analysis of the percentage of the popular vote amassed by Trump, correlations were computed with U.S. Census data for median family income in 2015 as well as the degree of increase in median family income from 2010 to 2015. In both instances, at a state-level the relationship of lower economic status and support for Trump was significant.[1]

In looking further at factors associated with the success of candidate Trump. His state-by-state percentage of the popular vote was found to correlate with the number of households at or below the poverty level in 2014, with lower relative gain in median household income over the past five years, and lower median household income in 2015. Also, candidate Trump took a larger share of the popular vote state-by-state as the percentage of non-Hispanic whites increased, based on the 2010 U.S. Census.[2] This largely fits with the economic duress argument many commentators have invoked since 11/8. It is worth saying again: it is not simply an economic observation but also a key aspect of dissatisfaction that has been linked to bigotry and stereotyping.

Polling data also show that the state-by-state percentage of households living under the poverty level in the 2010 U.S. Census was correlated with the percentage of voters who supported his candidacy. The economic argument for preferring Trump shows itself in states where he won the popular vote as having a progressively widening disparity in median income vis-à-vis the states carried by Clinton. This disparity in 2000 was roughly $6,000, $8,500 in 2010, and $10,500 by 2015. This information is summarized in Table 3.1.

Table 3.1   Economic, Demographic, and Hate Indicators by Electoral College Winners

	Trump States	**Clinton States**	**T Value**
2015 median family income	$51,776	$62,239	4.81***
2010 median family income	$47,129	$55,759	3.54***
2000 median family income	$38,226	$44,059	2.86**
2010 to 2015 MFI gain	$4,646	$6,652	2.41*
Families below poverty level	15.7	13.9	2.82**
2010 Census percentage whites	74.16	67.37	1.53
10-year (2000–2010) percentage white change	3.99%	4.49%	1.77
History of black lynchings (1880–1968)	110.6	6.4	2.95***
Ratio of hate crime reports 1992–2015	0.34	0.71	4.63***
Identified hate groups	19.93	13.8	1.19
Post-11/8 reported hate incidents	15	30.55	2.16*

*p < .05
**p < .01
***p < .001

Economic Privation and Hate Activity

The issue of what Don Green called almost 20 years ago the elusive relationship of economics and hate crimes remains . . . elusive. That is, while economic deprivation—such as poverty or unemployment—has been speculated to heighten the risk for hate crime perpetration, the evidence is unconvincing. The relationship between the decline in cotton prices and the perpetration of black lynching in the early 20th century had been proposed in the influential work of Hovland and Sears (1940) and Hepworth and West (1988). In a more recent study of lynching behavior, declining cotton prices, a staple of the economy of the region, was correlated with blacks being lynched, suggesting that economic duress in the region led to violence targeting blacks (Beck & Stewart, 1990).

This line of work had proposed a role for economic duress in intergroup violence, linked to the Dollard, Doob, Miller, Mowrer, and Sears (1939) frustration–aggression hypothesis. This hypothesis, when applied to intergroup violence has linked the experience of in-group economic threat with scapegoating or assigning blame to a denigrated social out-group. So as the farming and cotton-producing industries faced a downturn, so the frustration–aggression hypothesis argues, whites redirected their sense of helplessness and upset onto their black neighbors—individuals who one to two generations before would have been the slaves asked to work the cotton fields. This frustration of goal-response activates, purportedly, aggression toward the out-group.

Green, Glaser, and Rich (1998) found in their more thorough analysis over a longer period of time, the absence of a clear causal relationship of cotton prices and black lynch violence. They likewise sought to determine if gay bashing in the United States was related to economic downturns. They concluded that these very modest relationships of out-group violence and economic duress were due in part to the transitory nature of anger and frustration—at least as posited by the frustration–aggression hypothesis—and tellingly "the *absence of prominent political actors* affixing economic blame on target groups." This later concern, of course, would need to be reexamined in terms of the evolving social climate post-11/8 in which stereotype activation was a critical aspect of the election.

Curthoys (2013) also examined the economic duress–hate relationship. He observed a curvilinear relationship between unemployment and hate crime occurrence between 1996 and 2011. He reports that hate crime perpetration is infrequent in settings of low unemployment levels, and rises as unemployment rises to a medium level of unemployment, and falls as unemployment rises to relatively higher levels. I had in turn looked at community poverty and income status over a 10-year work period work and its relationship to subsequent hate crime occurrence. In comparing census tract economic change from 1990 to 2000 for Los Angeles County, I found that the role of unemployment levels, and households at or below poverty levels of households, over a 10-year period was unrelated to hate crime reportage (Dunbar, Wild, & Toma, 2016).

Psychology of the Follower: Urban, Rural, and Regional Political Orientations

> Travel is fatal to prejudice, bigotry, and narrow-mindedness.
> —Mark Twain (1859)

Another factor that emerged in the U.S. presidential elections was the distinction in voting patterns by region as well as between urban and rural voters. The voting behavior of individuals can be examined in terms of regional differences linked to state alignment during the Civil War. The attitudes of American voters have been criticized as being myopic and culturally encapsulated. This is supported by a 2013 study finding that more than half of Americans (54%) had never traveled outside the United States and a third (35%) did not own a passport (Peppers, 2013).

Urban and regional differences have been associated with shaping citizens' attitudes about government and racial prejudice. The implicit urban bias of political leaders has been associated with their manipulation of the resentment of neglect of residents of rural communities (Kurtz, 2004). Bates (1981) has attributed this urban bias of politicians in the developing world with promoting policies that economically disadvantage rural residents. Citizen racial bias has also been examined in relationship to place of residence. Lantz (1993, for example, in using GSS data, examined how community residence might influence racial bias. His results revealed that for adult respondents, their current urban versus rural place of residence had no significant relationship to racial bias, whereas where individuals had lived in rural communities at age 16 did. So, there is some evidence that suggests how rural marginalization and bias against racial minorities might play a role in responding to a political campaign predicated on a strain of xenophobic populism.

The appeal of Trump's culture wars platform as found in the 2016 election was importantly more favorably viewed by voters based on their (lower) educational level and economic privation. The survey analyst Nate Silver noted shortly after the U.S. presidential election that the role of voter educational level was significant in determining the outcome. His comparison of the 50 most educated counties (with a minimum of 50,000 residents) with the 50 least educated counties revealed how Hillary Clinton improved on President Barack Obama's 2012 electoral performance in 48 of the 50 (most well-educated) counties. In contrast, Clinton lost voter support in 47 of the 50 poorest counties vis-à-vis President Obama's 2012 performance—by an average of 11%. As Silver notes, "These are really the places that won Donald Trump the presidency, especially given that a fair number of them are in swing states such as Ohio and North Carolina.

Additionally, election results revealed a moderate correlation state-by-state between the number of white (non-Hispanic) residents, based on the 2010 U.S. Census, and the percentage of voters who supported Trump.[3] Also, at the state level, the decline of (non-Hispanic) white residents—as determined via 2000 and 2010 U.S. Census data—was negatively related to the percentage of the popular votes garnered by Trump. This would suggest that states that stayed (more) white went with Trump, whereas greater change of the state's racial composition at the start of the new century was related to lower levels of support for candidate Trump. So, in states with a greater proportion of white residents and those that had lower levels of racial change, the arguments of Trump about making America great again and building a wall resonated most forcefully. This allows for consideration of just how much deep cultural forces matter in the election of a candidate who engaged in explicit hate rhetoric and who has acted out his hostility toward women. The origins of the experience of being white in North America is therefore important in understanding what occurred in November 2016. Similarly, the role of regional differences of a war not yet over is also relevant to 11/8 and beyond.

> The Civil War is still going on. It's still to be fought and regrettably, it can still be lost.
>
> —Barbara Fields (Moore, 2015)

The regional patterns of voter behavior in the 2016 U.S. presidential election track reasonably well with the alignment of states during the Civil War from over 150 years ago. The 2016 election did, of course, witness the shift of several critical Midwestern states from a predicted blue or Union outcome for Clinton to support for the red Confederate candidate Trump. All the same, the culture war election of 2016 has a good deal in common with the shooting war of the 1860s. The characteristics of the Union states are presented in Table 3.2, which provide the correlations of economic and hate-identity variables with the percentage of the popular vote taken by Trump and significance tests for within-region states carried by Trump.

This Civil War analysis of voting patterns found that the Confederate Jim Crow Southern states—with the exception of Virginia—were all carried by Trump (92%), whereas Trump won 35% of the states of the Civil War Union and 75% of the unaligned states. So Trump's percentage of the popular vote was a function, in part, of the allegiance of the states during the Civil War. In the Confederate states a strong relationship between the number of families falling at or below poverty levels and Trump's share of the popular vote was observed. This relationship was

Table 3.2 Voter Behavior, Civil War Alignment, and Bias Indicators: Union States

Trump percentage popular vote: 44.8
Trump percentage of states carried: 35 (8 of 23)
Percentage white residents 2000: 79.62
Percentage white residents 2010: 74.93

	Trump	
	Percentage Vote	States Won
Median family income 2015	$r = -.68$	$t = 2.93$**
Median family income 2010	$r = -.31$	$t = 1.58$
Median family income 2000	$r = -.17$	$t = .99$
5-year median income change	$r = -.35$	$t = .78$
15-year median income change	$r = -.42$	$t = 1.25$
Percentage at poverty level	$r = .35$	$t = -1.35$
Percentage white residents	$r = .50$	$t = 1.50$
Change in white percentage 2000–2010	$r = -.39$	$t = 1.81$
Hate crime report ratio 1992–2015	$r = -.44$	$t = 4.88$*
Number of hate groups	$r = -.20$	$t = -.58$
Reported black lynchings 1880–1968	$r = .49$	$t = -2.90$*
Post-11/8 reported hate incidents	$r = -.41$	$t = .88$

*$p < .05$
**$p < .001$

more than twice as strong as that of the Union states. The poverty and Trump vote relationship completely vanished in the unaligned states. Interestingly, in the Southern states the relationship of Trump's share of the popular vote with the five-year median family income change was only half that of the Union states, suggesting that recent economic fortunes were less clearly related to a financial falling behind in the Deep South than in the pro-Clinton North. Tables 3.3 and 3.4 report the relationships of economic and hate-identity variables for the Confederate and unaligned states with Trump's popular vote and states that he won within each region.

As has been reported elsewhere, regional differences that have existed for the past several decades distinguish how law enforcement agencies

Table 3.3   Voter Behavior, Civil War Alignment, and Bias Indicators: Confederate States

Trump percent popular vote: 55.56
Trump percent of states carried: 92 (11/12)
Percent white residents 2000: 68.97
Percent white residents 2010: 64.58

	Trump	
	Percentage Vote	States Won
Median family income 2015	$r = -.77$	n/a
Median family income 2010	$r = -.80$	n/a
Median family income 2000	$r = -.85$	n/a
5-year median income change	$r = -.19$	n/a
10-year median income change	$r = -.43$	n/a
Percentage at poverty level	$r = .74$	n/a
Percentage white residents	$r = .54$	n/a
Change in white percentage 2000–2010	$r = -.67$	n/a
Hate crime report ratio 1992–2015	$r = -.19$	n/a
Number of hate groups	$r = .06$	n/a
Reported black lynchings 1880–1968	$r = .16$	n/a
Post-11/8 reported hate incidents	$r = -.63$	n/a

respond to hate violence. Specifically, the underreportage of hate crimes during the first 20 years of the passage of the 1992 Hate Crimes Statistic Act revealed significant differences related to the alignment of the states during the Civil War of the 1860s (Dunbar, 2017). These distinctions are found in Table 3.4 and reveal how blue, gray, and unaligned—at the time unincorporated—states differed from 1992 to 2012 in the ratio of reported hate crimes as a proportion of all crimes at a year-by-year basis. A singularly powerful predictor of underreportage of hate crimes was found in relationship to the number of reported lynching homicides against blacks over the period of 1880 to 1968 (Dunbar, 2017).

The deep cultural anchoring of racism in the United States and the manifestation of racial violence is revealed through the history of black

Table 3.4 Voter Behavior, Civil War Alignment, and Bias Indicators: Unaligned

Trump percentage popular vote: 53.01
Trump percentage of states carried: 73 (11 of 15)
Percentage white residents 2000: 75.4
Percentage white residents 2010: 74.1

	Trump	
	Percentage Vote	States Won
Median family income 2015	$r = .41$	$t = .94$
Median family income 2010	$r = -.60$	$t = 1.22*$
Median family income 2000	$r = -.46$	$t = 1.47*$
5-year median income change	$r = -.10$	$t = .54$
15-year median income change	$r = .02$	$t = .28$
Percentage at poverty level	$r = -.12$	$t = .34$
Percentage white residents	$r = .76$	$t = 3.18*$
Change in white percentage 2000–2010	$r = .05$	$t = -.19$
Hate crime report ratio 1992–2015	$r = .35$	$t = -1.16*$
Number of hate groups	$r = .10$	$t = .18$
Reported black lynchings 1880–1968	$r = .38$	$t = -.74$
Post-11/8 reported hate incidents	$r = -.42$	$t = 2.24*$

$*p < .05$

lynching. The underreportage also speaks to differences in how state-based institutions respond to bias crimes. As I have noted previously, "The inverse relationship of lynching activity state-by-state for nearly 100 years prior to the passage of the federal hate crime law additionally indicates the embedded nature of hatred and resistance to reportage of hate offenses. The linear relationship of higher lynching activity per state for over 80 years was significantly correlated to lower hate crime reportage when considered in terms of the lynching of blacks" (Dunbar, 2017). These deep structural traces from the lynching-underreportage link and the continuously lower reportage of Confederate states are in turn strongly related to the voting outcomes of the 2016 election as well.[4]

So what do lower levels of hate crime reportage for over 20 years have to do with a cataclysmic cultural change? Well, for one thing, the Deep South states revealed a negative relationship of the number of SPLC-identified hate groups and the percentage of Trump's share of the popular vote.[5] This relationship is again half that of the pro-Clinton Union states. It was also in the Union states in which reportage of hate crimes was related to lower support for Trump; this relationship was not found in the Confederate or unaligned states.[6] Also, interestingly, Trump's share of the popular vote in the Confederate states was only minimally correlated to the historical record of black lynchings—being roughly three times less related in the Deep South than in the Union states and also less related than what was found in the unaligned states. Also, Union and unaligned states that Trump carried were significantly more likely to underreport hate crimes in the 25-plus years prior to the 2016 election. Figure 3.2 reflects the 20-year historical differences in the ratio of hate crimes reported for the pro-Trump versus pro-Clinton states.

To look nationally at the support for the Trump presidency, two independent predictive models were computed. The first examined how economic indicators were related to the percentage of the popular vote taken by Trump. The second looked at the hate-Trump relationship. The first question computed how median family income in 2015, the five-year change (2010–2015) in median family income, and the 2015 poverty levels of families predicted Trump support. The second question examined how measures of hate crime reportage, history of black lynching, and the presence of organized hate groups were predictive of voting for candidate Trump.

These two predictive—multiple regression—models both explained voter support for Trump.[7] In the first model, predicting Trump's share of the popular vote, all three of the variables, economic level in 2015, median household economic change in the five years prior to the election,

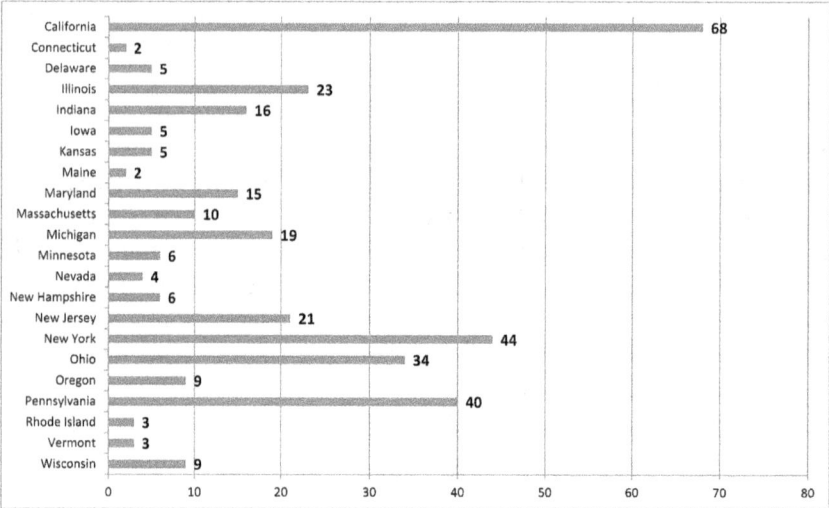

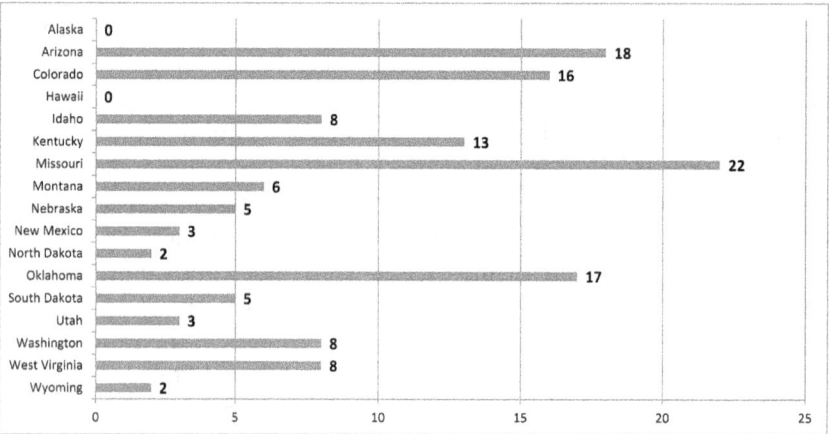

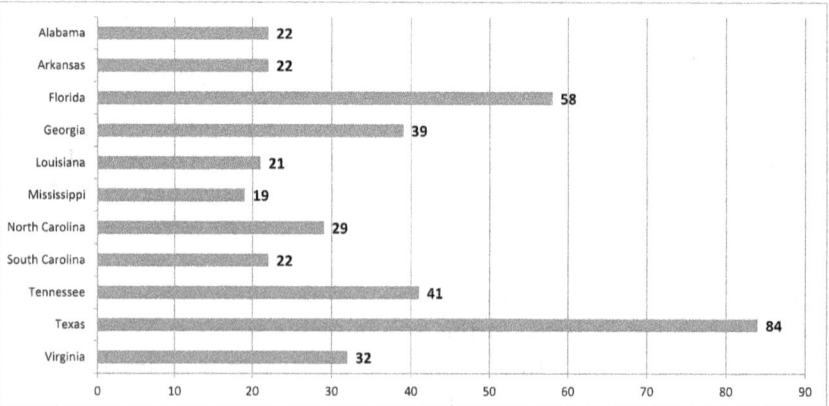

Figure 3.1   Civil War Clusters by Hate Groups in State

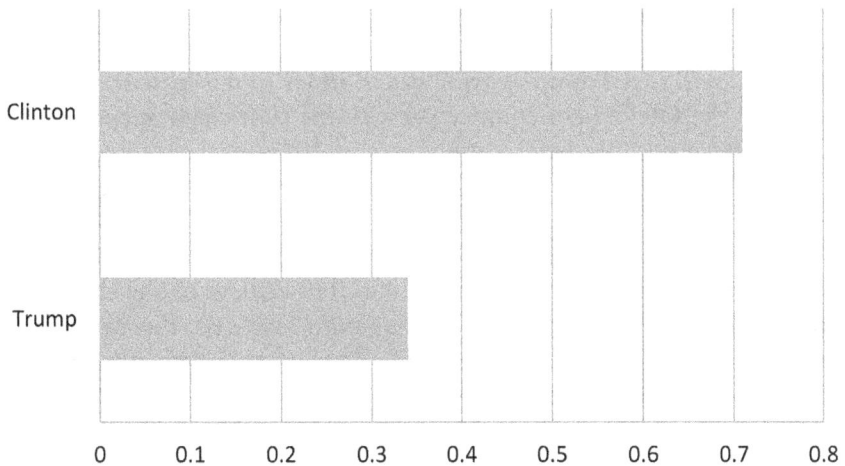

Figure 3.2   Differences for Clinton and Trump States and 20-Year Average of Yearly Hate Crime Reportage

and level of families living below the poverty level were significantly related to support for Trump. The results for the second analysis—the hate-Trump model—uniquely pointed to the history of within-state black lynching in predicting Trump's success with the voting population. That is, black lynching in the state from 1880 to 1968 was related to Trump voting support but not the near-term indicators of the presence of hate groups or level of reportage of hate crimes. The hate argument seems most linked to the deep cultural anchoring of racism, nationally, whereas the near-term economic privation argument explained support for candidate Trump.

Psychology of the Follower: Social Desirability, Implicit Bias, and the Ballot Box

Social desirability and expressed behavioral intent has been an issue of concern to professional pollsters, political strategists, pundits, and professors alike. Voting practices that have been found to significantly deviate from prior polling numbers have been of particular concern in the election of racial minority candidates. Referred to as the "Bradley effect," this phenomenon refers to discrepancies between voter opinion polls and the election outcome when Tom Bradley, the black mayor of Los Angeles, ran for and lost in his bid to become the governor of the state of California in 1982. The theory proposes that some voters who intend to vote for a white candidate would nonetheless tell pollsters that they are undecided or likely to vote for the nonwhite candidate. What the straight statistical data may have underestimated is the degree voters acknowledged that Trump's vitriol was contrary to the egalitarian social norms of the Obama-era country. As with the California gubernatorial election from decades before, the voters of 2016 may have been sensitized to the prospects of supporting an overtly racist candidate such as Trump.

Hopkins (2008) looked at the outcomes of 133 elections in the United States that occurred from 1989 to 2006. His review of the data supported the Bradley effect for elections up until 1996. For this period, the median polling-to-voting gap was 3.1%. Thereafter, the effect essentially vanished. His examination found an analogous effect for elections pitting a female candidate against a male was not significant.

The reliability of political polling, for all of its sophistication and effort to be objective, is still vulnerable to respondent factors—some of which might be as simple as access to pollsters, or as unique to the individual as their comfort with self-disclosure—which can be compromised by a desire to provide a socially desirable response. Issues of sampling differences and the subsequent misperception of actual voter behavior have been documented in terms of the role of face-to-face polling methods versus telephone or Internet surveys. This is summarized in the 2015 Pew Research study "From Telephone to the Web: The Challenge of Mode of Interview Effects in Public Opinion Polls," in which it was observed that a mean difference of 5.5% was found among differing "mode effects" or polling methodologies (Pew Research Center, 2015).

The issue of prejudice and voter behavior has been considered in terms of both social desirability and symbolic forms of bias. It has been observed in the review of preelection polling versus actual voter behavior that there is (in some instances) lower real support for black candidates. The issue of latent racism—or what McConahay and associates (1976) refer to as symbolic racism, may be an issue. The role of latent or implicit prejudice will be considered below. The issue of symbolic racism has been examined as a process by which racial bias is referred to in terms of social attitudes that signify a prejudice against racial minorities—and by extension women.

Dr. Sam Wang, a polling researcher, has commented on the evolution over time of the Bradley effect. "Polls did show a significant Bradley/Wilder effect through the early 1990s, which includes the period when Bradley and Wilder were running for office. However, Hopkins notes that the effect then went away" in campaigns he examined after 1996 (Wang, 2008). From this temporal perspective, as suggested by Hopkins, the "disappearance of the Bradley effect" co-occurred with the *decrease of racial code* (italics added) concerning crime and welfare. This is similar to what Green and his colleagues had observed about the decline in economic duress and hate violence 20 years ago. What is intriguing, of course, in terms of looking at this assumption in the aftermath of 2016, is the resurgent employment by the Trump campaign of exactly such hate rhetoric. In considering the Bradley effect to the results of the 2016 U.S. presidential election and the Brexit referendum we must invert the proposition.

The Bradley effect, when applied to the 11/8 election, suggests that in some instances, likely voters, when polled, reported a less biased option (e.g., support for a candidate other than Trump) because, similarly to the Bradley effect, the respondent, sought to present themselves as less-biased in their political choice. These nondisclosing Trump voters, in other words, are either consciously embarrassed by their support or do not recognize the power that their own biases hold in how they will subsequently behave. This has been referred to as a "reverse Bradley effect" (Perr, 2016). As Edsall commented in May 2016, "in matchups between Trump and Hillary Clinton, Trump does much better in polls conducted online, in which respondents click their answers on a computer screen, rather than in person-to-person landline and cellphone surveys" (Edsall, 2016). So, again, the question of how much a mode effect was at work all along should not be discounted. In face-to-face interviews or telephone interactions, it seems fair to assume pro-Trump respondents may have felt a need to present themselves in a more positive light, to appear more socially desirable, and to not endorse a candidate who espoused a hate-based worldview, as this may elicit disapproval from the other person. As the Pew study noted, these mode differences were consistently found how polling respondents when addressing issue of discrimination: "Considerable mode differences were observed on questions about societal discrimination against several groups including gays and lesbians, Hispanics and blacks, with phone respondents more likely than Web respondents to say these groups faced 'a lot' of discrimination" (Pew Research Center, 2015).

The mode effect was also observed within Republican and Independent Republican-leaning voters almost a year before the November 2016 election. The Morning Consult report of December 2015 (Drop, 2015) found the mode effect produced approximately 5% more support with Republican and Republican-leaning voters via online surveys than via live telephone interviews. With likely voters this increase jumped to 8% or 9% for online versus telephone interview results. This study further found that the mode effect was greatest with more educated Republican voters—individuals arguably more sensitized to and concerned about appearing socially desirable.

These findings suggest that pro-Trump sentiment is acknowledged by some of his followers as being socially problematic; this results in the employment of a socially desirous opinion suppression strategy in interpersonal interaction concerning political choice. This in turn leads many of us to underestimate the presence in the voting population of strongly held biases concerning social out-groups.

Psychology of the Follower: Gendered Opinions and Bias

A critical issue in the 2016 U.S. presidential election was the presence of Clinton as the first woman candidate of a major political party. The conflict of ideologies was based both in the issue of gender equity and the regressive backward-looking rallying issue of making America great again. As with Obama before her, Clinton's candidacy took on historical proportion in terms of establishing greater diversity in the possible leadership of the country. Unlike in President Obama's two successful campaigns, Clinton was pitted against a candidate who repudiated both the status quo of the political process and the acceptance of multiculturalism as a given in American electoral politics. As such the decision-making option that was provided to the electorate was significantly more divisive. This significant cultural gulf therefore presented U.S. society with its own referendum about gender and political power.

The study of gender bias provides insight into both the way people view political leadership and aggression targeting women. The psychological literature has included the work of Glick and Fiske's study of hostile and benevolent sexism. Hostile sexism quite literally involves the presence of negative affect and antagonistic attitudes concerning women. The negative and reactive aspect of the attitude is discernible by the observer. Hostile sexism is overt in the negative evaluations and employment of gendered stereotypes. Benevolent sexism is characterized by presumptions of women's vulnerability and hence need for protection, reification as objects of affection, and assignment of positive qualities of women to highly stereotyped roles as mother, caregiver, and the like. These seemingly positive evaluations all serve to control and dominate women, with a smile.

As operationalized by Glick and Fiske (1997), sexism is ambivalent in its manifestation of both negative and positive effects. In this sense, sexism is "ambivalent" given that sexism includes both negative and positive attitudes about women. Both hostile and benevolent sexism may be employed in viewing women as incompetent or inferior to men. In measuring gender bias Glick and Fiske (1997) employed the Ambivalent Sexism Inventory (ASI) to examine these two dimensions. Generally these two dimensions of sexism are moderately intercorrelated, meaning that experiences of hostility toward women and a more soft form of sexism co-occur for many individuals (Glick et al., 2000). Ambivalent sexists are not conflicted but rather maintain positive and negative forms of gendered bias as a form of equilibrium.

The context in which sexism in the U.S. presidential election exists reveals very high levels of self-reported harassment experiences in the general population. Klonoff and Landrine (1995) report that gendered discrimination is "rampant in women's lives"; with women of color reporting more incidents of gender harassment than white women. When gendered hostility reaches the level of criminality, base rates of domestic violence in the United States indicates one-third of women and one-quarter of men report being the victims of intimate partner violence at some point in their life span, with 20% of women being the victims of severe intimate partner violence in their lifetime (Black et al., 2011). Additionally, 1 in 5 women and 1 in 71 men in the United States have been the victims of sexual assault in their lifetime (Black et al., 2011). When we look at hate crimes, gender presents itself as a motivating factor in three specific instances. These include the very low base rates of gender-motivated hate crimes—in most studies yielding less than 5% of the total reported hate crimes for any sample—as well as hate crimes targeting lesbian and gender-bending victims. Importantly, there have become many instances in which religious hate crimes that are motivated by Islamic bias target women specifically; this is in offenders targeting women who wear the hajib, the traditional head covering of Muslim women. This later phenomena will be discussed more fully elsewhere.

There is some evidence that lower levels of Ambivalent Sexism as measured on the ASI (Blair, 2016) predicted in an online survey sample a greater intention to vote for Clinton. As she notes in her analyses, "The variable that played the strongest role in predicting a vote for Clinton was lower levels of ambivalent sexism, such that for every point decrease on the ambivalent sexism scale, individuals were 3.3 times more likely to indicate an intention to vote for Clinton. Higher levels of ambivalent sexism were also predictive of being an undecided or third party voter, such that for every step up on the ambivalent sexism scale, participants became 2.5 times more likely to be undecided or to pick a third party candidate."

Another study conducted in the months prior to the November 8 election also found the power of sexism in motivating individuals to support candidate Trump. University of Michigan researchers Carly Wayne, Nicholas Valentino, and Marzia Oceno conducted a study in June of 2016 with 700 adults; they questioned if endorsement of sexist statements was related to candidate choice. The team found that sexism was correlated with support for candidate Trump, even when the subjects' party identification and ideology was controlled for. This same team reported on experimental research conducted earlier in 2016. After priming the study subject's emotional state, they inquired how much they supported candidate Trump. Among respondents who were primed to feel afraid, the impact of sexism on support for Trump was smaller whereas for respondents primed to feel angry the impact of sexism was (slightly) larger than for subjects primed to feel relaxed (Aytaç, Rau, & Stokes, 2016). These findings underscore the power of sexism in potential voter attitudes about Trump.

In a study (Paul & Smith, 2008) with 500 likely Ohio voters, preference for male and female presidential candidates in the run-up to the 2008 election (inclusive of Hillary Clinton) found that male candidates were at a significant advantage when competing against a woman from the opposing party, rather than another man, respondent gender did not influence the results. Smith, Paul, and Paul (2007) additionally tested the attitudes of young voters in preference for male versus female presidential candidates. Supporting what they refer to as the gender-incongruency hypothesis, findings supported their prediction that simulated voting would support a female candidate for the U.S. Senate but not for the presidency, suggesting gender bias may be employed differentially depending on the level of power a woman seeks in public life.

Heilman (2001; 2012) has noted how gender stereotypes continue to result in negative evaluations of women in positions of leadership. She has identified descriptive gender stereotypes (defining what women and men are like) and prescriptive gender stereotypes (confirming appropriate "should be like" behaviors of women) as two components that negate perceptions of women's leadership competence. This effect is found in studies where both men and women were experimentally primed as being competent to hold a leadership role. Similarly, these results are found with millennial-aged male and female subjects. Rejection of women in positions of leadership is due in part to the prescriptive gender norms of leadership and the presumed attributes required to excel in senior leadership roles. Women who evidence their competence would in turn be seen as both gender atypical and ineffective as leaders.

Rudman and Fairchild (2004) determined via experimental study the backlash effect of when female leaders acted in atypical gender roles; in this instance, this implies acting in an authoritative and hence non-feminine manner. This backlash is in turn the rejection of women seen as competent but performing contrary to gender stereotypes. As in many experimental studies of social judgments, the conscious awareness of the subjects concerning their decisions is indeterminate. This actually explains one variant of gender bias, namely the oversocialized implicit bias individuals hold against persons of out-groups and individuals who function in a manner that violates social stereotypes.

Implicit gender bias may also have been a form of resistance to Clinton's candidacy. Research on implicit or automatic associations (Banaji & Greenwald, 1995) has frequently supported the notion of how over-learned bias shapes individual judgments at a preconscious level. Such automatic bias can counteract the individual's stated behavioral intentions. In terms of gender, the idea of implicit attitudes can lead to adverse judgments of women (Banaji & Hardin, 1996). This would suggest that support for Clinton would be compromised by implicit voter sexism. IAT research on gender and power differences (Richeson & Ambady 2001) found that men primed to be in subservient positions to women revealed negatively biased evaluative attitudes about women. By contrast, men primed to interact with a female equal-status partner or subordinate revealed attitudes that were biased in favor of women. The research on implicit bias would indicate that for men, support for a woman to have power over them—such as a woman being president of the United States—would lead to resistance to a woman presidential candidate.

It is worth considering some of the on-the-record statements Trump has made over the years concerning women. For example, he noted a quarter of a century ago in a 1991 interview with *Esquire*, "You know, it doesn't really matter what [the media] write as long as you've got a young and beautiful piece of ass" (Strochlic, 2015). In his audio-recorded Billy Bush interview from 2005, Trump states, "I've gotta use some Tic Tacs, just in case I start kissing her," Trump said. "You know I'm automatically attracted to beautiful—I just start kissing them. It's like a magnet. Just kiss. I don't even wait. And when you're a star they let you do it," Trump said. "You can do anything. Grab them by the pussy," Trump added. "You can do anything" (Lavender, 2016). In October 2016 in a speech in North Carolina he criticized a woman who said he had solicited her; candidate Trump commented, "Believe me, she would not be my first choice, that I can tell you. Man, you don't know, that would not be my first choice" (Rupar, 2016).

Politics, the Media, and Other Expletives

Let's acknowledge we are all ambivalent about the media. As Mark Twain said, "We are all ignorant, just about different things." Similarly, we all hate the media, just for different reasons. This ambivalent, if not always hateful, relationship of the individual to contemporary media is critically important to our coming to terms with the psychological and cultural fallout over the presidential election, as well as many of the ways social problems are depicted or ignored by traditional print and televised media as well as the expanding universe of social media. It would be impossible to have a modern society not approach the issues of politics and culture except via media outlets, which is where our problem really begins. The media has served to provide factual information about issues of intergroup relations, hate violence, public policy, and our aspiring future leaders who promise to address these seemingly intractable social problems.

In his campaigning for the presidency, Trump frequently referred to the media as not only biased but "crooked." His conspiracy theories of the mainstream media were further warranted when it was suggested that his opponent, Clinton, had been given debate questions by a member of the media prior to the second televised presidential debate. Again, if the candidate is running as an outsider, linking in the media as being an opponent—as a coevil force with the political establishment—makes good sense. This crooked and elite reference to the media not only resonates with the noted distrust of the media; it also plays to two important themes of hate, namely anti-intellectualism and anti-Semitism. The anti-intellectual aspect of hate is deeply embedded in the research on authoritarianism (Ezikoglu, 2016). As Altemeyer and others have argued, a core dimensions of what he terms right-wing authoritarianism is obedience (e.g., the abandonment of individual opinion and critical thought). As such, media analysis of "the issues" became suspect as symptomatic of the corrupt political stasis. Likewise, anti-Semitism and the suspicion of Jewish control of the media (the Jews controlling Hollywood), as the Anti-Defamation League notes, is a direct outgrowth of one of the more virulent conspiracy tracts against the Jews in our age, the "The Protocols of the Learned Elders of Zion" (Anti-Defamation League, 2006).

So what do we know about the media—this critical social portal about our society—and how the average citizen views it as an institution? If we consider this historically, North Americans used to have a reasonably favorable opinion of the news media. In 1956 the American National Election Study (ANES) revealed that more than one-half of Americans

(66%) felt that newspapers were fair with roughly one-quarter (27%) feeling newspapers were unfair. Before we dismiss this as being how people viewed the institution of media in a more serene age, consider that the study was conducted within a decade of the end of World War II, the explosion of the first nuclear weapons, the fall of China to Communism, the war in Korea, and the activities of Senator Joseph McCarthy of Wisconsin and the efforts of the House Un-American Activities Committee (HUAC). Hardly calm times globally or socially.

Importantly, the rise of broadcast and print media led to some people viewing the news media as an independent vehicle in providing checks and balances to the three branches of the U.S. government. The role of the free press became a principle of democracy in legal scholarship—U.S. Supreme Court justice Potter Stewart's "fourth estate" (Comegys, 1982)—and found its way into the standard IQ test as an item measuring social cognition ("Why is it important to have a free press in a democracy?"). To come more than half century forward in time, the 2014 General Social Survey (GSS), which is conducted by NORC at the University of Chicago, found that only 7% of adults expressed a great deal of confidence in the press and that only 10% reported a great deal of confidence in television news. What has occurred in the course of this half century is the fragmentation of news mediums (cable news, online news broadcasting, personal blogging, and independent investigative journalism) and new outlets into a veritable Tower of Babble, in which news and advertising is now tailored in the world of online media to the previous consumer behaviors of the individual.

There are numerous factors that have led to the loss of confidence in the media, from the manipulation of the message by increasingly more media-savvy public figures to the merging of entertainment with "straight" news, as well as to the value of providing a Babble-like targeting of news to fit the partisan attitudes of the consumer. What is more important is that these shifting attitudes toward the institution may also be shaping both how we view political arguments—and how we vote—on the one hand, and how the ultranationalist messaging and xenophobia is giving greater permission for explicit bias to become a benchmark for establishing voter behavior on the other. As Ladd (2012) has noted, the decline in the United States of trust in the media has contributed to the polarization of the American political system. In a 35-year retrospective study of political partisanship and attitudes toward the media, Ladd (2006) commented that "I calculate declining confidence in the institutional press could account for approximately 47 percent of the increase in partisan voting over the past 35 years."

As George Orwell explained in his *1984*, who controls the past controls the future, and who controls the present controls the past. In our post-*1984* age, we see how who controls the present is also the one who *creates* the present. I have suggested elsewhere (Dunbar & Blanco, 2013) that one of the great dangers of social media is the repackaging or rewriting of history to match the political needs of the state. As I noted "What is to be seen in the future study of media and intergroup violence is the way the organization of—purported—factual memory traces will shape feelings about cultural and national out-groups. The creation of emotionally significant associations to events outside of natural human memory will surely be a consequence of the new media. The formation of 'non-autobiographical' flash bulb memories of culture and violence awaits us." I now realize how wrong I was. The problem of re-creating history is not a risk for some future age; it is the risk we live with now, in our current time. The U.S. presidential election, as we have noted, was marked by dramatic and potentially voter-influencing "fake news" stories.

Fake News "поддельные новости"

The fake news problem that occurred during the campaign has been linked by the head of the U.S. National Intelligence Agency to Russian operatives. As director of national intelligence James Clapper stated at a U.S. Senate hearing, Russian cyberattacks are "multifaceted"—inclusive of fake news content. "This was a multifaceted campaign," Clapper said at the Senate hearing, "so the hacking was only one part of it, and it also entailed classical propaganda, disinformation, fake news" (The Daily Beast, 2016).

Moderating fake news with accurate information may not always prove beneficial. As Hopkins, Sides, and Citrin (2016) note, providing accurate information about immigration—as carried out in a series of survey experiments minimally influences individuals' attitudes about immigration, even when their subjects' misperceptions were explicitly corrected.

In the spirit of our interesting times, the Oxford Dictionaries selected "posttruth" as 2016's international word of the year, citing the role of the Brexit and U.S. presidential elections as exemplars of how inaccurate news feeds reformed social attitudes and voter behavior (Wang, 2016). The dictionary defines posttruth as "relating to or denoting circumstances in which objective facts are less influential in shaping public opinion than appeals to emotion and personal belief."

What do people who create this disinformation think they are doing? Are they all ideologues? As one individual expressed, it is simply a very well-paying job, making one writer over a quarter of a million dollars a year, which, if not carried out by them will be accomplished by someone else (Bill Brand, personal communication, December 14, 2016). This reeks of the "little man doing his job" rhetoric Eichmann employed to explain his role in the Holocaust, as observed by Hannah Arendt (1963), on the one hand, or the moment in Mario Puzo's *The Godfather*, when the mobster explains, "It's just business" as he prepares to drop an ex-associate into the East River, on the other. Evil can be a day job. Fake news is a gig that both pays well and works to undermine the democratic tradition. If we don't do it ourselves, then maybe the Russians will.

So 11/8 provided the Luddites among us the opportunity to disparage the media. The "truth" of course is that the political stump speech is traditionally rife with vagaries and half-truths. In a review of the accuracy of the two main U.S. presidential candidates their fact-checking found 26% of the statements of Clinton were partially or completely inaccurate. For candidate Trump this figure increased to 70% of his comments being factually wrong, with 4% being completely accurate and another 11% being partially accurate (PolitiFact, n.d.). The issue of how the receiver of this information is able to discern fact from fiction is, of course, important in the shaping of an opinion of the viability of the candidate. As Graham Greene has one of his characters remind us in *The Third Man*, it is dangerous to mix facts with fiction. As with fake news and leaked or partial news content, this misinformational process compromises how and what we discern as true or partially true versus what are willfully manufactured lies, used to shape what is implausible. This issue of cognitive load is worth discussing in terms of governance and hate violence.

The process of learning about social issues involves the detection of specific data bits or linguistic code that informs us of (hopefully) relevant information to follow, which will further specify the coherence and relevance of the message to us (Gilbert, 1989). This could be for example a message of "the economy is down" followed by "jobs are vanishing in your community," which signals issues of not only concern about economic privation but also immediacy to the listener. This process presupposes a capacity for sustained attention, as well as the ability to comprehend the linguistic code and its meaning. This working memory, if relatively intact, allows the receiver to then store and evaluate the relevance of the message to them. In political influence the presentation of information seeks to heighten awareness and openness to the message. If the messaging about jobs then continued to say "based upon changes in international trade agreements, the current climate of willingness to share in manufacturing processes intentionally between our two countries, may result in the retention of some semi-skilled jobs in the region and stop a complete abandonment of the manufacturing process in the state." This element of the message, which is qualified and more implicit as to the impact on the audience, creates a higher cognitive load. This typically results in greater difficulty in the accurate encoding of the meaning and invites greater distortion in the storage and retention of the message (Moreno & Mayer, 1999). The cognitive overload can be due to not only the complexity of the message but also the state of the individual(s) receiving the message.

There are several important implications from cognitive science about how we listen to political messages. For one, complex messages are more difficult to comprehend and retain than simple messages. Hence, the value of the tweet and sound bite are their brevity. Consequentially, fake news and intentional—and arguably in Trump's case habitual—dissimulation heightens the cognitive load. In learning the message we first must comprehend its meaning and then, as an additional task, appraise its inaccuracy. This requires more time, energy, and knowledge devoted to the fake signal detection—hence a higher cognitive load—which some listeners will not maintain. This furthermore means we must first encode the information with a consequence being that the fake content may be recalled even if the subject wishes to discard it (Lewandowsky, Ecker, Siefert, & Cook, 2012). Also, before I lose you in what I am saying here, keep in mind all lies are not created equally. More practiced liars—psychopaths and charismatic leaders fall into this category—are more competent at dissimulating than the person not practiced in willful deception. So the challenge to the individual's sustained working memory make rejection of "fake" and "con" arguments more difficult to detect. But this issue of competence to determine deception and inaccuracy in political arguments involves more than this. It involves the mental health of the listener.

The ability of the listener to determine the accuracy of political arguments can also predictably be compromised by their capacity to attend to, by the level of distress they are experiencing at the time, their level of arousal, and their vulnerability to activate intolerant stereotypes and attitudes. It is worth commenting on these issues. For one, as many observers of 11/8 note, a constituency that moved toward the Trump position and away from a democratic choice were individuals concerned about their economic welfare. This risk-taking shift when the alternative—Secretary

Clinton—seemed unlikely to help has already been noted. This is supported by the relationships of poverty and lower median family income in the Trump states. But as we have also noted, this economic duress has a psychological toll, most typically in terms of problems of lowered self-worth, depression, and low sense of personal efficacy. All of these psychological states are known to reduce cognitive capacity, openness to experience, and tolerance for complexity (Gotlib & Joormann, 2010). Additionally, problems of cognition due to learning problems, limited educational experiences for critical thinking skills, or the use of alcohol and drugs will further impair complex cognition and hence the ability to read the con. Under periods of extended unemployment and economic hardship, the capacity for voters to examine carefully the arguments of making America great again—an argument the listener, of course, wants to believe—is compromised. Trump may have connected with people both absent hope and absent the energy to think pointedly about what he suggested was the solution to their economic problems.

This leads to one more important point about both fake news and dissimulated arguments, namely the receptivity to stereotypes of out-groups and the activation of conscious prejudice of cultural out-groups. Frequently the language of intolerance is emotionally provocative—be it the use of classic fighting words or slang. Experimentally, stereotype activation has been linked to higher cognitive load and more punitive judgments of social out-groups, including more negative attributes being associated with the out-group (Van Knippenberg, Dijksterhuis, & Vermeulen, 1999). The themes we have reviewed, that Mexicans are rapists, Muslims are terrorists, and women are sexual objects, all strongly reinforce in the listener their internalized biases of social out-groups. Again, whether or not the source of the information is subsequently deemed false or simply a form of hyperbole, the impact upon the individual's association between the political problems to be solved and explicit intolerance is established.

Social media can also provide a "straight hate" story as well. Recently, following the June 16, 2016, assassination of Labor MP Jo Cox, ultranationalists celebrated her shooting and stabbing by a lone assailant who shouted, "This is for Britain." According to the *Guardian* on Twitter, more than 50,000 tweets were sent celebrating her murder and praising the assailant, Thomas Mair. Mair—a white supremacist who was opposed to immigration to the U.K.—was called a "hero" and "patriot" in the Twitter posts that appeared in the month following the assassination of Cox. According to analysis by Imran Awan of Birmingham City University, and Irene Zempi of Nottingham Trent University, the tweets advocating for the assassination of Cox came from more than 25,000 accounts. Their review of the more than 53,000 tweets sent in the month after the assassination of Cox found that words used to describe Mair were "hero," "patriot," and "white power," whereas his victim was referred to as "rapist" and "traitor."

As I noted previously, the psychological cloak of invisibility further enhances hate speech and hate ideology in the realm of social media. As I have commented: "The use of social media to promote hostility and bias is exacerbated by what commentators refer to as the Gyges effect. That is, the invisibility of the individual in cyberspace often emboldens them to levels of hostility that would not be replicated in face-to-face contact. The Gyges effect has been proposed as explanatory of online trolling— that is the hostile and anonymous provocation by one person toward another. Gyges refers to Plato, who wrote of the power of a man who, by wearing a ring that made him invisible, was free to engage in numerous illegal and immoral activities. When considered in terms of social media and hate content, the Gyges effect is explanatory of both the sender of bias-motivated broadsides, as well as the enhanced engagement of the viewer of such content. This constitutes an enhanced form of Allport's antilocution, made more powerful due to the anonymity of the means of communication. While some might think this is simply free speech, the point of the Gyges effect is the capacity to disinhibit the individual to engage in rhetoric that they would be disinclined to reveal in social interactions or in public contexts" (Dunbar, 2017).

Finally, in a market-driven society, news and social media are driven by profit. In the first two months of Trump's election to the presidency, there have been two examples of extremism being assembled as commercial products for the populace. One involves the online media critic Milo Yiannopoulos—who was taken offline by the social media outlet Twitter for his attacks on a black celebrity. Yiannopoulos, an editor with Breitbart News, signed a quarter-of-a-million-dollar contract for a book with the publisher Simon & Schuster (Bond, 2016), which was subsequently withdrawn (though he later released it under his own label). As the Huffington Post reports, "Threshold Editions told The Huffington Post in an email that the book will be called *Dangerous* and is set to be released on March 14, 2017. The imprint summarized the book by stating: "Dangerous will be a book on free speech by the outspoken and controversial gay British writer and editor at Breitbart News who describes himself as 'the most fabulous supervillain on the internet.'"

Another perhaps more provocative recent mainstream media foray into the alt-right marketplace was the eight-part Arts and Entertainment series "Generation KKK." This series consisted of interviews with members of the Ku Klux Klan in a classic reality television format. The series, which was announced after 11/8 and was to premier in January 2017, consisted of interviews with four families of members of the KKK. The program, which would have presented the ideas of the group members to millions of potential viewers, was to show the relationship between the group members and their families—some of who opposed their views (Ledbetter, 2016). Concern was expressed from many stakeholder groups after announcement of the program and led the network to pull the show. What is, of course, interesting is the program development time and execution, which would have occurred over several months, as well as the timing of the announcement within a few weeks of the Trump victory.

The role of media in how issues of hate and xenophobia are portrayed is critical in the aftermath of the 2016 elections. In the United States, the media is largely corporate-run and market-driven. In other societies, which typically are totalitarian or faux democratic, the media is state sponsored and controlled. By the nature of the U.S. marketplace model, ideologically based media outlets have a greater opportunity to play a role in shaping social attitudes, as well as catering to the ideology of a specific consumer base. So, theoretically, both civil society and ultranationalist organizations can find themselves an outlet for their political viewpoints. As is well-recognized some of the more hate-driven media commentators have had very successful, profitable, and influential careers, promoting ideas of nationalism and intolerance. Rush Limbaugh, for example, had an estimated worth between $430 and $450 million (Field, 2017), whereas Ann Coulter, another highly quoted and provocative pundit, has an estimated worth of $8.5 million from her books, columns, lectures, and media appearances (Celebrity Net Worth, 2014). The profitability of media-as-entertainment, when married with media-as-right-wing-propaganda is impressive. It also raises the point that individuals and political action committees (PACs) who can raise significant amounts of funds for political media programming are playing a big role in what is put into the mainstream public forum. The highly partisan—some people would say faux—news of a Fox media empire, for example, might have a great deal more impact on shaping public attitudes than a more militant media outlet such as Stormfront. As of the beginning of 2017 Fox News registers 135 million Google hits, whereas Breitbart records 10.7 million hits and Stormfront comes in at 2.27 million Google hits. The discrepancy between the mainstream right media of Fox via-à-vis the extremist media of Stormfront—with

Breitbart falling much closer on such a spectrum to Stormfront than to Fox—underscores how large segments of the media-consuming public may be influenced by less overtly if still significantly partisan right organizations than the in-your-face ideological outlets.

Not surprisingly, with the degree of influence and profit that corporate media holds, questions of objectivity and neutrality become hard to take completely seriously. Understandably, media executives have gone on record as saying they only produce content when there is an audience, in essence arguing that there is a bubble-up approach to content development. Arts and Entertainment Network developed their KKK series because there was a desire (or need?) for the issue and how it was produced. This "what the market will bear" argument is tautologically flawed; media is a socializing agent, and what is provided to the viewer/ listener primes future assumptions about the favorability of the media format and the content it provides. So, as consumption is conditioned, it is not unidirectional. As observers of the 2016 campaigns noted, the media created the personas of the candidates and by extension legitimized their use of both inaccurate information and, importantly, their free employment of stereotypes of social out-groups.

Finally, we need to consider the hundreds of millions of dollars spent in advertising and media content development to shape and promote messaging to the viewer. In 2015 in the United States more than $180 billion were spent in advertising (Romero, n.d.). An estimated $6 billion were also spent in advertising for candidates in the 2016 election (James, 2015). The candidates varied in how they used broadcast media. For the entire election cycle, Clinton aired 39% of all advertisements to candidate Trump's 12%. Also, 80% of broadcast television advertisements run by candidate Trump were negative or "contrast" pieces (Cook Political, 2016).

Summary

Nation states in the West that have functioned under a liberal democratic tradition have shifted their political center to a faux-democratic nationalism that is at risk of shifting toward a more frankly autocratic style of government. This transition has been accomplished via the mobilization of the voters to respond to deep cultural anchors of in-group bias and fears of "the other." The activation of old-fashioned xenophobia has proved to be politically expedient in the United States in the election of Trump. Similarly, there is evidence to suggest that voter prejudice against women—inclusive of overtly hostile, benevolent, and overlearned implicit bias—all worked against the candidacy of Clinton. Unfortunately, this invocation of bias has activated deep cultural divides that have been manifested in violence against public officials and the general public alike. There is a substantial amount of psychological research that would support the assumption that the success of Trump reflects the deep-seated resistance, or "racial fatigue," of many white voters to eight years of governance by a black man, whose policies would be carried forward by a white woman identified as a member of the social elite of political liberalism.

We have also found a meaningful if complex relationship between economic privation, hate violence, and a tradition of black lynch activity in the support for candidate Trump in 2016. What the analyses we presented here illustrate is that there were roughly one-third more organized hate groups in states carried by candidate Trump. In states won by Clinton, the ratio of hate crime reported by law enforcement was one-half, again higher than in the Trump states and that from the self-reported hate incidents identified by the SPLC were twice as high in the Clinton states. The data also show in states that have had a more significant decline in white residents since 2000 the number of hate groups within the state increases. It can be argued that the more multicultural the state is, the more effective they are at reporting hate crimes and that there are more prowhite hate groups. This reveals how multicultural states have traditionally had more effective law enforcement practices for identifying hate violence, have more fearful whites who organize into hate groups, and have higher median family income levels.

The loosening of both public trust in the news media and the whole cloth creation of partisan news, which provokes our deep-seated bias, has ushered in a powerful wave of ultranationalism that is at once antidiversity and antidemocratic. We will turn to the consequences of this anticulture movement in the following analyses and describe the potential threats to civil society, public safety, and carrying out good police work.

CHAPTER 4

How We Hate: From Social Intolerance to Criminal Motivation

I have spent more than 20 years conducting research on hate violence and clinically oriented studies on bias. I have addressed these issues with universities in different countries, with elected public officials, with law enforcement, in the courtroom, in crime labs, and in front of the media. On occasion, I felt I had some impact on the people I worked with; at other times, it felt like it was an exercise not to repeat. Sometimes, it was clear people really cared about what I was trying to get across, and then, of course, there were others who I could see were bored and occasionally visibly upset. I remember once getting shouted down at a human rights program, and, in another situation, I gave my presentation with two armed guards looking out at my audience—another exercise not to repeat.

Over this same period of time I have treated mental health patients who have been hate crime offenders, racial stalkers, hate group organizers, and clinically prejudiced individuals who were fearful of individuals with dark skin, offended by people with accents, and perplexed by the idea that there were people who had romantic attachments different from their own. It was hard to find some of these people credible in how they viewed the world, whereas others were quite likable. Some of these people had pretty awful lives that I would not wish on anyone.

As a clinician I have also treated people who have been harassed in their jobs and schools for their religion, their skin tone, their last names, their gender, their sexual orientation, and their being emotionally involved with a partner who wasn't the right type of partner to be with. There are also people I have worked with who were severely beaten up by hate gangs, stalked because they were gay, threatened because they were Jewish, bullied because they were the refugee kid, and traumatized for having the nerve to want to be who they are and have a normal life. I have learned a lot from these people in terms of "how to deal with the nonsense" of hate and get on with their lives. Sometimes it seemed hard to imagine there were people in my community who would put so much energy into making my clients lives so difficult, but it, of course, happened. It would also be very nice to say that the people I have known who were the targets of hate always got a whole lot better, but that is not how the world works.

People I have mentored as students have been gay bashed, sexually assaulted, stalked, racially profiled, and discriminated against because of their last name, their accent, their social class, their country of origin, and for just being the funny-looking kid in their classroom. Mentoring these folks has usually been very satisfying, personally.

I say all of this to explain that through my experience I find most of the working models of bias and hate to be useful but only partially explanatory of what has happened to the individuals I have known. I also must say at least once that the distinction between being a victim, an offender, and an advocate is not as absolute as we would wish it were, that, too, is not how the world works. So while it is true that, as Kurt Lewin said decades ago, "There is nothing as practical as a good theory," it is also true as Carl Bell once said to me, "Theories are like a toothbrush, everyone has one." So in the midst of a book about bias I would like to say that my bias is against a theory that can't be explained to a reasonably bright lay person or that has not been derived from being with people in the real world. Although I have conducted my own studies on social issues with undergraduate university students, I don't want to promote a psychological science of hate, violence, and politics that is found only in laboratory settings. Laboratory studies and simulations of hate victimization are questionable in terms of what some researchers describe and their insufficient "ecological validity" (Brewer, 2000).

So we will begin with a review of the factors that are characteristic of the intolerance that has surfaced in the 2016 election in the United States and that are representative of frequently nonviolent forms of hostility toward social out-groups. This will be followed by a discussion of the psychological dimensions of "hate" and "ideology" in the perpetration of bias-motivated violence, and, finally, I break down specific facets of how hate intentions can be identified in criminal infractions—and criminals—we see in our society today. In this microlevel of analysis I will observe where these markers are seen in the post-11/8 incidents that are part of the cultural cataclysm.

Factors of the New Societal Stasis of Intolerance

> When Fascism comes to America, it will be wrapped in an American flag and waving a cross.
>
> —Sinclair Lewis

In 2016, the Trump presidential campaign in the United States touched on many critical social problems and invoked strong biases against social minorities. As has already been noted, this intertwining of out-group bias, social problems, and a sense of cultural warfare escalated the issue of intolerance from an undesirable belief to a test of one's being on the winning side in post-11/8 America. If we examine this cultural cataclysm through a process of psychological inquiry, we can consider how the rhetoric of the campaign is related to the rise in hate violence leading up to and following the November election. What follows is a summation of the psychological models that were potent motivating forces in the shift in our cultural stasis; authoritarianism, ultranationalism, and xenophobia.

Authoritarianism

The study of authoritarianism was first made relevant in the psychological sciences in the period after World War II by Theodore Adorno and his colleagues Daniel Levenson, Nevitt Sanford, and Else Frenkel-Brunswik. Interestingly these individuals had their own experiences of persecution; besides Adorno, who had fled Nazi Germany, Frenkel-Brunswik fled Europe in 1938 to avoid anti-Semitism of the Nazis; whereas Sanford was fired from his professorship at UC Berkeley for refusing to sign a loyalty oath in 1950. In what has been referred to as the Berkeley School, Adorno and his colleagues produced a book in 1950 *The Authoritarian Personality*, which has become one of the seminal books in all of the psychological sciences. Based on case study and survey research with the F (Fascism) scale, the Berkeley School team identified nine traits of authoritarianism.

The formulation of Adorno and others working independently of the Berkeley School viewed authoritarianism as a personality construct, one related to bias and Fascism. What is now referred to as the authoritarian spectrum consists of deference to authority, subscription to dogmatic beliefs, group membership through obedience, denigration of nonconformers, and punishment of these nonconforming individuals. As was befitting the age of Adorno, a good deal of the thinking about authoritarianism was framed in terms of psychoanalytic theory. This pathologizing of a psychological and political construct has been most critiqued by Robert Altemeyer (2007, who has spent a significant part of his professional life examining the social psychological aspects of the authoritarian specter. Based on his own survey methods and laboratory work Altemeyer has carefully scaled-down the characteristics of what he has come to call "right-wing authoritarianism" (RWA) (Altemeyer, 1981, 1998). The core dimensions of RWA included submission to authoritarian norms, adherence to conventional social norms and values, and the engagement in aggression to force conformity.

In studies I have conducted, RWA has been related to anti-Semitism, racism against blacks in the United States (Dunbar, 1995), bias against Roma in the Czech Republic (Dunbar & Simonova, 2003), and opposition to human rights policies (Dunbar, Blanco, Sullaway, & Horcajo, 2004). In a study of correlates of personality and measures inclusive of RWA (Sibley & Duckitt, 2008), authoritarianism has been modestly correlated to personality traits such as lower openness to experience and positively to agreeableness. Interestingly, Ho (1994) found authoritarianism correlated with high levels of Filial Piety, a Chinese cultural value, a finding I replicated with U.S. Asian–Pacific subjects (Dunbar, Saiz, Stela, & Saiz, 1999).

Authoritarian Governance and Leadership

Governing by personal fiat is, of course, what authoritarians—and, for that matter, autocrats—do. The process of governance is not based on compromise but direct control—what French and Raven (1959) would refer to as hard forms of social power (see Chapter 7). Sometimes authoritarians have held significant influence without holding formal positions of power. Father Charles Coughlin and the aviation hero Charles Lindbergh are two examples of individuals in the public eye who held significant social influence in the United States in the 1930s—being proponents of anti-Semitism and a U.S.-brand of Nazism—without holding any formal role in government.

Authoritarian leaders have demonstrated a strong predilection toward state-sponsored genocide of their own people. During the Spanish Civil War and the following dictatorship, General Francisco Franco's civilian repression, the White Terror campaign, killed an estimated 200,000 civilians, heavily targeting writers, artists, teachers, and professors. Idi Amin in Uganda, Mao Zedong in China, Joseph Stalin in Russia, and, of course, Hitler in Germany all stand as examples of authoritarian or quasiauthoritarian leaders who committed atrocities against their own citizens. When not executing members of their societies, authoritarians employ stakeholders of the state—such as legal professionals, judges, and the media, to promote forms of social control via show-trials, fake news, and social ostracization.

The authoritarian state may force coexistence between socially discordant groups—as a strategy of uniform social dominance. The former Yugoslavia—under the control of Marshal Tito is one well-known example in which ethnic tensions were controlled. Historically totalitarian regimes have sought to control power under the figurehead of the state—the charismatic (sometimes) authoritarian (typically) leader.

Inherently, as a dogmatic system of political thought, authoritarian regimes are anti-intellectual. As the Fascist writer Giovanni Gentile (2011) commented "Fascism combats . . . not intelligence, but intellectualism . . . which is . . . a sickness of the intellect." The elimination of intellectual discourse and social criticism may include control of the media, restriction on the independence of the courts, and the suppression of the arts and humanities.

Forms of Authoritarian Control

Authoritarian control is not only revealed through executions, pogroms, and show trials. Authoritarian society is also characterized by the imposition of microaggressions and sanctions on the actions of individual citizens. The enactment of these social controls includes many forms of nonviolent coercive power. Historically, an example of a social sanction is found in the restrictions found under Franco's Spain. For example, men and women were forbidden from holding hands in public or engaging in what millennials refer to as public forms of affection. These almost imperceptible microaggressions become the experience of daily life when living under the authoritarian regime.

The notion of microaggressions was initially described by Chester Pierce (1970) as the hostile engagement by members of the dominant culture with a member of a nondominant social group. The acts are typically imperceptible to others or so habituated as to be seen as normative. Microaggressions also reinforce the power differential between the actor and the target. The targets of microaggressions often experience confusion, anger, frustration, or exhaustion (Sue, 2010). Additionally, microaggressions may occur in a social stasis that implies equity—arguably the social stasis until the 2016 elections. Under such conditions the target person may experience confusion and conflict as to their actual standing in the society in which they live (David, 2013). Microaggressions furthermore reduce the acculturation into the social stasis of the dominant culture. Berry and his colleagues, for example, reported that being the target of discrimination led to lower levels of adaptation to the new host society and resulted in a greater adherence to the cultural identity of an immigrant's country of origin (Berry, Phinney, Vedder, & Sam, 2006). Microaggressions and discrimination—two outcomes of authoritarianism—serve to further marginalize the marginalized.

In authoritarian states the occurrence of microaggressions is normative, resulting in a culture of victimhood and oppression as a way of life (Giroux, 2005). It is commonly noted in law enforcement that political refugees from authoritarian states are less likely to contact the police following crime victimization. The working assumption is that individuals from oppressive societies—habituated to microaggressions—do not view state agencies as being a source of protection following a crime.

Authoritarianism and 11/8

In our recent presidential election, obedience to the state was promoted by several candidates in addition to Trump. The use of punishment as a solution to problems of crime and immigration were frequently cited. Along with championing religious conservatism and militarism—signature themes of authoritarianism, the denigration of the media, and social criticism became signals of the importance of authoritarian obedience in the cultural war against liberal democracy. This was evidenced by Trump's championing of torture as a facet of the national strategy for counterterrorism. The campaign promised authoritarian sanctions inclusive of institutionalized forms of discrimination that could be levied on out-groups—specifically immigrants and Muslims. The actual manifestation of a postinauguration authoritarianism falls beyond the scope of the current project. Likely targets would include political opponents, his political predecessors in the Obama administration, proponents of a free press, and an independent judiciary. The balance of a top-down authoritarian dogma may prove challenging in dealing with a splintered legislative arm of government. In any case, the imposition of these "new norms" will likely remain tied to a conservative religious ideological doctrine; at least when it is consistent with the goals of the presidency.

The Mishegoss Relationship of Authoritarianism, Hate, and Terror Laws

The relationship of authoritarianism, hate, and terror laws is complicated. Authoritarianism as an organizing principle of the social stasis is fundamentally at-odds with the intent and enforcement of hate crimes as a unique infraction. The legal standards and strategies to address hate violence are relatively recent in their promulgation. In the United States, hate crime statutes were first enacted federally in the early 1990s—hardly old by the standards of U.S. law. The 1990 Hate Crime Statistics Act (HCSA) assigns the responsibility of the U.S. attorney general to annually gather data on crimes of prejudice related to race, gender and gender identity, religion, disability, sexual orientation, or ethnicity (Federal Bureau of Investigation, 2011). Subsequent legislation federally and at the state level defined these offenses as being a penalty enhancement due to the bias motivation found as a motivation in the perpetration of the offense. As I have noted elsewhere (Dunbar, 2017), "The advent of hate crime initiatives—e.g., the reportage of bias motivated infractions, the establishment of criminal enhancement penalties, the creation of victim response services, and the effort to create educational prevention programs—can all be seen as a part of the civil society movement (CSM). The CSM is a component of modern culture that is independent of the sitting government" (Kumar, 1993). Seligman (1998), for example, proposes that a civil society may serve as a sanctioned form of political criticism. As noted, an authoritarian government, logically, is in opposition to dissent, particularly from an organized nongovernment organization or as represented by legal standards that are contrary to the norms and practices of the state.

Our antiterror policies may keep us safe—"getting the bad guys" as a security expert once said to me—but also create a level of animus abroad against the United States that is difficult to quantify. The significant use of drone-based attacks in regions of Afghanistan under the Obama administration eliminated important "bad guys" but also killed innocent civilians. This is a reasonable consequence—from an authoritarian perspective—in the international terror campaign. For an authoritarian, this is a high-reward-moderate-risk proposition, whereas a civil society advocate would view this as a moderate-to-low reward proposition (there are always new Al Qaeda leaders, the argument goes) with a high risk (e.g., not wanting to be seen as a country of terror and violence abroad). Conversely, from the perspective of an authoritarian, hate crime laws offer a low-to-moderate reward (most of the victims of hate crimes are cultural undesirables) with low-risk—the perpetrators of these offenses are similarly marginal members of mainstream culture. So in the Manichaean worldview, authoritarian hate crime laws do not protect worthy citizens and are typically perpetrated by the unworthy. The law itself is an irritant in a winner–loser post-11/8 world.

So it is fair to say hate violence may be an inconvenient truth of an authoritarian shift in our culture. That being acknowledged, let me say this clearly, hate crime offenders are almost never authoritarians; they are criminals. Hate offenders are not hyperconforming or norm-supporting members of our culture. A gay basher may state LGBT persons violate social norms, but they themselves otherwise frequently evidence their own unsocial problems—alcohol abuse, poor employment histories, a preoccupation with sexuality, and, yes, violation of the rule of law—which is anathema to a true authoritarian. In a liberal democracy, hate offenders stand outside the social norms proscribed by the state. In the AUX-type society these offenders are at best actors who perpetrate the shared prejudices of the dominant culture against denigrated out-groups. At the current time, authoritarianism is, however, consistent with the attitudes of persons who support alt-right ideologies. The country does face the potential risk of the rise of a paramilitary authoritarian organization. We are just not there yet.

Ultranationalism

The concept of ultranationalism is not my own, and it is less used in psychology than in history, specifically in the work of Masao Maruyama (1914–1996). Maruyama argued that Japanese Fascism was not a cultural deviation but rather was arrived at as a consequence of an evolving political ideology that had its origins in the late 19th-century Meiji Period (Maruyama, 1969), when imperial power had assigned to itself the ultimate power to create and re-create cultural values, leaving the society in a state of obedience and submissiveness (Sasaki, 2012). I would suggest that this holds specific relevance to the movement currently occurring in the United States and elsewhere in Western governments. Specifically, ultranationalism is characterized by the movement (back) toward a redefining of citizenship that is predicated on exclusionary criteria of race or language. This affords a means of creating a class of "real Americans" or "real Brits" or "real Russians" in which immigrants and traditional ethnic minorities are then "not real" and are as such disenfranchised from the benefits of citizenship—or what might be argued is full citizenship. This is reflected in the media as a backlash in which conservative political beliefs are inherently racialized or at minimum "nationalized" members of the traditional ethnic/racial dominant group. This is also a refutation of modernism, international interdependence, and multiculturalism. Ultranationalism is as such an effort to return to a more homogeneous referent point of citizenship, one that often belies the demographic realities of a multicultural society.

Ultranationalism from a political perspective incorporates a highly authoritarian approach to governance, a need to frame policies in terms of a hypothetical tradition or past (frequently the "golden age" of the state), and a valuing of a homogeneous in-group that is the repository of power and privilege. Additionally, ultranationalism proscribes follower behaviors as asserting identity with the state, perceiving the standing government as embodying the traditional values of the core culture, and views intergroup relationships as inherently an arena of conflict. As a solution to citizen alienation, ultranationalism requires the sacrifice of personal liberties and autonomy. This working definition incorporates a good deal that is characteristic of a Fascist political system (Payne, 1996).

Ultranationalism and Social Dominance

A psychological model consistent with the study of ultranationalism is found in social dominance orientation (SDO) (Sidanius, Liu, Shaw, & Pratto, 1994). SDO refers to the psychological orientation of the individual in terms of intergroup status and power differences. Individuals who are high on rating scales of SDO seek dominance of out-groups. High-SDO persons view intergroup contact as inherently conflicted and based on intergroup competition. The extensive research on SDO has found that measures of this attitude are related to in-group preference and stereotyping of out-groups as well as responsiveness to cues to compete with members of out-groups.

In a cross-national study of SDO, Carvacho et al. (2013) found that deprivation experienced by people from low social classes heightened their perception of the world as threatening and competitive and in turn resulted in greater bias toward social out-groups. In this understanding of governance, SDO predicts that the state has as its core political agenda dominance over other societies. "We will build a wall and the Mexicans will pay for it," a campaign promise of Trump to his constituents, serves as such an example. The notion of social dominance was further emphasized in the anti-immigrant, make America great again, political rhetoric, which polling data suggested played particularly well with economically threatened and predominantly white voters.

Xenophobia

The term xenophobia connotes, somewhat technically, the fear or discomfort with that which is experienced as alien. With its origins in antiquity (Harrison, 2002), the term was applied to describe barbarian foreigners in Greece and Rome. In the contemporary language of the social sciences, the term is reflective of any form of explicit bias toward a national or social out-group. While this is all-encompassing, it is problematic in terms of a specific context or relationship. For the purposes of trying to describe the role of bias and the cataclysmic social changes of the recent past, such a broad-brush term however has its relevance. To again return to the language of candidate Trump, his stump speeches labeled Mexicans as rapists, Muslims as terrorists, and immigrants as criminals. This broad spectrum of bias—as we have discussed— extended even further to include a complicit media of a purportedly corrupt political system.

As a consequence of the 2016 election, xenophobia became part of the new normal of our political rhetoric. For the Trump presidency the post-11/8 xenophobic shift would require the support of federal legislators to radically change many of our practices of free speech and civil liberties. As of the time of this writing the "what and how" of such an institutional transformation is uncertain. However, the rights of women, of non-U.S.-born persons, and sexual minorities may well face legislative and presidential executive orders to restrict their civil liberties. As has already been suggested, the AUX-type government may also evolve into a totalitarian form of government. Under this form of rule the state ultimately becomes the hate crime offender. In such an extreme form of governance, the relationship of the state to minorities and out-groups is characterized by tasks of domination, elimination, and sometimes extermination.

A recent illustration of the new xenophobic rhetoric is found in the statements of a University of Nevada, Las Vegas, faculty member who stated he would inform on students he took to be illegal immigrants to the United States (Papenfuss, December 4, 2016). Mathematics instructor George Buch stated online to a student of his: "I would have to turn you into ICE," he posted. "I don't mind diversity . . . I mind criminals." When this incident received national media attention, Buch backed off, telling the UNLV student newspaper that he was "just kidding."

Historically in our culture, expressions of ethnocentrism and nationalism, even by-the-book authoritarianism, until amplified, have reflected the opinion of an individual, a social group, or people of a given community. It is how and why this amplification occurs that we should be mindful of, particularly when we see a collective rise in, for example, nationalism, that there is reason for concern and attention. As has been discussed, authoritarianism, ultranationalism, and xenophobia—what I have referred to as an AUX-type shift in societies away from liberal democracies to antidemocratic forms of governance—played an important role in the cultural cataclysm of 2016. What we will now look at are some of the underlying psychological factors that motivate individuals to perpetrate hate violence. So we will move from the normative forms of bias into more explicitly antisocial forms of hate aggression, all the while considering how these psychological motivators were present in the 2016 campaign and its aftermath.

Hate and Ideology in Bias-Motivated Violence

Our discussion of intergroup violence is frequently muddled by concepts that are treated as though they are interchangeable. Recent discussion of terrorism has been referred to as a "hate ideology" (Yanay, 2012); this suggests that out-group attitudes have become inherently more strident and ultimately more hateful. Implicitly this hate ideology hypothesis proposes that political violence is now explicitly moderated by a hatred of the targeted group. From this perspective it would be expected that prejudice, impulsivity, hostility, and bias are significantly one and the same. Indeed, much of our contemporary discourse on hate is based on research concerning social norms of bias and stereotyping. It might therefore be difficult to consider "hate violence" as occurring without the ascription to negative stereotypes of the target victim. Similarly it might be assumed that the acts of mass homicides that we witness in the more extraordinary forms of domestic terrorism constitute the sine qua non of hatred. But this may reveal more of how we feel about intergroup violence than how we conceptualize and examine the issues.

Legal Intersection of Hate and Terror Laws

There are significant legal commonalities found in the definition of a hate crime and domestic terrorism under federal law. These laws speak of both animus and collective harm, with the presumed psychological injury these offenses impose on the target communities in which the infractions occur. As has been suggested elsewhere (Dunbar, 2017), it is plausible to understand these acts as being highly interrelated. As Sullaway (2016) notes, although the terms "hate crimes" and "domestic terrorism" may be used interchangeably, there are differences in these terms as well. A central component of the domestic terrorism stand-ard is found in the presumed intent of the perpetrator to "intimidate or coerce civilian populations; to influence policy of a government by intimidation or coercion; to affect the conduct of a government by mass destruction, assassination, or kidnapping" (U.S. Patriot Act, Public Law no. 107-52). This intent to influence government is not essential to hate crimes and is frequently absent from documented hate infractions. So while government or societal coercive influence is an essential component in the motivation of domestic terrorists, it is not a requirement in the classification of a hate crime under federal law.

It is also worth noting that there is a fundamental difference in how these laws (hate and domestic terror) are viewed depending on the political orientation of the individual. As I have noted in reviewing national polling data: "Democrats were twice as likely to support hate crime laws as the antiterror Patriot Act. Republicans were almost as likely to support hate crime laws (60%) as the Patriot Act (57%), whereas Independents reported almost as much support for hate crime laws (69%) vis-à-vis the Patriot Act (37%) as did Democratic respondents" (Dunbar, 2016, 23). Again in reviewing polling data it was found that Democrats were 15% more supportive of hate crime laws than Republicans—who were 22% more supportive of the Patriot Act than were Democrats. So what we find in pre-2016 polling is that similar laws addressing at times overlapping problems are distinguishable by the respondents' political ideology.

Hate Violence and Factors of Motivation

As I have discussed elsewhere (Dunbar, in press), psychological science would suggest that hate is best considered as an affect state; a condition that is both transient and responsive to external stimuli (e.g., provocation). As with other emotional states, hate is mediated by both environmental stressors and the body–mind (metabolic and neurological) status of the individual. This implies that the hate element is itself malleable to situational (e.g., intergroup contact) and shifting psychophysiological (such as alcohol consumption) factors. A second factor in the commission of a hate crime is the belief or ideological assumption the offender subscribes to (Sullaway, 2004).

The occurrence of hate violence is mediated (in part) by current social and historical cultural forces. As I have noted (Dunbar, in press): "Violence which is attributable to hate and ideology occurs in a cultural, historical, and social context. This context establishes when violence is bias motivated. The identification of hate and ideology constitutes the 'cultural coherence' of intergroup violence. The coherence of the act is achieved when the norms and traditions of the ingroup explain—i.e., normalize—the habitual practice of violence that targets members of a specific outgroup. This means that the infraction, while a violation of the standards of a civil society, assigns meaning to acts of violence and is salient to the cultural worldview of the offenders' ingroup."

To conceptualize the impact of hate and bias ideology on the attitudes and behaviors of the offender, we can consider how these two factors identify differing motivational types. I would emphasize this is for giving us a means to think about the individuals who perpetrate hate violence. In actual situations the characteristics of the individuals who commit these crimes are far more complex; any effort to talk about offender types is, in actual practice, rubbish. So, reader beware, but as is depicted in Table 4.1 the interaction of hate and ideology underscores the varying forces at work in committing hate crimes. These motivational differences are summarized below.

Biased Follower

Let's consider the low-hate/low-ideology individual. As Ezekiel (1995) has noted, there are individuals who join bias ideology groups as a form of social bonding. This might be thought of as a specific form of social identity (Tajfel, 1981), in which the individual experiences a strong need for in-group membership, and conforms to group attitudes about the undesirability of out-group persons. The need for inclusion may typically be more important than a need to express strong negative effects or engage in hostile behaviors. Ezekiel discusses the fatherless young men he encountered who were the joiners of hate groups. These "follower" individuals might engage in hate violence as a means of establishing their group membership or as a function of being provoked by a triggering event. Outside of the context of the hate group, these low-hate/low-ideology individuals may be disinclined to engage in hate activity.

Table 4.1 Hate-Arousal and Ideology-Expressive Factors in Commission of Bias-Motivated Violence

Labile Bigot (low ideology/ high arousal)	Hate Extremist (high ideology/ high arousal)
Spontaneous hate behavior	Ideologically driven aggression
Explosive/aggressive response to intergroup contact	Violent acts of both reactive and symbolic intergroup violence
Biased Follower (low ideology/ low arousal)	**Planful Terrorist (high ideology/ low arousal)**
Need to identify with other bias-oriented individuals	Ideologically driven aggression
Compliant with hate-based leaders	Planned acts of symbolic intergroup violence
Engages in hate violence to establish group membership/status	

Labile Bigot

This high hate-arousal and low ideology-expressive state typically reveals problems of reactive hate aggression. The low stress tolerance of these individuals results in spontaneous forms of aggression in situations of benign intergroup contact. By this we mean that highly impulsive and biased persons may engage in conflict with persons who trigger them in situations that are not inherently conflictual. The poor tolerance of exposure to persons who are different activates a biased aggressive style. Some of these offenders may reveal clinical problems of mania, hyperactivity, explosiveness, or impulsivity. Such highly labile persons are likely reactive to a range of life stressors and not just situations involving contact with denigrated out-groups. Other individuals are at-risk for such spontaneous hate violence through the use of controlled substances and alcohol.

Planful Aggressor

Unlike the labile hate offender, these individuals are more self-contained and premeditated in their perpetration of bias-motivated crimes. The consistent level of bias ideology may result in the perpetration of crimes (such as racial stalking) that occur over time. The psychological goals may include the experience of in-group dominance and capacity to create distress in the denigrated out-group victim.

The stability of the bias ideology also poses challenges in managing such an individual in terms of the criminal justice system. Punishment that involves incarceration in which the offender is then ghettoized with other similar high-bias individuals will only strengthen the ideological perspective and increase in-group identity.

Extremist Offender

This individual evidences both high levels of hate-arousal and ideology-expressive traits. They are at once ideologically true believers and motivationally diverse in that they may be engaged with others in group-based violence or function as a classic "lone wolf" offender. Behaviorally they may engage in either planful or reactive (that is, spontaneous) forms of hate violence. These more complex bias-identified persons may also have prior histories of intergroup violence; in some instances these offenders may have lengthy criminal histories while in others the repeat offenses are largely related to hate violence.

From an individual differences standpoint many of these offenders may reveal antisocial or psychopathic traits and be particularly difficult to rehabilitate and less likely to desist from a hate-based lifestyle. These repeat offenders are likely as they age to become more socially alienated as they spend more time in and out of the criminal justice system. When incarcerated, they are likely to become more identified with a hate-based ideology and may become particularly challenging to manage on community reentry.

To test this model of hate perpetration, a sample of over 800 cases from a large metropolitan police department were reviewed and classified using rating scales for the bias markers (see below) used in the Bias Motivation Profile-Revised (BMP-R) (Dunbar, 2016)— and aggression— based on the Cornell rating scale (Cornell et al., 1996). The aggregated score for the BMP-R and a rating dimension on the Cornell scale for arousal in commission on the offense were used to establish a median cut-point, allowing the organization of offenders into four categories of high bias/high arousal (extremist), high bias/low arousal (planful offender), low bias/low arousal (follower), and low bias/high arousal (labile bigot).

When using this scheme to look at types of offenders with a sample of over 800 hate crime cases, the majority—nearly 50%—of the individuals fell into the follower category with slightly more than a third following into the planful offender group. Roughly 10% were in the extremist category and roughly 7% were identified as the labile bigot offender.

Differences in the nature of the offense were found for these offender categories. Violent hate crimes were roughly twice as likely to occur with the extremist and labile bigot types. Extremists also traveled further from their homes to target their victims—typically more than 10 miles from their residence where labile bigots engaged in highly reactive offenses that were frequently within one mile of their homes. Extremists were much more likely to perpetrate offenses of assault with a deadly weapon, to engage in simple assaults, to engage in verbal threats of hate violence, and generally perpetrate more severe forms of hate activity than the other offender types.

Follower types were much more (twice as) likely to engage in non-violent offenses—with infractions for vandalism and graffiti being more likely conducted by followers, who rarely engaged in verbal taunting. Followers engaged in more religious-motivated crimes but the planful offenders were much more likely to perpetrate anti-Semitic hate crimes. These planful offenders were also more likely to have planned their crimes for longer periods of time. The differences in types of crimes perpetrated found in this method are summarized in Table 4.2 below.

Table 4.2   Hate-Arousal and Ideology-Expressive Factors: Research-Based Distinctions

Labile Bigot (low ideology/ high arousal)	Hate Extremist (high ideology/ high arousal)
Perpetrates spontaneous and unplanned hate crimes	Commits more violent offenses—assault with a deadly weapon and physical assaults
Likely to commit hate crimes close to home	Perpetrates more crimes of verbal threats
	Travels outside of community to perpetrate hate crimes

Biased Follower (low ideology/ low arousal)	Planful Terrorist (high ideology/ low arousal)
More likely to engage in nonviolent offenses—vandalism and graffiti	Commits more anti-Semitic hate crimes
Engages in more antireligious hate crimes	Carries out planned and goal-directed hate crimes
Less likely to engage in hate crimes of interpersonal aggression	

Markers of Hate Crime Perpetration

Disentangling hate and ideology, to quote Lewin again, is a practical approach in the study of hate crime offenders. Ideological violence is almost always a precursor to premeditated violence. The presence of a bias-based ideology can on one hand motivate people to support an ultranationalist political candidate. It may also motivate an individual to engage in premeditated forms of intergroup violence or domestic terrorism. Similarly bias-based ideological groups may reflect recognized political organizations with strong in-group ideals or be a marker of violent gangs. Hate, by comparison, as a motivator can lead noncriminal individuals to engage in prejudicial behaviors. For antisocial offenders, hate may result in violent forms of out-group aggression. We get angry in response to some triggering event, which for individuals with strong social bias can be linked to intergroup contact or perceived between-group conflict. Of course, offenders who hold strongly to an ideology and evidence significant levels of hate and arousal pose particular risk to their communities. These issues have been important to crime investigators and legal professionals and will be further examined below.

Importantly the issue of measuring bias from a forensic psychology perspective has been largely ignored (Sullaway, 2004). Forensic psychology has recently paid a great deal of attention to determine the risk for criminal activity as well as the risk for recidivism, increasingly by examining specific risk factors for specific groups of offenders (Lewis & Doyle, 2009). What follows is an examination of the risk factors in perpetrating intergroup violence as found in specific historical and behavioral markers. These risk markers have been employed to identify the intent and motivation to commit a hate crime (Dunbar, 2016); they are summarized in Table 4.3 below. This strategy has been used to both review prior criminal histories and analyze a specific offense where bias is an element or in the context of a criminal investigation. This methodology is useful for investigating issues that self-reporting may not produce typically from an interview.

Presence of Hate Paraphernalia and Symbols

In several ways, symbols of hate may be present at the occurrence of an offense. These can include tattoos or clothing, for example. Importantly with tattoos, there is frequently an embeddedness of signs within the larger images that communicate varying messages to the aware viewer. For examples, some images specify a criminal gang membership whereas others may connote a form of white identity. Some images, which are

Table 4.3   Markers of Bias Intent: Bias Motivation Profile Dimensions

Presence of hate paraphernalia/symbols

Hate group or racialized gang membership

Articulated ethnic/race-based hate ideology

Punishment of sexually deviant behavior

Aggressive "sexual self-defense"/homosexual panic

Gender-bending aggression and hostility

Hate speech during commission of offense

Prior history of hate aggression/criminality

Articulated religious ideology-based aggression

Offense absent motive of material/extrinsic reward

Effort to defend turf or neighborhood

Victim unknown to suspect

filled in over time, may also message the level of violence the offender has engaged in. The issue of body images is that these are typically only known by members of the offenders in-group. Additionally, of course, messaging a hate belief may be based on hate literature found on the suspect. So the use of symbols and fliers may also indicate a hate belief system. I have also observed cases where racist images were found in the suspect's belongings—perhaps in some cases to be distributed in a victim community. Almost always these signs of bias are related to race/ethnicity or in some instances antifaith crimes, which are almost exclusively crimes against Muslims and Jews.

The imagery and representation of xenophobia may be more dynamic than our stereotypes of hate group members would suggest. Coester (2016), for example, notes how the image of Che Guevara, a Latin American Communist, has been integrated into contemporary German ultranationalist groups, as a rallying image of a revolutionary who sacrificed for his cause. Many contemporary ultranationalists have adopted a more reggae/world image to promote themselves to youths put off by the traditional severe uniforms of the classic neo-Nazis. Additionally, the appearance of U.S. alt-right activists includes a hipster haircut called a "fashy"—for Fascist (Silman, 2016); even neo-Nazis are slaves to fashion trends.

The presence of hate symbols—as found in studies I conducted with a California-based law enforcement agency—indicated that approximately 15% of the cases from a sample of over 800 reported crimes included the presence of hate symbols; in other samples I have found approximately one-in-four cases as inclusive of hate iconography or symbols.

Hate Group or Racialized Gang Membership

Membership in hate-oriented groups implicitly involves homogeneous race/ethnic membership and some essential element of criminality. Ideological groups that are not antisocial do not become engaged in hate violence. Typically, criminal gangs in urban settings engage in racial violence. This may be to control "turf" or to dominate some criminal activity, such as drug sales. In this sense the primary motivation is social bonding, financial gain, and social dominance. For this sense of group reward to include racial dominance is not unusual in criminal gangs. Also, what is meant by a hate gang or group is not applicable to spontaneously emergent groups—as might be found via an Internet-based rally where individuals with no prior relationship come together at a specific date and place to air their grievances. Rather, a hate group has shared goals of its members, has recognized leadership, and exists over some period of time. This has been borne out in cases I have worked where a violent hate group member was expelled from his criminal group for being too erratic and "crazy."

It is worth considering how the run-up to 11/8 also saw the importance of Trump "rallies" that were marked by the physical removal of persons of color and members of the news media. On occasion this was a function of candidate Trump shouting to his audience to "get them out of here!" In this sense, then, the election rallies became a place of defining membership in the "movement"—one that was not only ideological but also racialized.

From the baseline data of reported hate crimes, a good 30%–40% of the cases revealed offenders were involved with a hate-oriented group or a racialized criminal gang. Gang-based hate crimes almost always were related to racial/ethnic hostility versus that of religion, gender, or sexual orientation. The majority of the gang- or group-affiliated hate crimes were committed by suspects below the age of 25, with very few cases of suspects over the age of 35 having involvement with antisocial groups. Perhaps some youth groups that start around another activity, such as a sport like surfing or skateboarding, can evolve into hate-oriented groups, but this is rare.

A practical issue of gang-affiliated hate crimes is the greater likelihood of violence in the offense. Group-based offenses are less likely to be property offenses and have also been found to be cases where the victim is less likely to report the crime to law enforcement. This finding, which is in need of replication, may be due to concerns about retributional violence when there is a local criminal gang involved in the hate crime.

The 2016 election has been attributed as a motivator for the organization of new hate-based groups. According to the Southern Poverty Law Center (SPLC) about this increase, they note: "The number of hate groups in the United States rose for a second year in a row in 2016 as the radical right was energized by the candidacy of Donald Trump" (Southern Poverty Law Center, 2017). The increase in anti-Muslim hate groups was reported by the SPLC as increasing from 34 in 2015 to 101 in 2016.

Articulated Ethnic/Race-Based Hate Ideology

A frequent marker of bias motivation is reflected in the offender's articulated or otherwise communicated beliefs about in-group superiority, exclusivity, and the denigration of members of social out-groups. This ideological marker may be found in highly instrumental forms of inter-group violence—roughly 40% of the cases that revealed premeditation—and at an individual level reflects potentially enduring hate-based beliefs that are stable over time. This marker of hate intent was found in roughly one-half of all the reported hate crime cases.

Like with several of the other markers, ethnic hate ideology is highest with teenagers and then declines for offenders until people get over 35 years of age. This spike and decline into the 30-something aged group reveals how for many people their bias ideology falls away during the early adult years. Competing needs of employment, romantic involve-ment, and changes in social supports may yield competing ideologies that lead to a reduction—if not always desistence from—a bias ideology lifestyle. Additionally, persons who are engaged in hate violence after the age of 35 appear to be more ideologically entrenched—what I refer to as the true believer offenders.

Although this marker has been employed with criminal infractions, it similarly reflects some of the rhetoric employed in the hostility toward immigrants—the "Mexicans are rapists" argument, for example. This utilization of hate rhetoric, which is protected speech under the First Amendment, can also serve as a stimulating message to individuals who are vulnerable to the commission of violence. Popularly discussed as a permission-giving practice, this use of hate speech as a gateway to hate violence predates Trump and has long been a concern to persons track-ing hate violence.

Punishment of Sexually Deviant Behavior

In what could be thought to be an illustration of criminal right-wing authoritarianism this is a motivator of offenders who target sexual minorities and is only discernible through either interview of a suspect or explicit verbal or written declaration at the time of the offense, in this later case the hate speech aspect often occurs in context of violence—such as an assault. In the studies of LGBT hate crimes this characteristic is observed in roughly three-quarters of the offenses and is not surpris-ingly perpetrated almost always (9 of 10 times) by men. When this does occur, the hate offense tends to be more violent. The infractions where this is observed more frequently include cases of assault and violence employing a weapon or where the infraction included aggravated assault or assault with a deadly weapon.

As with the use of hate rhetoric in the political campaign, the spate of 2016 legislation at a state level to discriminate against sexual minorities and/or transsexuals was made famous by the North Carolina "bathroom bill" that restricted use of public bathrooms to specific gender groups. This area of legislation and policy, while potentially speaking for many members of a given community, also posed a risk for violence against sexual minorities. Once again, a marker of hate violence has recently found its way into the mainstream political practices of the United States in 2016.

Aggressive "Sexual Self-Defense"/Homosexual Panic

The gay panic idea is extremely controversial, and, in current legal practice, it involves junk science to argue against the culpability of an offender who targets sexual minorities. The self-defense strategy that employs panic has been outlawed in some states given the absence of any objective evidence of the condition constituting a legitimate psychiatric condition. Unless one is a historian interested in medical diagnoses then the issue of gay panic is a topic raised in the courtroom. In terms of our contemporary thinking, the contribution of Sullaway (2004) is important in drawing a distinction between gay panic and sexual advance—in the latter this concept is more frequently used in criminal defense. The sexual advance defense argues that the suspect had been provoked by the victim and that the aggression was therefore protective.

In the baseline data I have worked with, it is noteworthy that this marker is infrequently observed. With offenses motivated by LGBT bias this is found in somewhere between 5% and 10% of the cases. When this marker is in the apprehension of the suspect—typically via interrogation—the offense is quite often violent. The defense seems to be employed when the victim has been severely assaulted or where there is an attempted homicide or murder. Interestingly, in the crime reports I have examined, the presence of victim provocation of the offender is essentially absent.

Gender-Bending Aggression and Hostility

Individuals who are not gender-conforming in their appearance or behavior have been targets of aggression and hate crimes. In my studies this often happens in tandem with hate speech and punishment of LGBT victims; violence against gender-bending victims is almost exclusively committed by male offenders. This may also be the least common of the markers I have worked with in analyzing hate crimes, occurring in less than 5% of the cases I have examined.

Infrequency does not, however, mean culturally unimportant. Gender atypical and transsexual individuals are often the hate-based target of violence. In one recent review conducted by the Human Rights Campaign, 22 transsexual individuals were murdered in 2016 (Human Rights Campaign, 2017). An inordinate number of these victims were black transsexuals.

Hate Speech during Commission of Offense

I refer to this as the "hate crimes for dummies" marker. The presence of hate speech is the most frequently identified aspect of an offense defined as a hate crime (Dunbar, 2016). Many spontaneous and emotionally reactive forms of hate aggression include the use of language, often produced at the moment of escalation. These offenses are committed by men in roughly 80% of the cases.

In the post-11/8 period the vast majority of hate incidents involved the use of speech (see Chapter 5), much of which falls within the guidelines of hate speech; in many cases this may have been in the absence of another infraction and was therefore protected speech. In some instances there were explicit references to the president-elect. From a technical—and practical—standpoint, an offense using the reference "Trump! Trump!" is not hate speech. Pulling off someone's hijab may be simple assault or damage to property, for example, and simply saying "Trump!" is not conventionally considered a hate crime, as reference to a political figure is not a hate term. So we may see instances where the offense was a minor infraction but not conventionally deemed hate-based, even if there were a strong suspicion that this was the reference and intention.

We need to be honest here about something; a liberal democratic perspective on a political candidate's name being invoked during a hate incident would be horrifying to his or her supporters. For many individuals advocating for an AUX-type regime, this same incident might be seen as an assertion of their cultural ideology; one that would be at worst tolerated and at best championed. One person's hate term is another's stated belief.

Additionally, candidate Trump used gendered hate speech to objectify women and in his denigration of immigrants, so his name may for some individuals be equated with a hate ideology, an association Trump himself would reject. What makes this problematic then is both the observation that spontaneous hate speech may not prove to some individual's intent and the use of Trump as the sole reference is not properly identified as a hate term, even if it is recognized to have an ideological meaning.

Prior History of Hate Aggression/Criminality

This marker on at least one level makes the observation that past behavior supports future behavior viable. However, more to it, the recurring process of individuals perpetrating hate violence begins to suggest a more entrenched ideological perspective of intolerance. In the crime report research I have conducted, a good 25% of apprehended suspects had prior hate activity, though in many cases this was related to gang-on-gang violence. A more conservative estimate of prior hate violence may be 10% to 15% of the offenders had prior hate crime involvement. In some small number of cases this included extensive hate crime histories.

Articulated Religious Ideology-Based Aggression

Over the first 20-plus years of the Hate Crime Statistics Act, the most frequent category of religious hate speech was found for anti-Semitic crimes. Many of these offenses were property crimes. In the crime reports I have reviewed this may annually amount to 20% or less of the identified offenses in an urban setting in California. The FBI reported that from 2014 to 2015 the number of anti-Muslim hate crimes in the United States increased 67%—from 154 reports in 2014 to 257 in the following year. For the sake of comparison, 696—or 62%—of the reported religious hate crimes in 2014 were anti-Semitic incidents—compared to 11% anti-Muslim offenses.

In 2015 the percentage of anti-Semitic hate crimes constituted a 9% increase from 2014. Overall of the 1,402 religious hate crimes documented by the FBI in 2015 52% were anti-Semitic and 21% were anti-Islamic/Muslim incidents. This indicates the consistent but pervasive deeper hostility in the country in general against Jews than Muslims, but it also shows how the documentation of this hostility that is anti-Muslim/anti-Islamic is increasing rapidly.

The period in 2016 after the election saw community-based groups document a rise in anti-Muslim offenses. Some of this may be attributable to the infusion of alt-right religious intolerance into our cultural discourse. As has been discussed (see Chapter 2), the Trump campaign made frequent references to Muslims and radical Islam as significant threats to persons in the United States. This depiction of Muslims as a threat for terrorism within the United States has been studied for more than a decade now by Bail (2016). In his content-analysis of news media stories, he has observed how prosocial information about moderate Muslim organizations has been largely supplanted by attention to only extremist Islamic groups. Bail has noted that this practice by the U.S.

media has shaped a more hostile and fearful perception of Muslims, an issue that in terms of priming risk via mortality salience and stereotype activation has been occurring since 9/11. As will be discussed shortly (Chapter 5) how this conditioning of general social biases against Muslims came to the forefront in the period following 11/8.

Offense Absent Motive of Material or Extrinsic Reward

This marker in hate crimes is noteworthy for the lack of a financial motive in the commission of the offense. In my research on reported hate crimes, up to eight-out-of-ten cases are absent any financial incentive to the offender.

If the presence of hate speech during commission of an offense is the hate crime for dummies moment, then these cases where there is no material reward for the offender is a dummy-type infraction for the career criminal. As an offender once said to me, he did not "get" the point of hate crimes, in that there was nothing of value in committing an offense on a material level. Numerous times I have heard how an assault against a gay man is notable for the failure to take the victim's wallet or other belongings. Hate crimes as a class of criminal behavior are as much as one-half as likely to have a financial motive for the offense as all other types of crimes.

This marker is not related to how severe the offense is, nor to other factors such as distance from the offender's home or the number of offenders involved in the crime. Rather, many of these offenses involve hate speech and property crimes inclusive of vandalism.

Effort to Defend Turf or Neighborhood

These infractions have to do with classic community violence perpetrated against perceived outsiders. These relatively infrequent—perhaps 15% of cases I have reviewed—offenses often are committed by multiple offenders and are frequently violent. Experienced gang investigators have noted how these turf hate crimes are often part of the activity of racialized criminal groups. Examples of this may include cases of arson targeting a racial minority family (Dunbar, 2016) as well as black-on-brown gang conflict to control a neighborhood. Although these offenses often involve some degree of planning, the tit-for-tat nature of racial turf violence can result in a wave of community violence that involves victims who have no affiliation with criminal groups.

A somewhat different and at the same time infamous example of this protected neighborhoods idea is found in the Howard Beach hate crime committed in 1986. In this incident, which happened in a neighborhood in New York City, a group of white men—who lived in the community—attacked four black men who had stopped in the neighborhood when their car had broken down. In this case the white men pursued and assaulted their victims, one of whom died of his injuries. This spontaneous form of hate violence illustrates how perceived victim provocation—involving persons unknown to the offenders—can escalate into a lethal conflict in a matter of minutes.

The theme of "protecting our homeland" is an example how this same theme can be found in the political rhetoric ever since 9/11. What we will consider shortly (Chapter 5) is the frequency with which this theme of "America first" became a motivator for anti-immigrant hate speech and provocation post-11/8.

Victim Unknown to Suspect

As the interested reader may have deduced, hate violence, although perpetrated by individual offender(s), is largely motivated by hostility toward a specific out-group. In such group-based forms of violence, it is therefore not surprising that the majority of offenses occur in situations where there is no prior relationship between the offenders and their victims. As with the no material reward criteria, this marker is not on its face related to bias. The role of anonymity is, however, significant in that it has been observed in the vast majority of hate crimes, including over 50% to 75% of the hate crime cases I have reviewed. Additionally, as the offender reveals more of a complex bias ideology—as measured on the BMP-R—they are more likely to target strangers where there is no evidence of provocation prior to the offense. What this underscores is the detached and depersonalized nature of more seriously biased offenders from their victims. The targeted person is more of an object than an individual.

In studies I have conducted, the level of prior connection of hate offenders and their victims is very infrequent; with most samples, the anonymity factor was found to be present in around 90% of all hate crimes. I also find a slight gender difference, with men particularly likely to target strangers versus woman offenders who are, of course, rare in the offender group to begin with.

Normalizing the Abnormal

At this time of global retrenchment into ultranationalist political ideologies that are driven by fear and bigotry, we are contending with problems of heightened policies against immigrants, more overt racism in the general population, and political rhetoric that advocates xenophobia and isolationism. Given this increase in state-sanctioned intergroup conflict, there will continue to be a need for behavioral science research on the fall-out problems of hate violence. A cultural cataclysm inherently connotes a sudden change to the social order. As with other forms of homeostatic disruption, the resumption of a normal stasis is rapidly strived for. The effort at reestablishing a societal balance may consequentially normalize (i.e., make coherent) forms of bias (and bias-motivated aggression) that would previously not have been sanctioned by the larger society.

Permission-giving and the right to target minority persons have been going on for decades in our modern liberal democratic society. The intolerable has been tolerated. A dilemma of our open tradition to dissent is how the more outlandish and perverse aspects of society can be not only tolerated but also normalized. For example, when a Christian pastor, Terry Jones, stated he planned to burn 200 Korans to commemorate the 9/11 attacks, he gained national attention. Although an optimistic perspective is that this media attention led to his backing down, what is glossed over is the credibility and notoriety given to someone functioning as a political showman. The notion of self-promotion as being effective when it shocks and/or when it is bigoted may be obvious, but it is also changing how issues of diversity and terror are trivialized in our social discourse. There is something to be said for not giving extremists the attention they are seeking for their own personal gain.

What I have tried to consider is how social psychological factors of authoritarianism, ultranationalism, and xenophobia, which are characteristic of many persons in our society, can potentially lead to overtly hostile forms of bias and an ideological shift toward biased behaviors resulting in a permission-giving of antisocial persons to commit hate violence. The experienced social scientist will rightly observe that the three factors of AUX are all intercorrelated. That is, there is a good deal of research on intergroup bias that shows that authoritarians are inherently xenophobic, as are high-SDO-scoring persons. I feel it is indeed this overlap that is part of the problem. The linkage of identification with a traditional national culture with racist and anti-immigrant attitudes characteristic of xenophobia is a critical indicator of the cultural cataclysm we are witnessing.

Summary

The primary psychological themes discussed in gaining voter support for the dramatic and unanticipated results of the 2016 U.S. presidential election—authoritarianism, ultranationalism, and xenophobia—all have shown a strong relationship to intolerance of social minority groups. These normal forms of bias, as numerous studies have revealed, will under conditions of duress or threat support a shift toward a more overtly biased society. In shifting our attention from these models of societal bias to hate violence, the distinctions between hate-arousal and ideology-expressive factors were found to indicate the risk for pre-meditation and likelihood of violence in the bias-motivated infraction. This thinking versus feeling approach to hate violence can give us some insight into what leads persons to commit certain types of hate crimes and potentially what we can do in terms of remediation of the offender's level of risk.

In further examining the behavioral markers of offenders of hate crimes, there were common grounds found between ideological charac-teristics of offenders and the supporters of an AUX-type politics ideol-ogy. Common themes of in-group identification, out-group denigration, criticism of sexual minorities, and protecting a home turf were found in both groups.

What will be considered in the following chapter is what these studies of hate tell us about the fallout from the 2016 election and the period that led up to the inauguration of Trump in early 2017.

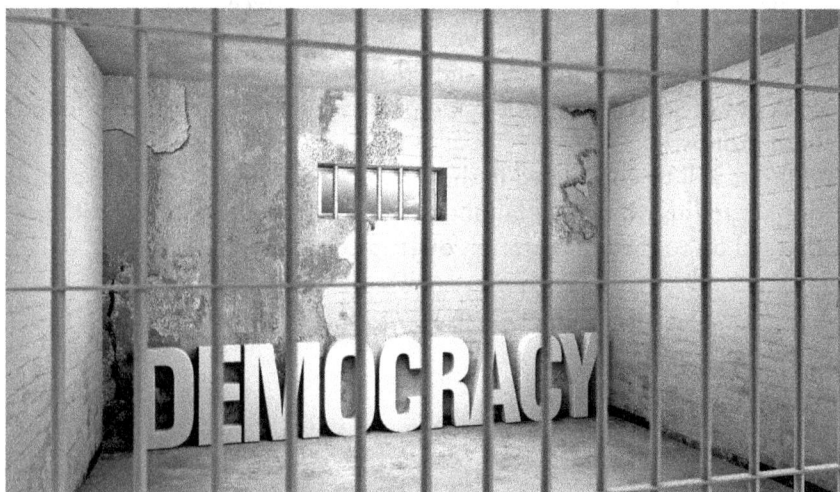

CHAPTER 5

The Fallout of Hate after 11/8

The results of the 2016 presidential election revealed the deep social and cultural divisions of the country. The election of Donald Trump, contradicting most all of the polling data, was framed in populist versus establishment ideologies, and politics versus entertainment. For professionals working in the area of hate crimes and domestic terrorism, however, the defining characteristic has been the freely employed use of ultranationalist or "alt-right" rhetoric that was employed to excoriate immigrants, persons of color, intellectuals, sexual minorities, and readers of the *New York Times* (Lichtblau, 2016). Societally, these "problems" have been linked to arguments for building a wall along the border of Mexico, for racially profiling Latinos for deportation, and for the religious/cultural exclusion of Muslims. As we see it, these culture wars themes served as motivational triggers for the perpetration of hate violence, the "fallout" of the election. We examine information from nongovernmental organizations (NGOs) that monitored the rash of hate crimes between the 2016 election and the 2017 inauguration.

Activating Events That Spike Hate Violence

An important question for stakeholders who fight hate crimes (one that precedes 11/8 by a few decades) concerns how societal events led to an escalation of bias-motivated crimes, which will be referred to as the activating or "triggering" events of hate violence. These include instrumental-messaging triggers, awareness-reactive triggers, and retaliatory triggers. These triggers involve the activation of the bias attitudes of members of society in regard to a specific out-group and convey a tacit permission-giving of powerful others or the ruling government to the perpetrators of hate violence.

Instrumental-Messaging Triggers

Planned "messaging" triggers consist of appeals by powerful others to their followers. These appeals seek to activate stereotypes, propose acts of intolerance, and condone aggression against denigrated out-groups. In some infrequent cases this is observed after explicit appeals for the commission of intergroup violence. This was the case of white supremacist Tom Metzger in his encouragement of violence by his followers, which led to the murder of an Ethiopian man in Portland, Oregon. This instrumental messaging is a form of propaganda that seeks to instigate intergroup violence. Implicitly this is the thesis of how the cultural cataclysm of 11/8 has impacted the United States in terms of the escalation of hate activity in the period following 11/8.

Awareness-Reactive Triggers

These reactive triggers are characterized by the individuals' adverse response, secondary to exposure to actions of a denigrated out-group that are identity-affirming or advocating for social equity. These acts might include public pronouncements of out-group leaders, public events celebrating the denigrated out-group, or temporal markers—religious holidays or historical events. These events may motivate both organized groups and lone wolf perpetrators. The triggering activity relayed via media outlets is experienced as provocation by bias-oriented individuals.

In one review of print media and hate crime activity, conducted before the wide-scale use of the Internet, my research team examined news stories that dealt with cultural topics, broadly. We pitted media coverage of diversity events such as Cinco de Mayo, Martin Luther King Jr. Day, and the LGBT Los Angeles Pride Festival against hate crimes reported by law enforcement. What we found was a modest relationship of media coverage of the Pride Festival, which garnered print and television coverage locally, with an LGBT hate crime spike in the following week. None of the other community events, or their coverage by the media, had any relationship to near-term hate activity in the metropolitan area. This media-hate activity linkage may be more effectively influenced by partisan and propagandist media outlets.

Retaliatory Triggering Events

The triggering of bias aggression may function as a form of retaliation for perceived infractions by an out-group, particularly in situations of chronic intergroup conflict. The most noteworthy example of retaliatory hate triggering in North America was the fallout after the 9/11 terror attack. In the data compiled by the FBI, the number of anti-Muslim hate crimes increased for calendar year 2001 to 481 offenses as compared with only 28 reported cases in 2000. Southern California law enforcement agencies reported an escalation in anti-Muslim have activity that lasted only a few weeks after 9/11. These events consisted largely of hate speech, verbal threats, and property damage, such as graffiti. In examining hate violence in the United States prior to 11/8, there are examples of both instrumental messaging and patterns of supposed retaliation against Muslim persons. The 2016 election has pushed this issue to the foreground and will be discussed in what follows.

Campaign Rhetoric and the Triggering of Hatred

The occurrence of hate violence targeting Muslims had significantly escalated prior to the November 8 election. Eric Lichtblau of the *New York Times* commented: "Hate crimes against American Muslims have soared to their highest levels since the aftermath of the September 11, 2001, attacks, according to data compiled by researchers, an increase apparently fueled by terrorist attacks in the United States and abroad and by divisive language on the campaign trail" (Lichtblau, 2016). This constitutes the instrumental triggering through the rhetoric of anti-Muslim ideology that was a prominent part of the campaign, which had been picked up by more reactionary parts of the press.

Consistent with our thesis of the cultural cataclysm, the pre-11/8 discourse on anti-Muslim sentiment moved from a debate about difference of policies to a potent activating message about Muslims posing a clear and present threat to public safety. The messaging of "Muslims as terrorists" was inconsistent with the available crime data. Importantly, the argument that the mainstream political leadership was weak, at the least, and arguably complicit in feeding into Islamic ideology was driven home by the employment of the term "radical Islam." Many of the Republican presidential candidates employed this as a rhetorical device to establish a dividing line with the soft policies of a liberal democratic model of governance. The reluctance of Secretary Hillary Clinton to use this phrase pitted her against Trump, who was able to label her as part of the ineffectual leadership in Washington. President Barack Obama had, of course, in choosing not to dignify the issue as worth debate, resisted the term and had been vulnerable to the "birther" conspiracy theory that he had been born outside of the United States and was a closeted Muslim. The choice between democratic and Republican ideologies became again an issue of a cultural war rather than a choice between candidates.

There were also incidents that fit the older tradition of antiblack, Deep South violence, such as the arson attack in 2016 of a black church in Greenville, Mississippi; the "historically black church was targeted in what authorities believe was an act of voter intimidation, its walls spray painted with the phrase 'Vote Trump'" (Southern Poverty Law Center, 2016, November 29). "Trump" became part of the graffiti in many places after the election results were in. Some of these offenses also constitute the commission of what are called "copycat crimes"—the perpetration of acts that recur and are carried out by diverse offenders.

An array of studies conducted after the election noted that the United States experienced a surge in racially motivated assaults, property crimes, and incidents of hate speech as part of the fallout of 11/8. This rise in hate incidents has been documented by the Southern Poverty Law Center, which collected information on 437 incidents that occurred in week one; this will be more fully examined below. Before we look at the statistical evidence, three examples of the individual experience of the 11/8 hate fallout will be considered.

Post-11/8 Victimization: Case Illustrations

In the first week after the election two individuals described to me their (unreported) hate crime victimization in Los Angeles—a blue city in a blue state; meaning a heavily democratic city in a region that over-whelming rejected the Trump alt-right rhetoric. A third case illustrates the consequences of the anti-Muslim rhetoric in action.

Interracial Aggression

This first case occurred within the first 48 hours of the declaration of Trump as the president-elect. The case reveals several of the subjective classic aspects of hate victimization: unpredictability, confusion, arousal, and (subsequent) comprehension. The incident involved a white woman who had gone into a coffee shop near where she worked. While there she encountered a former coworker—a dark-skinned multiracial man—and they struck up a conversation concerning what they had been doing of late. After getting their to-go coffee drinks they both walked out onto the sidewalk on a busy Los Angeles street. As they were standing there continuing to talk, a car pulled to the curb. The driver, a white man, then started shouting and swearing at them. The driver said something to the effect of "You can't do this anymore!" and "What are you doing, why are you with him?" He then shouted, "You could be shot for doing this!" and drove off. The man and the woman looked at each other startled and confused. The man quickly said "I better go" and dashed off. The woman later relayed this incident to her family.

Of note is that the woman was an attorney and, upon reflection, considered how this probably met the criteria for a hate crime. As with many crime victims, and particularly crime victims where bias is a factor, the sense of what to *do* about the incident was troubling. She also noted that her ex-colleague, a very demonstrative and "out" gay person, had said to her after the driver pulled away "Was it me?" meaning did this out of control man *know* he was gay? The confusion for the two individuals was one of "why us?"—was it the man's behavior, his easygoing flamboyance? Was it he was too dark and she was too light, was it they were too different to stand and talk? And, implicitly, the timing of the event, at least to the woman, meant that this was not okay to do *now*, now that the election had happened. A cynic would say simply that this event was because of someone being a bit crazy and belligerent. Although this may be true, it leaves the individual to sort through "Was it me?" and "Why now?" We will come back to this and consider what this fallout of hate does to the individual.

LGBT "Out" Violence

The second case had its own direct corollary to the question of individuality and how to function in an oppressive environment. Within the first week after the election, an adult gay man found himself feeling very distressed about what the election meant for him and his friends. Was this a signal the world was now less safe? Was he supposed to become more ghettoized and stay in WeHo—West Hollywood, a gay-friendly neighborhood—the rest of his life? Was he supposed to go back into the closet? He stated he decided to dress out in "as faggy a way" as he could think to and just go out. While sitting in his vintage convertible in a busy part of Los Angeles, a man walking in the crosswalk, looked at him, gestured, and threw a large ("big gulp") cup of soda on the victim and shouted "How do you like that sweetie!" and then ran off. After he pulled over and cleaned himself up he thought about how here he was again being threatened for his queerness.

In this case the victim—who was raised in a Deep South Confederate state—said he had been targeted because he had dressed-out to be gay after deciding he could not just hide in the closet because of the election. His experiences with his immediate family in the Deep South were to hear how Trump would replace the "nigger president"—including from a family member receiving medical care from a black physician under Obamacare. For this victim, who suffered minor injuries in the assault, he concluded that his family felt he had this coming because of his lifestyle.

The fallout issue for many individuals continues well after the incident itself; for example, this individual had difficulty maintaining a relationship with his extended family to have his concerns about the Trump presidency understood. This illustrates again the differences of political choice as a cultural wars flashpoint. It was not concerning attitudes about Clinton but rather a potent dividing point in a family. As one of his (older-generation) family members said "You know, I don't see what the problem is; you know you can always act straight if you want to!"

Anti-Muslim Violence

A nationally recognized post-11/8 incident that took place in December in Brooklyn reveals several of the key elements we see in our cultural cataclysm: spontaneous incidents between strangers that appear predicated on an anti-Muslim sentiment in which the sole provocation is the appearance of the victim. Officer Aml Elsokary, wearing her hajib, and her teenage son were threatened, and, in her son's case, assaulted by a man who had approached them and shouted at her "ISIS [expletive] I will cut your throat, go back to your country" (C. Kim, 2016).

Elsokary, a Muslim NYPD officer, had previously been recognized a few years before for her efforts in saving a baby and grandmother from a burning building. Her hate victimization is a consequence of the triggering activity we have discussed. The incident with Officer Elsokary came days after a teenage Muslim girl in New York City had reported being harassed by three men on a subway train who shouted "Donald Trump" at her. This story, which received national media attention, became one of the few fake news hate crimes post-11/8 (Eversley, 2016). What we do not know conclusively was whether the fake story motivated the actual offense against Officer Elsokary or not.

Making Meaning of the Fallout

An influential body of work has considered how victim processing of personal responsibility may aid in recovery from the crime (Janoff-Bulman & Frieze, 1992). Put simply, if the individual can determine how they had been vulnerable to the crime occurring, they can then take steps to reduce the risk of future victimization. Janoff-Bulman (1989) has proposed a schema model of recovery from trauma in which the rebuilding of a healthy self-concept is proposed. Specifically behavioral self-blame ("I can't put myself in a situation like that again" or "I will stay in places with people I trust from now on") may help in developing a positive postincident recovery from trauma—versus that of a characterological ("I am a loser and I got what I deserved") form of self-blame. This healthy self-blame thesis is not consistently born out in the literature; however, Kushner, Riggs, Foa, and Miller (1993) found that the victim's perceived controllability of crime perpetration reducing assault severity was only partially supported.

So what do we know about hate crime victimization and how it impacts the individual? A study conducted by Herek, Gillis, and Cogan (1999) made a useful observation about the sequelae—symptoms of depression, anger, anxiety, and posttraumatic stress—reported by LGBT hate crime victims were more severe than with crimes against this same community that were not *perceived* (italics are mine) as being bias-motivated. They also noted that lesbian and gay respondents in their community sample reported more crime-related fears, had a lower sense of mastery, and felt more discriminated against because of their LGBT status. What Herek et al. get at is that the bias element worsens the impact of the offense itself; which also—potentially—makes the event more difficult to recover from. As I have also noted, it may be impossible to reduce one's being at-risk if the crime is perpetrated because of our skin tone, gender, or age; an issue found in the first and third cases (Dunbar, 2001). It is also fair to say that to abandon one's religion or sexual orientation may simply be unthinkable as a viable strategy; an issue raised in the second case. Getting beyond hate may indeed be harder than getting over a "vanilla" crime, even one of violence.

Janoff-Bulman (1992) has referred to the process of trauma and recovery as the "Shattered Assumptions Theory" in which experiencing traumatic events changes how one views themselves and the world. Specifically, the theory concerns the effects that negative events have on three interlinked assumptions: the benevolence of the world, meaningfulness one derives from living in such a world, and the individual's self-worth in being in this (safe) context. This model may make persons raised as visible ethnic minorities in much of the United States, or persons who have lived in totalitarian countries, quite uncomfortable in terms of the implicit cultural encapsulation found in the model. Many people are socialized from a young age to see themselves as unsafe. However, the proposition that acute hate victimization changes our worldview is implicit to most of the work done in the field and is pregnant in the advocacy practices found in reducing intergroup violence.

One of the tasks for these individuals is, of course, to create new assumptions or modify their old ones in order to recover from the traumatic experience. I have referred to this as *identity reformation*, a process that is best engaged in after the acute phases of trauma have been treated (Dunbar, 2001). Danieli, Norris, and Engdahl (2016), in examining long-term effects of hate trauma—the Holocaust—noted that survivors and family members of genocide reestablish a sense of coherence via the process of restorative justice (Danieli, 2009) and repairing identity via attachments to community, place, and history.

To come back to our three case studies described above, in the first case, confusion over what the incident was predicated on may have led to it being comprehended differently for the two victims and may therefore have led to differing self-management assumptions going forward. The second case begins with a decision to be identity-affirming that is then undercut by the lack of support from family members living in a conservative "red" state world. The third case provides us an example of how even doing everything right still leaves you vulnerable to the oppression of the larger social environment. If Muslims are terrorists, as the Trump people seem to want us to believe, Officer Elsokary shows she is there to protect the public good by putting her own safety on the line. Unlike her assailant, she did not do an identity check to decide whether or not to save the baby in the burning building.

In shifting our attention from the individual to the national perspective, we will examine findings of post-11/8 hate activity. This will include review of the work conducted by the Southern Poverty Law Center (SPLC), the Human Rights Commission (HRC), national media coverage of hate incidents, metropolitan Orange County data on hate incidents, and results of the online survey on adjusting to post-11/8 America.

Reports of Postelection Hate Victimization: SPLC Project

The SPLC tabulated reports received nationally starting the day after the election (Southern Poverty Law Center, December 16, 2016). During the first week, the number of self-reported incidents, which were reported via phone interviews and social media communiqués, of hate-based intimidation and harassment reached 437. The SPLC report found that the incidents that occurred between November 9, the day after the presidential election, and the morning of Monday, November 14, were related to anti-immigrant bias (136), antiblack (89), and LGBT bias (43). Forty-one cases—10% of their sample—involved pro-Trump references, such as the pro-Trump vandalism of a "unity" sign in Connecticut. SPLC also reported 20 incidents that were because of anti-Trump bias. These incidents most frequently occurred in school and work settings; 99 incidents occurred at kindergarten to 12th-grade schools, 67 at colleges and universities, and another 76 in the workplace.

The high frequency of school-based incidents is telling in that a significant amount of public opinion polling has shown over the past decade a steady decline in out-group hostility by millennial-and-younger aged persons. As I have commented (Dunbar, 2017) elsewhere, "social attitudes have substantially changed to become more supportive of equity under the law for gay, lesbian, and transsexual persons (Pew Research Center, July 2012; McCarthy, 2016). As of 2015, 35 of 50 states in the U.S. have legalized gay marriage" (Winning in the States, 2016). So, although the number of young persons in general who hold animosity is declining, the initial wave of events, arguably carried out by a relatively small number of individuals, makes itself felt in a population that is otherwise on the average and in the long-run more tolerant than their elders.

A follow-up on the SPLC data collection at roughly one month after 11/8 produced a total of 1,094 reported hate incidents. All reported incidents to SPLC were tabulated in the period from November 9 to December 12, 2016. Of the 1,094 reports filed in the first month after 11/8, the most frequently targeted group was immigrants ($n = 315$). Other high-frequency reports of hate victimization were tabulated for antiblack ($n = 221$), anti-Muslim ($n = 112$), and anti-LGBT ($n = 109$) incidents. It is noteworthy that two of the frequent target groups—blacks and sexual minorities—were at best secondary targets of the campaign rhetoric and not explicitly the ground zero scapegoats targeted in the Trump campaign. This wave effect—of pulling in a range of targets to hate—extended to the more fringe supporters, as reflected in the distribution of hate organizing propaganda immediately after his election. The SPLC report also found a very high spike in hate literature—57 independent events—that was distributed in the first week following his election. As they noted, "We've also been tracking the reported distribution of white nationalist (47), KKK (7), and anti-Semitic (3) posters and fliers" in the weeks after 11/8.

An example of the type of incident reported to the SPLC includes the following: "I witnessed an apparently inebriated older white man in the park make an obscene gesture at two women in hijabs in a public park. The women scurried away and the man turned to me perhaps under the assumption that I shared his enmity. He made remarks about Ohio and, to the effect, that Muslims are subhuman and that 'President Trump got his work cut out for him.' We exchanged words but I avoided an altercation and left the scene" (Southern Poverty Law Center, December 2016).

What do the SPLC cases tell us about hate crimes and the hate-arousal and bias-ideology distinction (Chapter 4) that has been proposed? Well, in a word, that many of these offenses are high on the arousal-hate dimension and largely absent a strong ideological element. This means many of the perpetrators of these offenses have acted-out their hostility in a manner that is in many cases low in the ideology-intent dimension and is rather characteristic of the labile bigot type we have discussed. It is almost fair to say that these events occurred as a function of having been given the message that this was an opportunity to hate.

The use of candidate Trump's name further has the Orwellian–Big Brother aspect of the authoritarian belief system; offenders committed the hate act with the endorsement (e.g., permission giving) of Trump; an example of instrumental triggering. The zeitgeist of the thing is Trump-inspired. As the SPLC noted in their report: "Around 37 percent of all incidents directly referenced President-elect Donald Trump, his campaign slogans, or his infamous remarks about sexual assault."

Relationship of SPLC Reportage to Voter Support for Candidate Trump

In working with the SPLC report and linking it to the election findings, a clear pattern emerged nationally. It was found that the occurrence of post–November 8, 2016, hate incidents was related to states where candidate Trump received a smaller percentage of the popular vote.[1] Additionally, more hate incidents were reported in states with a lower percentage of white residents.

Relationship of SPLC Reportage to Civil War Status

How does the pattern of state Civil War alignment relate to hate incident reportage during the period after 11/8? What was found was that states that were part of the Union had an average of 30 reports between November 9, 2016, and January 20, 2017, which was three times greater than the unaligned states, with an average just over 10 reports.[2] The Confederate states in this case—unlike in the reportage of hate crimes—were in a middle range, with an average of 21 reports.

The relationship of self-reported hate incidents post-11/8 was not related at a state-level to the overall pattern of law enforcement documentation of hate crimes from 1992 to 2015.[3] It was found that hate incidents reported by the victims of these events were also unrelated to the historical marker of black lynch activity from 1880 to 1968. Victim reportage was, however, related to the number of SPLC-documented hate groups in each state. Importantly, an increase in victim-reported hate incidents by the victims was negatively related to both the percentage of white residents in the 2010 census and the percentage of votes cast for candidate Trump.[4] In Figure 5.1, Civil War clusters by reported post-11/8 hate incidents are summarized.

Taken together, what we find is that the process of victim self-reporting is related to regional factors inclusive of greater race/ethnic diversity, a less politically conservative populace, and more organized antidiversity groups. The pattern of victims reporting hate incidents was unrelated to historical factors of black lynching and to the lower reported statewide hate crime reportage by law enforcement personnel. In other words, the more multicultural and politically liberal the state, the more hate activity was reported—or, at least reported to the Southern Poverty Law Center. Where history did matter, however, was in the higher reportage levels in the Union states, which mirrored the findings of the 20-plus-year pattern of law enforcement reportage.

Postelection Hate Victimization: Human Rights Campaign Study

An online study of teenagers was conducted by the Human Rights Campaign (HRC) from mid-December, 2016, to January 10, 2017, to assess experiences of adolescents impacted by 11/8. More than 50,000 young people aged 13–18 (mean age was approximately 16 years) from across the United States participated in their online solicitation (via HRC online media sources) and included a diverse range of respondents in terms of gender, sexual orientation, gender-expression, race, ethnicity, and religious background.

Of the usable subjects ($n = 50,619$) pulled from a pool of over 90,000 responses, roughly 50% of the respondents noted feeling nervous "most or all of the time" since 11/8. For transgender respondents (11% of their subjects), the HRC report noted that "about half of transgender youth reported feeling hopeless and worthless most or all of the time, and 70 percent said that these and similar feelings have increased in the past 30 days."

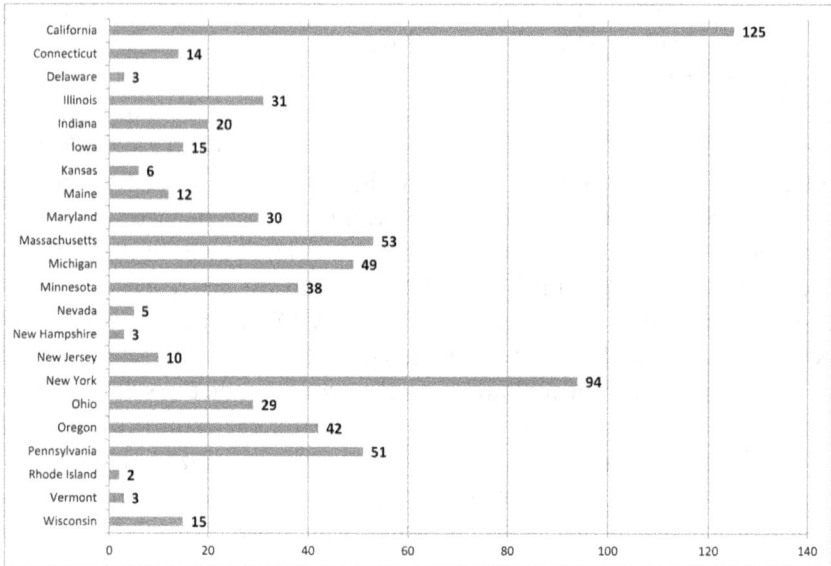

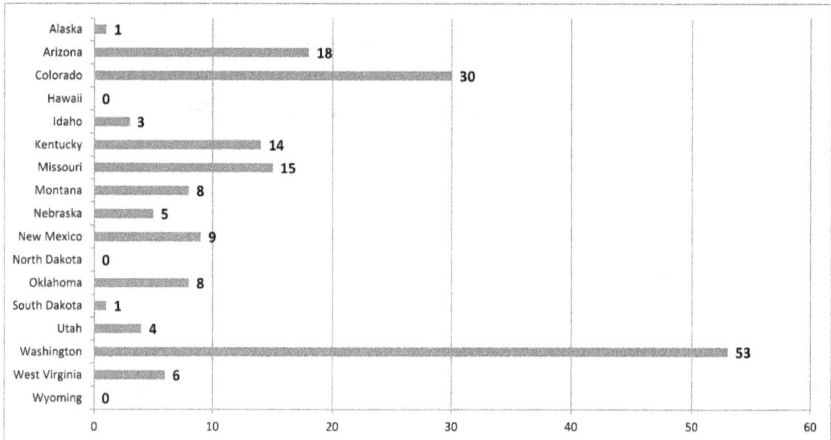

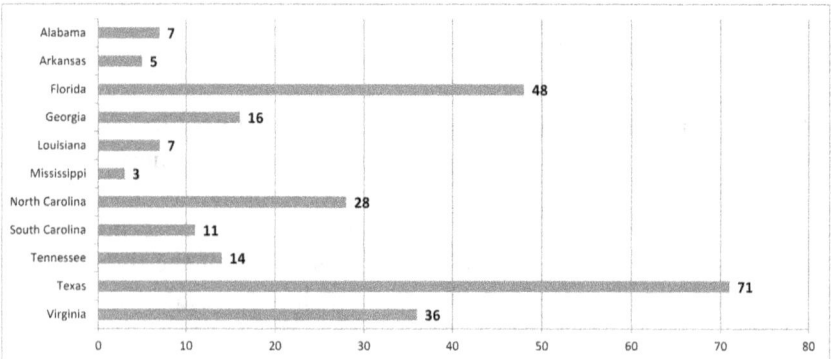

Figure 5.1   Civil War Clusters by Reported Post-11/8 Hate Incidents

Being the target of hate activity—defined in the report as bullying and harassment—was reported most frequently for victim status of race/ethnicity (70%) and sexual orientation (63%). Fifty-nine percent of the reports included being targeted due to immigration status, with 55% for including bias related to gender. As noted by Allison Turner, the HRC assistant press secretary, "Our biggest takeaway was that 70 percent of all respondents had witnessed bullying, hate speech, or harassment since the 2016 election." It is important to note that, according to the SPLC study, the most common place of hate victimization in the month after 11/8 was the school setting. Almost a quarter of the SPLC locations ($n = 226$) were hate incidents that occurred in school settings. In spite of this, virtually none of the news stories tracked in mainstream media during this period of time discussed the experiences of young people.

Analyzing Media-Reported Post-11/8 Hate Activity

I conducted a review of hate activity post-11/8 by conducting an online media sweep of published stories and posts reporting hate incidents and hate crimes from November 9, 2016, to January 19, 2017, the day before Trump's inauguration. This approach looked at the frequency with which media reported on the spike of hate activity, and further considered what the target groups were and the nature of the offense in terms of constructs of hate- and ideology-motivated violence discussed in Chapter 2.

The varying data collection activities of the post-11/8 period were reviewed using some of the ways of distinguishing between ideology- and hate-driven aggression discussed in Chapter 4. Examining media-reported hate incidents post-11/8, we found 60 unique infractions were identified. These reported hate incidents included 10 infractions that were hands-on violence, including two homicides, which revealed a hate motive. The remaining 90% of the infractions were related to hate speech (16.7%) and property crimes (55%). These national media-reported incidents included more acts of violence proportionally than the SPLC and human relations projects (see below) observed. Media attention to more sensational and violent hate acts is not a new phenomenon. What this has led to in this specific situation, however, is the obscuring of the high proportion of hate incidents perpetrated by individuals who were not engaged in criminal activity. Implicitly, what the SPLC and Human Rights studies note is the frequency of hate activity by noncriminal members of the community, which is in turn motivated by the election of Trump as the incoming president. What these other data sources point out is the normative nature of hate activity since 11/8.

Alt-right involvement was noted in nearly one-half (43.3%) of the incidents, and 46.7% of the reported incidents had explicit references to President-elect Trump in the commission of the infraction. What this demonstrates is how the 11/8 election served as a high-activating event for individuals and groups perpetrating hate crimes. In the short history of hate crime prosecution in the United States, there has never been an elected public official who was routinely cited as a motivator in the perpetration of hate violence, let alone the president-elect of the country. No matter what the rhetoric of Trump has been in the period leading up to his inauguration or his statements on hate crimes since becoming president, the invocation of his name in the commission of hate activity makes clear the ideological alliance he has formed with bias-motivated offenders in our country.

Many of these incidents reported in national media were related to anti-immigrant attitudes—being commented on in 45% of the cases. The alt-right aspects of the offenses were not, however, indicative of more violent forms of hate activity. From a conceptual standpoint many of these acts of bias revealed spontaneous forms of conflict with little premeditation—typically being linked to hate speech in public venues. Most of the premeditated acts were property crimes that had some form of messaging—be it pro-Trump or anti-Islamic terms and images. Few of the events revealed both a strong ideological and high level of aggression or violence. So the analyses of the actions themselves indicated many of the acts were committed by individuals who adhered to a biased belief system but were unlikely to (in most cases) engage in criminal infractions. Therefore, many of the high-identity incidents were crimes against property and less frequently against the person whereas the high-hate incidents were perpetrated by individuals who were confrontational but not violent. This is not to say these forms of violence are not powerful. It can be argued that being harassed by a seemingly noncriminal individual—the soccer mom or person in business attire—may create a unique form of threat, one that implies it is not simply antisocial youths but the typical member of society who might target the vulnerable individual. As a victim of a religious hate crime once put it, "The problem is it could be anyone, at any time." The experiences recounted by the media after 11/8 support this concern as valid.

Orange County, California: Documenting Post-11/8 Hate Incidents

Another source of information on hate activity post-11/8 is found in the work of the Orange County Human Relations Commission (OCHRC).

Human relations organizations in the United States have served for more than half a century to monitor and intercede in situations of intergroup conflict (Dunbar, Wild, & Toma, 2016). The OCHRC served as the point agency in documenting hate incidents after the 2016 election. This will be discussed further below. In tabulating hate incidents from November 9, 2016, to January 20, 2017, the OCHRC recorded 44 cases that were found credibly to be a bias-motivated. The agency noted a marked (e.g., nearly 50%) increase compared to their data collection for the same period from one year earlier.

In the cases that were documented in a historically conservative and at the same time multicultural city, the vast majority were characterized by spontaneous hate speech. The majority of the victims were members of groups that were targets of the Trump rhetoric; Latinos, nearly 40%, and Muslims, another 25%. At the same time, more than 10% of the targets of hate speech were Asian-Pacific persons; a similar number were gay or transsexual victims.

Motivationally, 25% of the cases included specific reference to President-elect Trump with roughly 20% of the perpetrators referring to anti-immigrant attitudes. Nearly one-half of the cases made reference to the victim(s) getting "out of the country." Situationally only one of these offenses indicated any prior relationship between the offender and the victim. The majority—three out of four—offenders were adult men. Behaviorally the offenders were modestly agitated. None of the reports indicated that provocation had occurred prior to their hate behavior. Most of these incidents took place in public domains, city streets, commercial establishments, and schools. Only one of the incidents involved property damage and one other involved burglary.

Analyzing Online Survey Responses

From the online survey research I have conducted post-11/8, a significant number of Wave One subjects (the first two months after the election) expressed a concern that their community faced a significant risk (40%) for an increase in hate crimes and another 34% (n = 140) felt there had been somewhat of an increase. Additionally 20% (n = 69) of the respondents felt a "significant increase" in terror risk and another 107 (30.5%) felt "somewhat" of an increase in risk of terrorism in their community since 11/8. The survey respondents reported that 12% of them had been the target of hate speech after 11/8.

For respondents who completed the survey in the eight weeks following 11/8 (i.e., prior to the presidential inauguration), concern about the welfare for friends and family members was higher than that reported by the individual for themselves. Concern of friends/family being the victim of racial hostility was 66%, for ethnic hostility 70%, and for LGBT friends/family the perceived risk was 77%. For friends being the target of gender-based hostility the percentage of concern was 68%, for hostility due to immigration status, 48%. The risk of being the target of religious hostility for friends or family members was endorsed by 57% of the respondents, for disability 43%, and for nationality 48%. The perceived risk of friends/family being at-risk for terrorism was 34%.

In Wave Two ($n = 1,555$), conducted during the first three weeks following the January 20, 2017, inauguration the perceived community risk for hate crimes was seen as significant for 39% of respondents and somewhat greater for another 37%. Terror risk perceptions after week one of the Trump presidency found 30% feeling a significant increase in risk for terrorism and another 24% feeling somewhat of an increase in risk for terrorism.[5]

Findings from the online survey conducted after 11/8 and again after the January 2017 inauguration were compared for supporters of Clinton vis-à-vis all other candidates. Concerns about friends and family being vulnerable to harassment experiences were found in nearly one-half to three-quarters of responding Clinton voters. There was little variation on the risk ratings between Wave One and Wave Two. The lowest area of concern in both samples was that of being a victim of terrorism; this was reported for one-third of the Clinton voters in both survey periods. In Table 5.1 the frequencies for Wave One (postelection) and Wave Two (postinauguration) concerns are summarized for the Clinton voters.

Respondents who voted for candidates other than Clinton reported significantly fewer concerns in the weeks after the election and during the first month of the Trump presidency. In Wave One the expressed concern fell in the range of one-in-five voters, with lower concerns for immigrant harassment or deportation risk—two issues candidate Trump had been connected to. Generally there was a moderate increase in concerns for friends and family in the postinauguration sample, though the level of expressed concern remained far below that of the losing Clinton voters. The survey results for the non-Clinton voter group are found in Table 5.2.

Community Response: Government and NGO Initiatives

The wave of hate activity, as the SPLC report notes, started to swell immediately after the 11/8 election results were in. At both state and local

Table 5.1 Comparing Postelection and Postinauguration Survey Concerns—Clinton Voters

	Wave One (*n* = 357) November 14, 2016– December 31, 2016	Wave Two (*n* = 978) January 29, 2017– February 16, 2017
Risk to friends/family:		
Deportation risk	49%	58.7%
Terrorism risk	38.4%	31.8%
LGBT harassment	88%	68.4%
Race harassment	74.7%	77.6%
Ethnic harassment	79.5%	74.4%
Gender harassment	77.4%	61%
Religious harassment	63.7%	55%
Immigrant harassment	53.8%	67.6%
Disability harassment	48.8	37%
Age harassment	42.8	35%

Table 5.2 Comparing Postelection and Postinauguration Survey Concerns—Voters for Candidates Other Than Clinton

	Wave One (*n* = 292) November 14, 2016– December 31, 2016	Wave Two (*n* = 157) January 29, 2017– February 16, 2017
Risk to friends/family:		
Deportation risk	18%	24.3%
Terrorism risk	14.8%	26.1%
LGBT harassment	26.2%	43.9%
Race harassment	22.6%	33.5%
Ethnic harassment	21.3%	53.5%
Gender harassment	16.4%	31%
Religious harassment	26.8%	41.4%
Immigrant harassment	18%	52.9%
Disability harassment	14%	11.2%
Age harassment	13%	21.2%

levels the issue of how to respond to this unanticipated outcome was cha-otic. An interesting example of how a metropolitan region of the country responded to the rise in hate is found in Orange County, California.

The OCHRC actively responded to the fallout right after the election results were in. It should be noted, as with other forms of public safety organizations, the leadership with OCHRC was prepared to launch preventive initiatives ahead of any signal of civil unrest. The response strategy can be reduced to four planks: (1) incident information collec-tion, (2) promoting and discussing with the public the experiences of hate crime victims, (3) a media-based public education campaign, and (4) sponsoring law enforcement–community member dialogues about intergroup and hate crime concerns. These are briefly described below.

Community outreach occurred to gather information on hate crimes and forms of harassment, given the concern of immigrant groups; a particular emphasis was made to engage at-risk groups who would be reluctant to contact law enforcement agencies. This resulted in the iden-tification of 16 hate crimes and 51 hate incidents following the Novem-ber 2016 election.

Educational programming occurred to share information on hate inci-dents. Examples of the types of events identified in the community out-reach efforts included the following:

- A Muslim woman who was walking in the park had her hijab yanked off her head from behind and was smashed in the face with a metal water bottle;
- A group of elementary school children in a privileged community chanted at their Latino custodian in the school cafeteria, "build the wall";
- An African American family who had first a watermelon left in their yard, then chicken bones in their mailbox, and finally a swastika painted on their automobile; and
- A Korean American church that had swastikas painted in red on their church.

A public awareness campaign was started through social media, #Hate-FreeOC, to counter the narrative that these hate crimes represented our community, emphasizing and celebrating the diversity of the communi-ties of Orange County.

Police–community dialogues occurred to bring line officers together with grass roots community members including immigrants to build positive relationships and enhance safety. This later initiative sought to allay concerns of non-U.S.-born individuals as to the opportunity for help and protection from uniformed officers.

Additionally, OCHRC continued longtime practices of: (1) supporting hate crime victims with calls, visits, and assistance in navigating police and social service systems, (2) teaching about the special nature of "hate motivated" crime to law enforcement officers, in the New Recruit academy as well as block training, (3) compiling data for publication of an annual report on hate crimes in Orange County, this involved collaboration with law enforcement and community groups, and (4) conducting community presentations about hate, implicit bias, and building intergroup relations (Rusty Kennedy, personal communication, March 21, 2017).

One of the significant targets of the intolerance of the cultural cataclysm was undocumented persons. On December 7, in response to the promised federal efforts to deport undocumented persons, the Santa Ana City Council voted to designate the city as a sanctuary city. The city—with one of the largest Latino populations in the nation—provided the first clear response to the Trump victory.

Long-Term Hate Fallout of 11/8

A great deal could change in the near future in terms of how hate speech is viewed, of what law enforcement is asked to do about hate violence, and the real possibility that federal oversight of hate crimes will all but vanish. The issue of the underreportage of hate crimes has for decades been recognized; this will become more problematic with the promised changes to our federal government and the Department of Justice. A challenge going forward for agencies responding to hate violence is how does (or, why would) an oligarchic or authoritarian government monitor hate activity? As we have stressed, hate crime laws are a consequence of the civil society movement, which is intimately associated with the liberal democratic political system. Our cataclysmic cultural change of 2016 has moved our society into a faux-democracy model of governance, one that may ultimately teeter on the verge of an autocratic state. How can our government, after such a shift on its ideological axis, be expected to enforce policies that support the civil liberties minority out-groups?

Going forward, will state-based hate crime data collection take on greater significance as a political statement? That is, will the regions of the United States that adhere to a liberal democratic model of governance continue to actively document and respond to hate violence? By comparison, will regions dominated by antidiversity political norms move away from documenting this special class of criminal offenses? What will the psychosocial stress be for communities with escalating hate activity and governmental indifference? In the dynamic and some may say chaotic times the Trump presidency promises, it is important to both identify the near-term consequences of an ideology of intolerance and to anticipate what might happen if this shift becomes more stable and enduring in the United States.

Efforts that examine the long-term impact of state-sponsored intolerance are therefore relevant to our evolving social stasis. The work of Danieli (1998) has sought to articulate the impact and forms of coping intergenerationally with hate violence—what she refers to as "Trauma and the Continuity." In looking at long-term trauma she has described adaptive forms of coping as characterized by "victim," "numb," and "fighter" styles. In a study with 422 adult Holocaust survivors, she found that her respondents reported how the parents' (intensity of) victim, numb, and fighter posttrauma adaptive styles impacted the psychosocial status of the family. Danieli and her colleagues note that problematic, "broken," generational disruptions and living in more supportive sociocultural environments—in her study Israel—were related to both higher and lower levels of transmitted trauma symptoms. On one hand, this research points to the risk for immigrant families living under a regime of greater intolerance and the threat of deportation and, on the other, suggests what longer-term experiences of societal oppression can do to family and child functioning. As she notes, recovery from oppression requires the recapturing of meaning, identity, connectedness, and community attachment.

As we have suggested, the experience of hate victimization in our post-11/8 society pose several challenges for how citizens view their government, importantly in terms of belief in social justice, protection under the law, and the mental health needs of victims of hate. The threat of hate violence in our communities has increased as a consequence of the cultural cataclysm. The use of intolerant rhetoric as a political device is also a powerful trigger that motivates individual actors to perpetrate hate violence.

The social environments in which we live are more unpredictable. Many of the hate incidents that have been documented since 11/8 revealed a highly reactive form of aggression that occurs in our places of work, association, and learning. The majority of these noncriminal hate incidents appear to have been perpetrated by otherwise law-abiding individuals. These perpetrators were apparently otherwise not engaged in criminal activity (i.e., there was no co-occurring infraction in these incidents). This lowering of the bar of biased behavior has activated—triggered—individuals to engage in hate speech in what were benign contact situations.

What this further underscores is that *we are all at risk*—although many of the targets of the recent spate of hate activities are immigrants and Muslims, others singled out are sexual minorities, black Americans, and Asian-Pacific persons; in other words, individuals who *even stereotypically* are neither illegal entrants to the country nor individuals motivated to violence due to "radical Islam." Anyone can now be a victim, even citizens who voted for candidate Trump.

The federal government of this administration will not help. A direct consequence of the cultural cataclysm is the indifference of policy makers to the civil rights of persons who are historically marginal members of a Eurocentric society. This government will not help us—that is the hard fact of the matter. We will need to deal with this one ourselves.

Summary

Hate behavior across the country appears to have been exacerbated by the rhetoric of the 2016 presidential race. This resulted in a brief escalation not unlike that seen in the aftermath of the 9/11 terror attacks. The triggering of hate violence has been linked to planned political campaigns that fueled the perception of a Muslim threat to the homeland as well as galvanized opposition and hostility toward immigrants from Central America. The activating of bias has been a specific outcome—and arguably a goal of the Trump campaign and his public rallies. The diverse data collection by NGOs since 11/8 underscores this rise in anti-Muslim and anti-immigrant bias. Our case study on this reveals how doing public good as a law enforcement officer does not exempt an individual from being the target of an anti-Muslim hate crime.

The fallout from 11/8 reveals a range of motives in many cases carried out by persons who apparently acted spontaneously and independently of any organized group. Many of the perpetrators of the noncriminal hate incidents acted in a highly spontaneous fashion. These incidents underscore the heightened animus found in the general population against groups that have been messaged to not trust and to disdain. The diverse efforts to document this hate crime spike revealed a significant number of incidents in school settings that targeted our youths.

Online survey research revealed a significant level of concern among respondents about the risk for hate victimization of their friends and family. Longer-term challenges for hate crime documentation are of great concern given the shift in our federal justice initiatives. This raises the important challenge of how culturally regressive regimes view human rights laws in general as inconsistent with the goals of the state. Our data collection efforts remain poorly integrated, even in this time of great need for logic and accuracy to debate the erosion of civil rights.

If we are seeing the beginning of a recalibration of tolerance for formal and informal forms of bias, we must also look at how hate victimization may become more rampant and chronic for at-risk groups in our society. The study of intergenerational trauma becomes one illustration of this area of concern. Our society may be moving into a period of a retrenchment of civil rights that poses a unique challenge to living under a xenophobic and potentially autocratic form of government. The threat to free speech and individualism is a consequence of living during this period of the cultural cataclysm. In the long term this may be seen as a dark period of society in which intolerance became a cultural norm while the society became increasingly multicultural.

CHAPTER 6

Political Persuasion: Debating and Engaging Hatred

Propaganda is not a matter for common minds but rather a matter for practitioners. It is not supposed to be lovely or theoretically correct. I do not care if I give wonderful aesthetically elegant speeches, or speak so that women cry. The point of a political speech is to persuade people of what we think right.

—Joseph Goebbels, 1934 speech

You accomplish more with a smile, a handshake, and a gun than you do with just a smile and a handshake.

—Al Capone (though some believe this quote is erroneously attributed to him)

As has been argued, a signature characteristic of the U.S. presidential campaign was the employment of a rhetoric of intolerance. In the run-up to 11/8, the chronic, even mind-numbing, use of virulent identity politics infused our political discourse. As Herr Goebbels and Mr. Capone would have to agree, this alternative platform of intolerance to the liberal democratic tradition proved its effectiveness. The 2016 elections resulted in the presidency of Donald Trump and Republican control of the U.S. Senate and House of Representatives—which in turn guaranteed confirmation of the Republican president's nominee for the ninth justice of the U.S. Supreme Court, leading to presumed Republican control of the Supreme Court for years to come. Why have a Reichstag fire when you can win at the polling booth?

Underlying the outcome of the 2016 election as well as being a critical element in the debate over human rights are the forms of persuasion that are practiced to shape public opinion. The study and application of principles of social power are essential to egalitarian discourse as well as authoritarian forms of control. What follows is a brief summary of the practice of persuasion and propaganda as applied to social attitudes, inclusive of hate crime laws. We will then consider what influence tactics can be employed by the vanquished in response to 11/8. In moving against a quasiautocracy, a critical question then is what constitutes a strategy of influence for the politically powerless?

The Psychological Science of Power and Persuasion

In 1959, French and Raven published a paper, "The Bases of Social Power." In the subsequent decades their work on forms of social influence led to a range of applications in leadership studies, organizational psychology, and interpersonal relationships. French and Raven posited: "Our theory of social influence and power is limited to influence of person, P, produced by a social agent, O, where O can be either another person, a role, a norm, a group, or a part of a group." Additionally, an essential part of their thinking emphasized how specific forms of influence could be identified and characterized as being either "hard" or "soft" in their application. Their work (French & Raven, 1959) identified five primary forms of power; these are: (1) Coercive power in which the object is influenced to comply via material, physical, and emotional threat. Coercion can result in physical harm, although its principal goal is compliance. Demonstrations of harm to others may be employed to establish the legitimacy of the threat. This form of influence is employed often by authoritarians, despots, and bullies. (2) Reward power includes both material and emotional forms of influence. Reward power may also be realized via punishment (e.g., "Do this or else"). (3) Legitimate power that is typically signified via formal position titles. The legitimacy of influence is contingent on the influenced person assigning credibility to the position of authority. Legitimate power may also be inherently coercive. (4) Referent power relies on shared membership between the influencer and the object. This form of influence may employ shared cultural norms or experiences or be evidenced via the charismatic influence exercised by the influencing agent. (5) Expert power reflects the influence of the object by the assertion or demonstration of expertise by the influencer. This is a form of influence useful in organizations and in contexts where information and knowledge are vital.

Of interest to the issue of hate crimes, of course, is how social influence may serve to promote human rights and policies (such as hate crime laws) that protect the rights of social out-groups. The study of social influence may also shed light on opposition to civil liberties and oppression of minority groups. French and Raven's work continued the thinking of Lewin (Raven, 1999) in terms of recognizing the essential roles of leadership and power in the maintenance of a social system. Likewise the notion of influence proposed by French and Raven was consistent with the research of Asch (1952) who experimentally examined the dynamics of group pressure and the members' reactions to conformity and submission to group norms. The examination of social attitudes as characterized by Kelman (1958) is largely congruent with the power model discussed here. For Kelman, the process of attitude change is reliant on the influencing agent as being competent to exert power over the follower, that they are (culturally) viable and attractive to the influenced object, and that their request for control is seen as inherently credible.

Studies on Persuasion about Hate Crime Laws

A series of studies using the French and Raven model was employed to examine the psychological characteristics of persons who sought to change another's beliefs about social issues such as hate crime laws, women's rights, the rights of ethnic minorities, and attitudes about antiterror "patriot act" laws. Conducted in both the United States and Spain by a team of researchers (Dunbar, Blanco, Sullaway, & Horcajo, 2004; Dunbar & Molina, 2004; Dunbar, Sullaway, Blanco, Horcajo, & de la Corte, 2007; Dunbar & Blanco, 2015, the observations revealed a significant level of consistency in terms of endorsed strategies to advocate for and against human rights laws. Opposition to hate crime laws, particularly, has been rooted in arguments that the laws are ineffectual, require the law enforcement officer to read the mind of the suspect, and are inherently divisive if not discriminatory (Jacobs & Potter, 1998). As has been enumerated (Dunbar & Blanco, 2015), specific argumentation points against these laws further infer that all crimes are crimes of hate, that the laws restrict First Amendment rights of free speech, that these laws are the product of special interest groups, and (generally) that these laws constitute an infringement of civil liberties. In these studies on how human rights were perceived, a consistent pattern emerged. We found that the individual's' political conservatism was consistently related to their rejection of human rights and hate crime laws. This in and of itself is not surprising, but what is important is that these studies were all based on university-educated samples. This is wholly consistent with the interesting work of Stephan Lewandowsky and colleagues that found opposition to global warming science is not a product of educational level or science knowledge but of such factors as political conservatism and "free market" political views. In this sense it would seem that a preference for nonregulatory political practices were a motivator in rejecting science-based arguments. Importantly, Lewandowsky et al. also found that free market conservatives questioned the scientific study on the link of HIV to AIDS and the relationship of tobacco use to lung cancer (Lewandowsky, Oberauer, & Gignac, 2013). He and his colleagues have since explored how this conservative free market orientation is linked to ascription to a range of conspiracy theories (Lewandowsky, Oberauer, & Gignac, 2013).

In addressing these concerns, the most important aspects of the Dunbar et al. studies revealed that politically conservative individuals, and those who endorsed more of the beliefs in authoritarianism, adhered to the use of force (emotional coercion, formal power, and material rewards) to attain the agreement of others to accept their beliefs about hate crime and human rights policies. So, although the skepticism about human rights on one hand and scientific problems on the other are adopted by the conservative individual more readily, what has also been consistently found is the need to get *others to comply* with such a belief system.

Another finding across the Dunbar and associates studies was that both gender and gender attitudes contributed to opposition to hate crime laws and laws protecting the rights of women and ethnic minorities. This gender effect for greater bias orientation has been discussed previously (Carter, 1990), as has the role of a male-dominant "machismo" worldview. Results have found that men more favorably endorse the use of material and coercive forms of influence, that is, the use of hard influence tactics. Likewise, conservatively oriented individuals endorsed more coercive and forceful tactics to influence another's beliefs about human rights. This liberal-woman-soft influence versus conservative-male-hard influence distinction was unaffected by the specific human rights issues surveyed or by nationality. Again, across specific study or locale, it was observed that ideological issues—specifically right-wing authoritarianism—were related to hard influence tactics even after political orientation or other demographic factors such as gender had been considered. We will now discuss in some detail the issues of hard and soft persuasion as political strategies.

Harsh Persuasion, Political Instability, and Ultranationalism

What will it take, to whip you into line?
A broken heart?
A broken head?
It can be arranged.
It can be arranged.
—From "Mr. Blue" by Tom Paxton

As has just been discussed, bias and opposition to the civil liberties of others is evidenced via the endorsement of harsh forms of social influence. Experimentally, many individuals with biased worldviews will impose their beliefs on out-group doubters via tactics of coercion and force. The influencing of the nonconforming person—Mr. Blue in the Tom Paxton song—will be dealt with from a position of power and punishment. Attitude influence of members of an in-group, by comparison, can be accomplished through employment of relational power, stereotype activation, and softer forms of hate speech. It is worth going back to Allport's classic 1954 text *The Nature of Prejudice* in which he discussed antilocution as the most benign—and personal—level of prejudice. For Allport, this entailed the sharing of hostile speech of out-groups between members of racial and ethnic in-groups. The bias was acknowledged as a mutual presumption between members of the in-group. Today, we see the use of personal hate speech in print, electronic, and online media. The once inherently private is made public.

As Allport's (1954) classic work and the efforts of others have observed, intergroup bias is a potent means of destabilizing a society. As Feierabend and Feierabend (1966) proposed, societal instability is characterized by the frequency that aggression is directed against individuals or groups, targets members of political groups in opposition to the state, or through the perpetration of aggression against figurehead leaders of social out-groups. An example of this splintering of a societal stasis is found in the recent Argentinian experience, in which the standing president Cristina Kirchner engaged in policies to divide the populace by proposing a faux populism. Referred to in the country as *la grieta,* the process was one of creating a separation, as is seen in a brick wall, to separate the populace and turn citizens against one another. Argentina, a country accustomed to relativizing everything, reached a point for many that was found to be unbearable. As one writer described it: "Every Argentine can tell an anecdote of when he went to a marriage and the Kirchners were on one side of the aisle and the anti-Kirchners were on the other" (Falchi, 2016).

As social commentators have noted, one of the more problematic consequences of the use of hate speech as a form of political discourse leading up to 11/8 is the permission-giving that is communicated to the individual to embody—and potentially act on—state-sanctioned xenophobia. Personally I think of how such sanctioning of hatred may compromise public safety. For example, 10 years ago I served as an expert witness on a criminal trial involving a hate-motivated homicide, in which the defendant argued he killed an Asian man "because the government doesn't mind." At the time this was viewed as a marker of the psychiatric disturbance of the assailant. In our new alt-right world such a line of argument can be warranted by the speeches given by our elected president. Our new normal is now incorporating the once abnormal; Muslims are terrorists, Mexicans are rapists, families of veterans are even suspect.

From a multicultural perspective we need to consider how the 11/8 political shift may lead to a more overtly intolerant societal stasis. As proposed by Dunbar and Blanco (2013), the acculturation to hatred occurs societally when there is a recasting of the legitimizing myths (e.g., Muslims come to the United States to perpetrate terrorism) to make bias-motivated violence more palatable, or when our social norms are populated by stories of harm done to the homeland by outsiders (Elwert, 2003); this may result in agencies of the state acting to indoctrinate the populace about a new normalization of intergroup violence or risk for harm. Tilly (2003) has proposed something similar to this when he argues that collective violence, a process he sees as complex and volatile, is realized via the use of narratives and policies to divide groups and relationships. As he commented, this occurred "when Bosnian-Serb leaders radicalized the line that separated them from their Muslim neighbors with whom the Bosnian-Serb descent had long mingled, married, traded and collaborated" (Tilly, 2003).

Another manifestation of social power to be reckoned with concerns how splinter groups function as proxy enforcers of cultural and political hegemonies. To say this simply, in many societies hate groups have served as informal surrogates to act out the prejudices of the state. I recall how a Czech politician discussed with me his knowledge of how many police agencies in his country viewed the neo-Nazi groups as helping to oppress the Roma minorities, a job that the police themselves could not overtly carry out. Similarly in Arthur Dong's chilling documentary *Licensed to Kill*, an incarcerated homicide offender of gay men states blankly that the police did not care about gay bashing in his community. More formalized examples of the hate violence by proxy is found in the ethnographic work of Davies, Blanco, & Miron (2016), as they describe the actions of far-right paramilitary groups in Columbia during the conflict with the FARC guerrilla forces. These groups perpetrated terror in their communities, targeting leftist guerrillas and citizens alike; these actions otherwise violated the scope of activity of the standing army.

The harsh-influence tactics of these groups inherently rely on classic authoritarian principles of obedience and punishment of dissension. Although this has already been discussed in terms of follower behavior, it is important to recognize the extension from authoritarian ideology to action found in these violent groups. It would be inaccurate to think of the members of these hate groups as being (uniformly) ideologically motivated: in the Davies study, many members of the death squads had no other economic opportunities; furthermore, many members of racialized criminal groups belong to the group for social bonding motives and are essentially bereft of a hate ideology. These proxy groups use coercive force to socialize their members to be obedient and compliant with the hate beliefs of their leadership. As social psychology has shown, that does not mean authoritarian followers view themselves as being slavish to a party line. It is rather that the coercive control and cultural norms make questioning a belief system of the group problematic. To come back to Kelman, if we find a source credible, or a group as desirable to be a member of, we will align ourselves with the respective ideology of the group, authoritarian or not.

Soft Persuasion and the Liberal Tradition

> But you can't make people listen. They have to come round in their own time, wondering what happened and why the world blew up around them. It can't last.
>
> —Ray Bradbury, *Fahrenheit 451*

As French and Raven have told us, social influence and change in liberal democracies are based on logic-driven decisions, relationship-based discourse, and the recognition of expertise gained through practice and reflection. Facts are respected, even when they are inconvenient truths; they are not alternative facts. Further, as the Bradbury quote emphasizes, soft strategies do not force the opinion change on the other.

Logic and the scientific method are crucial to the running of a liberal democratic society. Empirical fact-based techniques to examine issues of social policy are employed and relied on by political leadership. The effectiveness of programs to divert substance users from prison, of early childhood programs deemed useful for the development of literacy, and medical treatments that can extend the life expectancy of patients all utilize the scientific method. This same process of examination and fact-finding has shaped the (better) work in the area of discrimination and hate violence. The liberal democratic tradition relies on—even overrelies on—expertise, knowledge-based programs of inquiry, and the intellectual capital of academia to shape governmental policies.

One of the shining examples of psychology's contribution to social justice is found in the work done of Kenneth and Mamie Phipps Clark, which proved influential in the 1954 Supreme Court ruling in *Brown v. Board of Education of Topeka*. This watershed moment in soft persuasion—one that drew on psychological research—played a role in achieving a critical outcome of a civil society. The Clarks had studied the adverse impact of school segregation on black children, which they detailed in a 1950 report. This was presented as evidence of the deleterious effects of racism on child development and contributed to school desegregation and the overturning of the separate-but-equal argument upheld by supporters of racial segregation.

In contrast the passage of the Voting Rights Act a decade later was the consequence of a more dynamic process of progressive social change. Public protest and civil disobedience as practiced by Martin Luther King Jr. and other black civil rights activists demonstrated that influence was accomplished through in-group bonding, via the media of television, and by the enactment of transformative experiences—both for the followers and the observers of black activists. The logic-driven discourse practiced before the Supreme Court in *Brown v. Board of Education* by Thurgood Marshall and others was supplanted by mass action and charismatic leaders. From a theoretical perspective, the civil rights movement revealed the power of charismatic discourse. The combustibility of the argument was made powerful via the symbolic linkage of the advocate/ leader and their audience (Burke, 1969).

The process of soft attitude change, in the liberal democratic tradition, is characterized by inquiry and engagement. The form of influence is realized via positive and equal contact, which in turn allows for a respect-based give-and-take about social attitudes. A good example of this soft form of engagement in how to combat stereotyping, for example, is found in the Anti-Defamation League (ADL) booklet on confronting anti-Semitism. As they comment: "If someone says that Jews own everything, emphasize that Jews are individuals like other Americans and need to be looked at as such. Even though certain high-profile individuals in an industry may be recognizably Jewish, that does not mean that the entire industry 'is controlled by Jews.'" Challenge assumptions: Ask if there's a "_____" way to run a bank or produce a movie. There isn't a "_____" way, and there isn't a Jewish way. You could respond with, "Why shouldn't Jews be involved in the media or finance?"

Soft Influence and Cultural Relativism

The challenge of engaging the issue of intolerance is nicely captured in the film *Manhattan* by Woody Allen, in which people in the publishing world discuss their lives at a dinner party:

JERRY: *(chuckling)* I—I heard you, uh, you, uh, uh, quit your job.
IKE: I, uh—y-yeah, a real self-destructive impulse. You know, I wanna write a book so I—so I . . . *(sighing and changing the subject)* Ha-has anybody read that the Nazis are gonna march in New Jersey, you know? *(Helen and Polly shake their heads no)* I read this in the newspaper. *(waving his fist)* We should go down there, get some guys together, you know, get some bricks and baseball bats and really explain things to 'em.
JERRY: There was this devastating satirical piece on that on the Op-Ed page of the *Times*. It was devastating.
IKE: W-e-e-ell, a satirical piece in the *Times* is one thing, but bricks and baseball bats really gets right to the point down there.
HELEN: *(overlapping)* Oh, but really biting satire is always better than physical force.
IKE: But true physical force is always better with Nazis, uh . . . because it's hard to satirize a guy with, uh, shiny boots on.

The Allen character, Ike, struggles to find a value in satire in confronting xenophobes in his society. To his friends he appears agitated and unreasonable. Ike runs the risk, of course, of being just as vile and Neanderthal-like as the Nazis he complains about. His dilemma is that of wanting to have an effective response, one his friends find inappropriate. For them, biting discourse wins.

A more nuanced form of liberal persuasion has been practiced in the advocacy for the federal hate crimes laws. Arguing about hate crime laws involves the use of cultural symbols and assumptions about the problems these laws seek to address. From a perspective of the theory of modern discourse, as found in the thinking of Baudrillard and others (1983), the challenge of influence becomes one of whether individuals can identify with the relevance of hate crimes and human rights laws irrespective of their own sense of vulnerability. To consider this in terms of the psychology of persuasion, the issue becomes what are alternative forms of influence other than the invoking of mortality awareness and terror threat? From these other perspectives the intention of media is the creation of a sense of being in a given state or status by which attitudes are changed. Questions of logic and ethics aside, does the receiver of the message envision him- or herself as being in an "as-if" state as Melanie Klein might have said? This status creation is inherent to the feel-good advertising strategies we encounter. Through media-primed consumption, the individual shares certain experiences with celebrities and a lifestyle associated with heightened social status (keep in mind I have already suggested that this was one of the forces that had poor whites identify with candidate Trump and his largesse). Herein becomes a challenge for liberal democratic advocacy: Can media advertising prove potent enough to create a prosocial other-oriented perspective about human rights, while the individual potentially experiences the need for these social policies as being for someone other than themselves? Additionally, can an individual enter into a state of prosocial beliefs via modern advertising, while at the same time their sense of economic uncertainty is being activated by the isolationist and ultranationalist arguments of the opposition party?

A further challenge to the positivist dialectic approach to social influence is found in the emerging neuroscience of political attitudes (Haas, 2016); this line of research implies how overlearned and biologically based processes influence all of us in a semiconscious manner on political decisions. The argument has been made that we *feel* our political choices rather than *think* about them. Although surely oversimplistic, this lays out the issue of whether we can engage in a logic-based inquiry that is largely independent of neurocognitive processes of fear induction, implicit attitudes, or forms of self-serving bias. This field of cognitive research may lead to a redefining of the notions of political choice and political persuasion.

As has been suggested, the differences in conservative and liberal influence styles may in many contexts allow for healthy if not always efficient engagement. One of the underlying observations about the process of regime change in the 2016 U.S. presidential election is the abandonment of a middle ground in favor of a winner–loser cultural war. Debate is replaced with threat and revenge. These hard tactics become both a symbol and a tool of an ideology that is at once anti-intellectual and authoritarian. To paraphrase Douglas Adams "discourse is useless."

So the liberal dilemma, then, becomes one of deciding what to do if the traditional forms of logic and soft power to effect change are ineffective. There is a further issue, which we will go to now: Is the liberal democratic tradition more attuned to seeking to create a focus of hope, to inspire opposition, or to engage fact, which may be far more depressing?

Positivism vs. Psychological Fact-Finding

In writing this book I had several interesting conversations with stakeholders involved in hate crimes, one of which was with a young filmmaker who had worked in the fields of LGBT and ethnic minority issues. After she patiently heard what I was doing, she stated firmly, "You need to give people hope! This is important! Who do you want to read this, people have to feel good and not get depressed over all of this, we need hope! Write about hope!"

As an American, one of my thoughts was "I get it." At the same time, if I hold true to the principle of the scientific methods of inquiry, observation, and analysis, then "giving hope" becomes a form of contamination—consciously or otherwise. The point instead seems to be to try and be informative and open to alternate perspectives than whatever my own might be. So this issue of providing hope as a tool for advocacy makes good sense, it just does not jibe with the pursuit of fidelity to theory and inquiry. In the face of the current political situation, it would be reassuring to suggest that people will resolve their differences and naturally wish to connect around a common identity; it would also feel good to assume that logic and respect would resolve the problems we are now facing; finally, it would also be desirable to think there was nothing nefarious about the way the election was conducted. But, as psychologists who try to conceptualize behavior and culture in tandem, the acceptance of complexity is a given. Do we give people hope or does this become a personal decision to be arrived at? Do we enter into a practice of creating an alternative narrative to inspire or to minimize a sense of vulnerability?

What our cultural cataclysm makes clear is that classical positivism may not provide a workable solution to the situation we are facing. Logic, observation, engaged discourse, and a sense of concerted effort can accomplish a great deal. Racism and hatred in any of its forms is inherently moderated by emotions and primitive needs of the organism. Hope, logic, and good will may not answer to the tactics that have hatred or Al Capone's handgun as a form of attitude change.

Practiced Catastrophization

A striking alternative to the modern-day forms of positivism is exemplified by the notion of "catastrophic imagination" as proposed by the journalist Masha Gessen. For her, this is the practice of identifying the viable extension of a current threat into future scenarios: as she would say, the notion of imagining the unimaginable as actually happening— and accordingly establishing a course of action to mitigate the risk. This is clinically intriguing, in that a great deal of the work of talk therapy has sought to alleviate the ruminative worry of the patient with more complex and diverse conceptualizations to replace the core "neurotic" fears of catastrophizing. Gessen, a Russian journalist who expatriated from Russia as she observed the danger posed by Vladimir Putin, commented that her personal family history led her to comprehend this notion of the unimaginable as something to engage as real. As she notes, "I looked at Putin and was terrified from the very beginning. That makes me look very prescient because he actually turned out to be exactly the monster that I thought he was. I could also have been proven wrong, but I wasn't." In 2012, Gessen published her analysis of the rise of Putin in Russia in her acclaimed book, *The Man without a Face: The Unlikely Rise of Vladimir Putin.*

The practice of catastrophic imagination is perhaps, less a giving over to a passive fearfulness but rather dialectic method made of survival. As one person suggested, a paranoid is the person with the facts. So this is less a process of worry and more an honest and skilled appraisal of risk, one to be engaged in by the average citizen. Gessen's dictum, while close to Murphy's Law of "if something can go wrong it will," is more one of both taking autocrats at their word and applying the implications of this to the individual and their circumstances. I take what Gessen argues for as a legitimate form of influence. As a clinical psychologist I view this as a means of active problem solving, which typically increases a sense of personal control. Additionally, however, I view this as a strategy to influence public awareness as to what and how to deal with the death spiral of the liberal democratic form of government and the risk of the loss of civil rights under the law.

It is important, furthermore, to question whether Americans are equipped to perceive the risk of the political shift that has occurred. It is worth considering who we have been and what is being asked psychologically of individuals to adjust to this new form of being governed. Francis Hsu (1981) compared U.S. and Chinese society and identified what he referred to as his postulates of U.S. culture. His influential ideas helped to shape a generation of researchers interested in psychological anthropology. Hsu's observations significantly pointed to the values of equity, individuality, and fairness as being highly esteemed by Americans. If we indeed are operating from such a set of basic assumptions, then are we culturally competent to conceptualize the heightened risk of autocracy? Gessen acknowledges learning how to think in this forward-looking fashion from her family members who survived totalitarianism. To draw a comparison of political resilience to immunological functioning (see Chapter 8), it can be argued that Americans are deficient in the cultural—or, if you will, immunological—memory to anticipate this cataclysmic shift toward intolerance and autocracy. The recognition of such a fundamental shift in our form of government would indeed change the postulates of being an American. It also would, unfortunately, establish that the United States is no longer a safe haven for persons like Gessen, who have left totalitarian regimes to come to a place to exercise personal rights and liberties. In this sense, then, the impact of our cultural cataclysm is not a national problem but one that impacts the world community.

What Constitute Useful Strategies of Advocacy?

What does psychological science offer, then, in terms of how to advocate for human rights and hate crime laws? Under our evolving post-11/8 societal stasis this becomes particularly challenging. Critical social issues are being debated, based on heavily emotion-driven arguments. In the balance rests the risk of an increasingly authoritarian approach to governance—one that might leave many citizens vulnerable to hate- and terror-based violence.

Political Protest

Although there is limited empirical evidence on the effectiveness of political protests, there is a long-standing understanding as to what motivates individuals to protest. Earlier studies of political protest proposed that individuals participate in protests to address grievances concerning injustices or inequities (Berkowitz, 1972; Gurr, 1970). More recently, in a meta-analysis of studies examining protest and perceived deprivation, Van Zomeren, Postmes, and Spears (2008) found that a combination of cognitive and affective factors motivated individuals to engage in political protest. As such, both personal judgments and feelings lead to involvement, as does a perception of group inequities that result in feelings of dissatisfaction and indignation. Interestingly, even if individuals feel their efforts are unlikely to prove effective, involvement continues in protest movements as a form of group bonding and the enhancement of the individual's sense of group identity (Drury & Reicher, 2009).

So although we have some insight into the motivation for protest, the issue of its efficacy has been rarely examined. A recent survey in the United States observed that young adults—a.k.a. millennials—were proportionally more likely to have recently gone to a protest and were polled as finding such actions as more influential (Ruiz-Grossman, 2017). A study by Madestam, Shoag, Veuger, and Yanagizawa-Drott (2012) examined the role of Tea Party conservatives. They found that "our results show that protests can build political movements that ultimately affect policy making, and that these effects arise from influencing political views rather than solely through the revelation of existing political preferences."

Product Boycotting

A form of protest that is linked to the contemporary market place involves the boycotting of products or organizations that violate norms of a social group. The origin of the term comes from a protest involving landowner Charles Boycott who in the 1880s was targeted by the Irish Land League for his business practices. The resistance of local workmen to farm his lands led to financial penalties for Boycott in drawing on other human capital to both harvest his crops and protect the activity from potentially riotous locals. In contemporary society boycotting may involve corporations, small businesses, and celebrities.

In a study by Klein, Smith, and John (2002) of the practice of corporate boycotting, it was found that factors that predicted boycott participation included an individual's desire to make a difference, the increased sense of self-enhancement and self-efficacy, counterarguments that inhibit boycotting are the perceived cost to the boycotter by their constrained consumption. Kozinets and Handelman (1998) reported that boycott participation—much like on-the-ground political protests—is a collective effort with affective rewards and enhancement of personal expression and individuality. A very recent illustration of this tactic, one that gets at a deep Trump value, money, is found in the boycotting of his products and those of his daughter, Ivanka. In the autumn of 2016, Shannon Coulter and Sue Atencio started the #GrabYourWallet boycott of Trump products. Their grassroots initiative is an example of a tactic to convince companies to stop selling Trump-branded products (grabyourwallet.org).

Engagement with the Opposition

I hope it is clear that *society does not fight hate violence by isolation and disengagement*. Likewise our communities cannot achieve a safe new stasis through balkanization and intergroup mistrust. The contact hypothesis of Gordon Allport remains a source of guidance in forming viable intersections—perhaps to now reflect the reality of social media—between diverse communities and stakeholders. One recent example was a request—which was not responded to—by Muslim police officers to meet in December 2016 with President-elect Trump to express their concerns about his proposed policies (Papenfuss, December 11, 2016). The New York City officers, including Officer Aml Elsokary, herself a victim of a hate crime (see Chapter 5), requested the meeting to discuss the spike in anti-Muslim hate violence. The officers were also supported by Brooklyn borough president Eric Adams who wrote a letter to Trump in December supporting the officers' request and detailing the dramatic rise in hate violence in New York City.

This action of engagement incorporates two principles I have applied several times with victims of hate; these are to document the transgressions and collaborate with other stakeholders. Briefly the principle is to not get habituated to oppression; this will only lead the victim to normalize the experience. People need to clearly articulate what the infraction was and be prepared to relay and relive this with others. Advocacy can be undercut by our losing focus and losing faith in our own experience. Similarly we need to collaborate with other stakeholders in responding to hate violence. As the poet Kenneth Patchen once said, "No one ever works alone"(1968); the experience of hate is inherently divisive and in many cases leaves the victim isolated. Connecting with diverse stakeholders is one of the means of influencing the larger social context and addressing the collective injury. However, this practice of bridging differences cuts both ways. I personally knew a white power organizer who tacitly agreed to communicate grievances with a member of a black criminal gang to foment black-on-brown gang violence in Los Angeles. Both parties felt racial violence was needed to change the problems they perceived in the city. Neither held any positive regard for the other.

Question Everything

With an incoming administration that has argued for a dismantling of the institutions of the federal government and has an inner circle who is affiliated with extremist media, it is fair to be a practiced skeptic. More than that, the work of psychological science in dealing with terrorism and hate violence is particularly needed. It is not that a fact-based approach to issues of hate crimes and human rights will sway right-wing extremists. Rather it is that such evidence is needed to articulate a clear alternative ideology to the proponents of misinformation. It is also to determine what does work. Several critical social issues related to hate violence have been compromised by the intolerance of the recent election. The draconian approach to immigration reform, for example, as well as the shift in attitudes about the rights of sexual minorities, and the reproductive rights of women, have been made more problematic and will likely erode public trust of stakeholder groups. As is referred to in the field of community psychology, the "help-seeking" of vulnerable individuals is now placed under greater strain. Persons who are sexual minorities, for example, have had a long and conflicted relationship with local police agencies, who may in one situation be allies against and in another perpetrators of hate violence. Similarly undocumented persons who are crime victims may now view going to an emergency room as being a risk for being apprehended and deported. It is almost as if we are back at the starting point of having to argue anew the rationale and need for antihate laws.

Perhaps the lesson to learn is that, while convincing this administration of the importance of hate crime laws may be pointless, those who advocate for hate crime policies need to make this a policy of inclusion. That is, in this time of heightened xenophobia, human rights advocates need to deal head-on with the traditional resistance of seeing these laws as catering to special interest groups. In some of our communities, frequent victims of hate violence are white men. This does not get picked up by our media. Similarly, as the SPLC and HRC studies revealed, many of the victims of, and many of the people most impacted by, hate crimes are young persons. Advocacy for the enforcement of hate crimes needs to focus on common needs for protection of all members of society. To make this point, a research-based approach on how to advocate for hate crime policies needs to emerge. It is time we engage people of many diverse social backgrounds to emphasize the risk we all face of intergroup violence.

Coping with Fake News

A somewhat different question is how we can identify, challenge, and disengage from propagandistic media that is tossed off as objective news. For example, in a matter of a few weeks after the presidential election, a news piece found its way onto social media indicating Hillary

Clinton and one of her senior campaign staff had been involved in a child pornography ring in the Washington, D.C., area. In what came to be referred to as "Pizzagate," alt-right sympathetic news sources indicated that the staff of Clinton used code to communicate about child sex. This bizarre news piece, which lingered on the fringe region of social media, motivated a man to drive from North Carolina to metropolitan Washington, D.C., in early December and discharge an air rifle in a pizza parlor in response to the claims this was true.

Although hardly representative of the real issue of misinformation, the Pizzagate story gives some insight into the great challenge for news sources providing either faulty information or engaging in an intentionally dishonest practice in providing news stories to both established new services and alternative social media outlets. I would argue that fake news will not change our fundamental opinions, at least in most cases. Rather, doctored or whole cloth lies that we perceive as credible will reinforce biases we already hold. In other words, this will activate a process of confirmatory bias and strengthen the beliefs we held a priori. If there is any real strategy behind the fake news approach it seems to be to lock down the base to whatever social ideology the story is targeting. Fake news makes us more of what we already are.

Dealing with fake news requires some degree of awareness of social media and a capacity for critical thinking. As Steve Inskeep has noted, there are many signals when a news source is less than trustworthy; these include: Does the source cite alternative perspectives? Is there an editorial body that oversees the author? and "Does the headline match the content?" (Inskeep, 2016).

Create Transformational Experiences

If the thesis of this book is largely accepted, that is, that the 2016 U.S. presidential election is a moment of transformation from a liberal, participatory form of governance to one of coercion, intolerance, and anti-democratic principles, then the practice of social advocacy by necessity must also evolve and abandon liberal practices as a business-as-usual approach. The "what and how" of such an evolved form of political engagement is a significant issue. What I would like to propose as one means of beginning to address this is to recognize the inherent transformative nature of community dialogue, of citizen protest, and, perhaps most important, of the assumption of the individual's responsibility to have influence on the state as an institution and the standing government as a broker of this relationship of the populace to the state. What the recent past has resulted in is a reduction in wealth of the majority of the citizens of the United States, a reduction in the relative health and welfare of blacks and Latinos in our society, and the installation of two presidential administrations in the past 20 years that were not elected by the majority of participating voters.

I will not seek to describe a general political philosophy or even what a revision of the U.S. postulates of the citizenry needs to look like, rather what can be proposed is the establishment of a process of redefining cultural and social identity that is inclusive and demanding of active social involvement. To be more specific, this may come to be seen as a process by which individuals engage in new forms of community experience to pursue social change. Let me not be vague. This is a large question and one I only wish to point to now. I would hope to address this more substantially in the near future, as we need something new and different.

Chapter 3 began with recounting experiences of individuals that led them to feel something important or historical was happening. This is what is needed—not leadership retreats or training students to be legislative lobbyists (nothing wrong with either of these practices but this is part of the status quo, which has failed to be enough); individuals need to be emotionally engaged as a collective to be open to a new approach on how to not fight hate but transcend such forms of intolerance and to begin to address the social problems they experience in their lives. To respond to the cultural cataclysm of fear, shock, and awe, we need to collectively feel a process of involvement and responsibility to act. In the early moments of the new administration, efforts such as the Women's March on Washington and the advocacy of U.S. representative John Lewis suggest there is a desire to not fall asleep; so the question is can we stay fully awake to respond to intolerance.

Create Transformational Knowledge

It is worth commenting that in this period of cultural change, the need for a dispassionate and science-based study of cultural change is needed. Examining the role of media, social persuasion, and political power in the negotiation between a new model of democratic governance and the continued slide into an autocratic form of authoritarianism is needed. The alternative to ultranationalism may be quite different from what went before; likewise we may come to see how the citizenry views political truth and governance as being shaped by distinctly differing psychological and sociological forces. Going off of old scripts and old theories of government may no longer work.

Summary

The dramatic and contentious experience of the 2016 election underscores how important the practice of persuasion is. Social influence research has long distinguished between the use of forceful or "hard" and interpersonal "soft" tactics. This model of persuasion has also been shown to have cross-cultural utility in showing how individuals employ these tactics to argue for their attitudes about hate crime, antiterror, and social justice issues. Hard tactics have consistently been shown to be related to authoritarian attitudes, to endorsement of anti-Semitism, and ethnic bias. More tolerant advocates of human rights have shown a tendency to use information, personal experiences, and the quality of their relationship with their peers to advocate for antihate policies.

The issue of how intolerance may influence the attitudes about the role of hate crime and antiterror laws going forward is unclear. However, there are notable political differences between support for antiterror laws, and attitudes toward hate crime policies. The fallout of hate and the realignment of social attitudes that have come out of our cultural cataclysm underscore the limitations of conventional forms of positivism and reasoned debate. There is also a real need to determine what tactics in the emergent political climate may prove effective in bridging the significant differences about intergroup relationships. Going forward, these may include a more serious appraisal of how far of a shift in civil liberties may occur in America, a determination of the capacity of the average American to assess the risk of the loss of their personal rights, and how an active form of social protest might curb further erosion of the rights of vulnerable members of our society.

CHAPTER 7

You Can't Go Home Again: Interpersonal Conflict and the Erosion of Social Cohesion

It didn't take me long, actually. I had my first disagreement about the U.S. presidential election at 6:30 a.m. the morning after the election. I was getting my gear together from a yoga class I had just finished and a fellow I had known for a few years said, "So how about the election?" I think I simply made a face. He then said, "I didn't like anyone, but I really can't stand her." I think I again frowned. I then said, "Well you can't have voted for *him,* could you?" Then he frowned. I said, "You're ex–Air Force; do you want his hands on the nuclear button?" The other fellow then said, "But I just can't stand her." I then said, "Look, he has never worked for anyone in his entire life; I don't think he can do the job." He then said, "Who has she worked for?" I said "Well, the president of the United States." He said, "That doesn't count!" I rejoined, "I don't see how an ex-military guy can want a guy in the White House who thinks Vladimir Putin is a great guy." He said, "Trump said he is a great leader for *his* country." I didn't say anything else and walked out.

There is no definitive estimate as to how many people have argued about the 2016 election, but it is probably a good many of us. In what follows we will review the emotional divide that is experienced by people in our uncivil post-11/8 society. The concerns, problems, and experiences of how we are separated interpersonally will be examined. This will be followed by a series of vignettes that serve as thought exercises to examine the triggering issues in our post-11/8 relationships.

As a clinician, since the election I had been saying, "Be closer to those you are close to"; and to the writers, film professionals, and artists I know, I have said, "Consider how your art can engage the problems you are seeing." However, we do not know where this rhetoric of intolerance will take us. For many we come back to the tearful plea of the late Rodney King, a black man beaten by a dozen Los Angeles police officers: "People, I just want to say, can we all get along? Can we get along?"

We have considered previously the psychological factors that can fuel hate-based attitudes and broaden societal divisions. A consequence of this social polarization is the adverse impact on personal relationships and the conflicts experienced between friends and family in grappling with what in many cases are shared needs, experiences, and concerns. What has been suggested by UC Berkeley sociologist Arlie Hochschild (2016) in her interviews with conservative voters in Louisiana—often self-referenced as "Tea Party conservatives"—is that many of their concerns were not that far removed from their left-of-center counterparts. Importantly, many of her working-class interviewees described their deep sense of alienation from the standing government and that the country was moving toward a more racially and ethnically diverse sense of nationality. Many of these individuals expressed a sense of frustration and despair that their economic prospects were bleak. Her subjects voiced their misgivings about an economic insecurity, one that was compromised by a new world order of globalization, changing social norms seen as promoting the rights of minority groups—immigrants, gays, and visible ethnic minorities—as well as a government that had become seemingly indifferent to the problems of the white working poor. Hochschild documents the resentments her interviewees expressed as to government concerns about global warming or international human rights, which they viewed as supplanting the importance of religion or traditional family structure. Implicitly many of these individuals were resentful if not suspicious of educated elites of any political persuasion. The alienation of these individuals was discernible well before the 2016 campaign season. Many rural whites had long felt they were societal losers in the status quo social structure (Huntington, 2004). For them the cultural divide was not an outcome of 11/8 but rather a situation that had befallen them decades earlier.

Recognition of this winner–loser dichotomy was only amplified by the 2016 campaign; the recognition of the cultural war became more salient with the Trump victory. This social chasm is signified by a rhetoric of intolerance that serves to distinguish the victors from the vanquished. For the winners there is an expectation of a return to a classic American way of life that is reestablished by the control of our borders, the eradication of illegal residents, and the detection of potential terrorists in our midst. The populism of the winning side is also fueled by an anticipated resurrection of older industries (such as coal and manufacturing) and an isolationism from world society and world commerce. Inherent to this political ideology is a moving away from multiculturalism and a return to a dominant-race/dominant-culture society. By comparison the losers fear a reduction in civil liberties and environmental protection, as well as skepticism of an economic revival under an administration that appears aligned with the wealthy rather than the working classes. Culturally, the threat for the losing side varies in terms of the individual's race, gender, sexual orientation, and age. On the losing side, childbearing-aged women and persons of color, for example, are facing a reduction in reproductive rights, employment rights, and the further erosion of voting rights. For some ethnic groups—most notably Muslims and Latinos—the rhetoric of intolerance additionally suggests a new level of hostility, one that would be sanctioned by the leadership in Washington. These, and related concerns, have become the basis of the day-to-day conflict that Americans have come to encounter.

Online Survey of Post-11/8 Interpersonal Conflicts

To consider this issue of contention and interpersonal conflict, I will again turn to some of the online survey work that has been referenced previously.

Online Survey Results—Six Weeks after the Election

In the Wave One online survey with 357 respondents a series of questions about interpersonal conflicts was reported. Within the first six weeks of the election 120 (33.6%) respondents stated they had been in an argument about the election, while 62% of respondents indicated they avoided other people because of political differences—with 155 (43.4%) respondents indicating they had "unfriended" people they had known via social media. Arguments with coworkers (7.3%) and conflicts in primary relationships (7%) were less frequently reported. When these reported situations were aggregated, it was found that the experiencing of conflicts about the election varied by the age range of the individual. It was found that there was a steady decline from the 18- to 30-year-old group downward to the 60-plus group.[1] The use of avoidance tactics in the Wave One respondents was highest for the 30- to 40-year-olds and lowest for the under-30 and over-60 respondents.[2] Figure 7.1 compares the survey findings of Clinton and other-candidate voters in terms of conflict tactics employed in the first month after the election. This appears below.

This pattern indicates how in the first few weeks after the election people responded to interpersonal conflict related to 11/8 in terms of

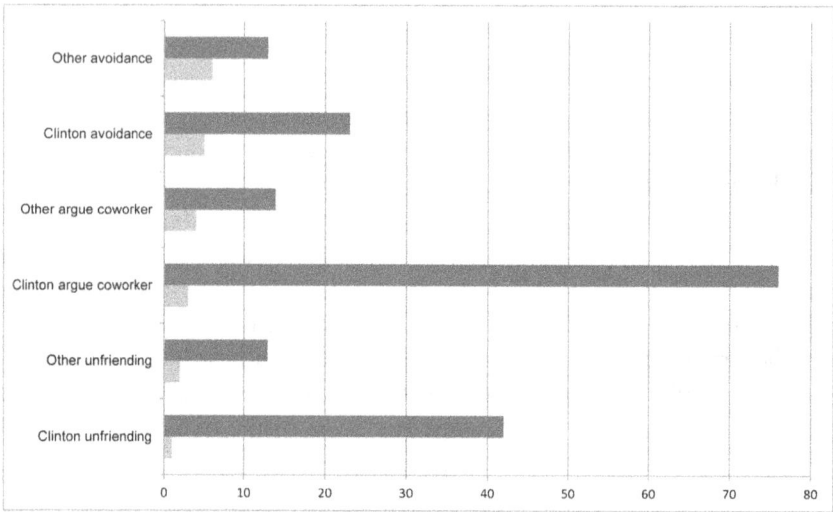

Figure 7.1   Clinton Voter and Other Candidate Voter: Interpersonal Conflict
Tactics

both assertion and avoidance, which varied based on their age.[3] The
young adult group reported more assertive and conflicted interactions
and were less likely to avoid others about issues of the election, whereas
older subjects reported being less likely to argue or avoid others because
of the election outcome. The issue of gender was also meaningful, with
women more likely to experience interpersonal conflicts and to engage
in coping styles using avoidance.[4]

Online Survey Results—One Month Postinauguration

The subsequent online survey ("Wave Two") again surveyed experiences
of interpersonal conflict concerning 11/8 during the first month after the
Trump inauguration. We found that the 11/8 and 9/11 association was
related to self-reported detachment from others and a perceived negative impact of their politics on their relationships. Symptoms of acute
stress, indicated by higher ASDS scores, were related to reported arguments or fights with coworkers and intimate partners.[5] Higher acute
stress ratings were also correlated with avoidance to manage conflict
and detaching (unfriending) from others who were provocative.[6] The
symptoms of acute stress on the ASDS were also correlated with subject
age, gender, and perceived threat of hate crimes and terror acts in the
subject's community.[7]

Table 7.1   Online Survey Results: Reported Interpersonal Conflicts

	Wave One (*n* = 357) Percentage Endorsed	Wave Two (*n* = 1,155) Percentage Endorsed
Negative impact on relationships	73%	74%
Got into arguments	33.4%	43.9
Argued with coworkers	6.8%	11%
Got into physical altercation	0.5%	1.2%
Argued with intimate partner	7.1%	9.2%
Unfriended someone on social media	43.3	38%
Avoided persons with contrary opinions	62.6%	56%
Target of hate speech	13.5%	12%

Comparing conflict patterns post-11/8 and after the January 2017 presidential inauguration revealed a modest reduction in avoidance and unfriending tactics and a similarly modest increase in arguments, particularly in the workplace. Hate speech and arguing with an intimate partner was similar in both survey samples. These findings are summarized in Table 7.1.

Characteristics of Interpersonal Conflict in Our Cultural Cataclysm

In discussions with mental health consumers, review of the online survey work, and by observing our social commentary, there are four specific factors related to conflict between individuals attributable to the 11/8 election. These are: (1) relational failure, (2) collectivistic attributions of the conflict, (3) the influence of amplifying factors, and (4) a capacity for contention. These will be briefly detailed below.

Relational Failure

Conflict as we are discussing it is found in situations where the parties experience a failure to sustain a healthy tolerance of a social or cultural difference. This difference may or may not be expected and in and of itself may not result in significant conflict between the individuals. Relationally, the conflict may entail a failure to mirror the shared assumptions of the other, when the presumption is cultural similarity of the parties. When there is a significant cultural difference in, say, race or age or gender of the parties, the conflict is more likely characterized by stereotype activation that occurs between the individuals. In the former, the conflict may be unanticipated by both parties; when there is anticipated value similarity there is less self-monitoring and the realization of significant differences may be both surprising and disorienting. In the latter, between-person differences may be presumed before contact has occurred. The premise of stereotype activation is after all a means of simplifying the cognitive appraisal of the differences of the individuals. The utilization of stereotypes provides a viable means of presuming differences, even when subsequent evidence may argue against such discrepancy of the individuals.

Collectivistic Attributes

The political argument, while experienced interpersonally, is linked to social norms and cultural postulates (e.g., employment rights, free speech) of the individual's social group. Importantly, out-group bias and forms of prejudice are inherently collective. Bias is omnipresent in our collective conflicts, as is the minimization of personal decision making. Since 11/8 political debate is not only ideological, but broadly cultural. The individual's beliefs are contested in terms of their cultural identities and not simply their political preferences. As has been described, this cultural wars thesis transforms interpersonal discourse into intergroup conflict, one that occurs in the context of there being winners and losers. So the conflicts we encounter are not simply personal but rather collectivistic. We are potentially put into roles of becoming the voice for "our side." Furthermore, criticism of our social group may result in us having to argue for positions that we may not subscribe to.

Amplifying Factors

Individual characteristics may result in heighted aggression, hostility, and animus in political discourse. Individual and situational factors may incite disagreement or escalate a difference of opinion into significant conflict. These factors may be contextual, as in the temporal or locational features of the interaction. *When* we disagree happens in a context—one that is moderated by external events, such as hate violence or acts of terror being perpetrated in our communities. Other amplifying factors may include personal events that have happened prior to the current conflict—these could include experiencing microaggressions of bias or identity-affirming experiences that strengthen our personal identification with a social group—such as attending a political rally. Similarly, biopsychological factors such as alcohol consumption or psychiatric symptoms (e.g., mania) or problems of impulse control may escalate the contention to overt hostility. Additionally, the use of hate speech may amplify the disagreement into overt hostility and aggression.

Capacity for Contention

What, finally, is critical in terms of the type of relationship-damaging behaviors I have seen is the willingness of the (opposing) parties to be committed to political debate. Many situations occur that we abstain from engaging in, due to a lack of salience or capacity to rejoin a political argument. Conflict may escalate from simple differences of belief to a level of contention that perpetuates the stereotypes of the opposing party and enhances the win–lose nature of the conflict. This means that all parties involved would have to care enough to argue. This entails a recognition of the salience of the issue, a sense of one's collective identity as making us ready to be an exemplar of our groups' cultural values and norms, and positive reinforcement for our identity affirmation by engaging in political argumentation.

Forms of Empathic Failure Post-11/8

Let me give a few brief illustrations of the impact that is being experienced in relationships in the United States.

Familial Alienation

The alienation from immediate family members over the political and cultural differences we have discussed is a damaging experience for many of us. This process of family removal and rejection came into play predominantly around the holiday season of 2016 when many adults had to decide whether or not to spend extended periods of time with one another. In close relationships, the fallout of the cultural wars is always in the context of the prior personal and ideological history of the unique relationship. This may include ad hominem arguments or reifying a family member as being a member of a denigrated political group. For some individuals the conflict surrounding 11/8 is simply a confirmatory experience of prior hurts and forms of rejection of the individual from their family member(s). In such circumstances the recovery may be more problematic in that there were other similar events and points of contention that had occurred prior to the election. In such cases, recovery and resumption of a family connection may be sabotaged by prior infractions that were never properly dealt with at the time.

Losing Connectivity via Social Media

Politically based unfriending was a very real problem for many people well before the November 2016 election. The use of social media has allowed for the rapid sharing of political information—some of which is inflammatory in its tone. Many individuals report being frustrated when a family member or an old friend sends them extremist forms of social commentary. In some instances this is seen as an intent to provoke and engage based on a social belief; in others it may simply illustrate the evolution of an individual's social attitudes over a period of time.

The erosion of social support for many individuals is made much worse by the hit-and-run hate and depersonalized nature of xenophobia found in our social media. The story from Plato of the *Ring of Gyges* has been employed as a reference to heightened aggressive speech via social media and to the amplification of hate speech particularly (Dunbar, 2016). The story refers to the notion of individual invisibility—accomplished by the character Gyges by wearing a magic ring, leading to more antisocial and aggressive actions by Gyges. In terms of our contemporary world, this has been applied to the notion of Internet trolling and to "flaming" via hate speech and stereotype activation.

The Gyges effect affords the interpersonal conflict via social media and fosters the amplification of rhetoric of all sorts. It is ironic that a medium such as social media, which allows for immediate and continuous communication between persons geographically removed from each other, has also resulted in the termination of older and in some instances otherwise stable relationships. Our rhetoric of intolerance has become a means of a new form of social ostracization.

Political Shaming

The experience of being told "you voted wrong" can readily bifurcate into "you should not have voted for candidate Trump," on the one hand, or, "you voted for the loser," on the other. Shaming has several important social psychological consequences that include establishing a level of power in close relationships, assigning blame for failure to others, and the solicitation of empathy from others (Tangney & Dearing, 2003). So shame both keeps us in line in terms of social conformance and keeps us in a state of (uncomfortable) equilibrium in close relationships. Shaming would be most expected in a political context in which a blue individual resides in a deep red community or the red individual in the deep blue community. These individuals would likely engage in tactics to avoid shame in benign contact situations; in closer relationships political shaming would be experienced as negatively reinforcing attitudes about the dominant and oppositional political ideology of others. Many individuals would put effort into avoiding situations in which shaming could lead to greater alienation. Political shaming, of course, may also show itself in terms of experiences of discrimination in work relationships or isolation in social settings; others may feel that they "do not need to work with someone who holds extremist views."

You Cannot Go Home Again

A consequence of the conflict we have witnessed is the decision to not return or visit communities they had lived in, based on cultural and political differences. Individuals have disconnected from old friendships via social media and have chosen to remain disconnected from familial contexts and communities of one's childhood. Familial alienation is a consequence of the employment of avoidance tactics, particularly the disconnection and elimination of face-to-face interpersonal contact. Such global avoidance tactics results in removal of the individual from family ceremonies, holiday events, and situations of familial crisis. This became more evident in the December holiday period of 2016 in which many individuals first definitively decided to not go home to their families—for these people this is where the divide became real.

Fallout of 11/8: Loss of Social Cohesion

The fallout in our relationships reflects the loss of societal cohesion and social support that has occurred through the 2016 election. Support of people we are close to is part of a core human need for connectivity. In the fields of health psychology social support is viewed as one of the important contribution to well-being. Social support includes emotional, material, informational, and cultural reinforcement to the individual.

Our social connections are critical in dealing with depression, recovery from major illness, and adjusting to economic duress. Numerous studies have looked at social support and health status (Berkman, 1985) across the adult life span—such as the Framingham Heart Study (Fowler & Christakis, 2008) or the Alameda County study (Berkman & Syme, 1979). Social support also protects us against forms of interpersonal conflict—including experiences of hate victimization. The process of social support under periods of societal duress is particularly important.

So the inherent problem for many Americans is that at a time when we particularly need the connection with friends and family, issues of bias and politically based xenophobia (or should we say *xenophobically based political attitudes*) are driving us apart. What is happening below the radar is the unfriending of persons from one another, based on their political beliefs, the heightened sense of vulnerability many persons feel by the loss of these relationships, and for many Americans who have moved away from the heartland of the country a sense that "you can't go home again." As we approach these new political realities many Americans are rethinking the prospects of spending time confronting these differences within their family and in the communities of their childhoods. It has led some individuals to question what in this new age of abnormality constitutes family. Is it genetics? Is it where you live? Is it shared values? Is it simply being with people who do not denigrate you for what you believe in? What is happening, perhaps imperceptibly, is the reconsideration of who *we* are and who *we can get along with*.

What has to be emphasized is that this *cultural and emotional* bifurcation of our place of belonging is not a matter of hurt feelings; rather it is a public health problem. Poor social support has been repeatedly linked to morbidity risk (Berkman, 1985; Berkman & Glass, 2000; Mookadam & Arthur, 2004) and is a critical component of suicide risk (Heikkinen, Aro, & Lönnqvist, 1994; Compton, Thompson, & Kaslow, 2005) particularly for middle-aged men (Cobb, 1976). Social support has also been seen as a buffer for mood disorders and risk of autoimmune illnesses (Cohen & Wills, 1985). Support from friends and family is also a critical buffer in how adults adjust to problems of work stress and unemployment (Johnson & Hall, 1988). We can say social support is not only getting along with others but also how we keep going as individuals.

So there are real consequences in the breakdown of the social connectivity of our country. For a foreign dictator who views the United States with anger and contempt, this dissolving of the social stasis into overt intolerance would be highly desirable. Strategically for the Putins,

Erdoğans, and Jong-uns of the world there is a tactical advantage to there being an ideological civil war in the United States. A breakdown in faith in the electoral process, a loss of faith in the ruling government, and a growing ambivalence about what the role of the country should be in our highly interdependent world all play to the needs of totalitarian leaders abroad. The ultranationalist and xenophobic themes of our culture additionally further erode the role of our country as a human rights watchdog on the global stage. What we are all struggling with is not simply an ambivalence about how we are governed, it is about how we feel about each other. It is therefore critical how people deal in the situation with this growing alienation from one another. An individual's coping is impacted by their sense of social support, their sense of legitimacy as a citizen in society, and their perceptions about the availability of assistance from stakeholder groups (police, medical, and legal professionals, for example) in resolving conflicts of intolerance.

In studies I have conducted with victims of harassment, it is fairly clear that engagement with the provoking party is often a desirable course of action. Many persons who encounter biased behaviors feel better for having engaged with the problem. This is not to be presumed for situations of intergroup violence, however. So, to note here briefly, experiences of intergroup conflict that are not inclusive of violence or the threat of violence can be responded to by direct engagement and by the process of victim help-seeking, which often is via informal social networks. In Chapter 8 coping with political and cultural conflict is examined more fully.

Thought Experiment: Argumentation Points

There are numerous topics concerning cultural differences that the 2016 election elevated to conflict not only between in-groups and out-groups but within otherwise demographically homogeneous groups. These fighting issues are worth articulating and considering as points of engagement in our cultural wars of post-11/8. The following are some of the prototypical issues that are being debated and argued over in our homes and places of work.

1. If rape involves the targeting of victims in terms of their gender and often age, then are sexual assaults hate crimes?
2. Does the president have the right to say Mexicans are rapists?
3. When Dylann Roof planned and carried out a multiple-victim homicide, he targeted blacks who were members of a black church. Roof,

an avowed white supremacist, wrote a manifesto proclaiming his ideology and intention to create a race war. Should this offense be considered a hate crime or a crime of domestic terror?

4. If the federal crime data indicates Muslims are no more likely than other religions to commit terror-motivated acts of violence, then what are the legitimate reasons to ban these persons from entering the United States?

5. Are a reallocation of federal funds away from social programs and toward projects to build a wall along the border with Mexico and an increase in the military budget effective means of dealing with terrorism and keeping America safe?

6. Is tolerating political regimes that engage in human rights violations and suppress free speech, like Russia, an acceptable trade-off to make America a more economically successful country?

7. Is promoting stereotypes about immigrants okay if it helps to improve the American economy?

Characters of the Cultural Cataclysm

In my discussions of this writing project with filmmaker Arthur Dong we hit on the notion of character types—people who are encountered along the political spectrum—in the upset and fights that have occurred since the conclusion of the Trump–Clinton presidential race. As in many movie scripts, these characterizations depict individuals we can identify with or react against; this is in some fashion what we all are experiencing now, as we negotiate our interactions with friends, acquaintances, coworkers, and strangers in our daily lives.

Let's consider some of what we have been discussing by examining prototypical individuals and how they might interact around the issues of the 11/8 election. The following stock characters are people we have met and whom we (implicitly) anticipate holding certain beliefs in alignment or conflict with our own.

1. Larry: 40-year-old black law enforcement officer with large city police department. Background in U.S. Army; married with children in public schools. He has been diagnosed with diabetes and is under medical care for this; his spouse is active in their church.

2. Donna: 60-ish feminist white women with a background in arts and crafts, reproductive rights, and community organizing. Limited economic resources and involved in a co-operative for many of her basic needs. She has an adult daughter who is an out lesbian who is married to her partner of many years.

3. Louis: Former Afghanistan combat veteran in his early 40s who is active in mental health treatment for vets with PTSD and facilitates groups on suicide risk of postcombat vets. Currently works in a health club and has limited financial resources.

4. Ron: American living abroad; has lived abroad in Mexico running a small business and has a non-U.S. wife. Generally apolitical, concerned about how Americans will be seen abroad. His parents are retired in the United States; a younger brother died in the war in Iraq.

5. Luis: Victim of a hate crime since November 8, 2016. Latino man who is in his late 20s who was assaulted by two white men in an urban neighborhood. Lives with an aunt and works as a delivery driver. U.S. born; many of his friends are undocumented.

6. Valerie: Female social progressive millennial; she is college-educated and from a middle-class background. Has worked for Planned Parenthood and is considering going to law school—she is concerned about taking on over $100,000 in college debt. She has several close friends who are minority and LGBT individuals.

7. Manny: Man of Puerto Rican heritage, he is an unemployed machinist in his 40s who has had an inconsistent employment history, having worked at companies that have closed down and moved out of state. He lives with two roommates; he receives financial support from a family member who runs a small business in another state.

8. Jack: Political progressive living in a deep red state; 50-year-old male with background in community affairs, limited economic resources. Purchased health care via exchange—a.k.a. Obamacare. Has lived most of his life in rural parts of the country.

9. Dale: Self-employed white man in his 40s with successful life insurance business. He is married with a stay-at-home wife, is an NRA member, champions Sean Hannity and Fox News, and volunteers as a part-time law enforcement officer.

10. Lito: White gay Republican man in his 60s, medical doctor with significant financial resources. Married to his partner of 15 years. Interested in opera and international affairs; describes himself as a follower of the ideas of Ayn Rand.

11. Maria: Marketing professional, U.S. born, her Filipino family resides both in the United States and back in the home country. She is married to a spouse who works in the chemical industry. She has two elementary aged children in private school.

12. Alejandra: Undocumented person, female in her 20s with limited formal education and work in service-sector jobs. Her family is in

Los Angeles and in Central America. Lives with three other undocumented women; she is six months pregnant.

13. Kathi: Retired military widow, late 60s, lives off her SSI and deceased husband's veteran's benefits. Has multiple health problems and relies on Medicare for her health needs. Has had a lifelong involvement in the Catholic Church and the Republican Party.

14. Ronnie: Moderate Christian working in private educational institution. Married with family and middle-income with minimal resources. He has a brother with autism who lives in a board-and-care in another city and lives on Social Security disability funding and Medicare.

15. Greg: General contractor, male self-employed with health care purchased on the Obamacare exchange, he is a member of the NRA and volunteers as an auxiliary officer with his community police department. He is divorced, and struggles to pay child support. Minimal financial resources, active in his congregational church.

16. Stuart: Academic, tenured professor in public health. Late 50s with advanced degree and reputation in his area of research. His spouse is a lawyer; they have two children attending Ivy League universities. He is active in his synagogue and supports charities involved in Israel.

Contrast Culture Exercise

The technique of exposing basic cultural assumptions has been conducted in the exercise referred to as the "Contrast Culture" technique. Bhawuk and Brislin (2000) have discussed how this technique can assist a trainee in identifying their personal cultural assumptions in intergroup relationships. Drawing attention to the process of comparisons (the "contrast" part of the exercise) can assist an individual in understanding and anticipating how social group norms will impact the cross-cultural relationship.

As applied here, the between-individual differences we are concerned with are linked to the self-attributions and stereotypes that influence the political argument and lead to conflict in interpersonal relationships (Cikara, Bruneau, & Saxe, 2011). What is particularly relevant is how perceived between-individual differences activate adverse out-group stereotypes and hence reduce the cognitive load of the individual (i.e., the need to consider the arguments of the other individual is reduced by ascription to the stereotype). Out-group stereotyping is explanatory of the ensuing conflict (rather than hearing the potential legitimacy of another's argument). This means that objective differences of social group categories in amplifying political argumentation are less predictive of the process of debate than the assumptions fueled by the stereotype activation. In the post-11/8 discourse this employment of stereotypes and the turning of personal beliefs into issues of intergroup contention turn the individuals into exemplars of their social group. We are as such deindividuated and reified as a spokesperson for our cultural group. In our relationships we are experienced by the "contrast other" individual not as a unique person but rather a representative of a denigrated out-group. This political and cultural reification simplifies how we are viewed and also restricts us in how our personal attitudes are appraised.

Moderator Factors

Social psychology has frequently studied how manipulating social environments and social interactions can shift attitudes and behaviors of the individual. Below 11 interpersonal interactions—scenes—are proposed, which can allow for a contrast culture analysis or for self-study or training in dealing with differences related to the current political climate of the United States. We then consider the factors that fuel conflict in the scenes.

A. Imagine what would happen if Louis, Luis, and Manny were all getting drunk in a bar. Louis says that he would support religious profiling of Muslims and would support "locking them up by opening a camp to put the terrorists in." How would the others most likely respond to this comment? Consider if in the above scenario the discussion was about "locking up" undocumented persons instead of terrorists?

B. If Valerie had just had an argument with her right-wing uncle about the elimination of environmental regulations, how might she respond to Kathi if they got into a debate about funding of women's health services?

C. How would Dale, Ronnie, and Ron respond to news the Trump administration was eliminating the Department of Education to build a wall along the border of Mexico. If Ron demanded to know what the others thought about this, what is likely to happen next?

D. If Dale was a member of the same church as Kathi and Greg and he said he had just lost his health care and blamed it on the ending of Obamacare, how would Greg and Kathi probably respond?

E. Assuming all three people are members of a 12-step group how would Greg and Lito likely respond if Ronnie disclosed he was gay and pressed to know if the others supported gay marriage?

F. Imagine Stuart, Jack, and Louis were in a business meeting and heard that a terror-related shooting had just happened in Michigan. How would the others respond if Stuart said "we had it coming?"

G. If Maria and Greg were both friends of yours, and Greg said he wanted to become romantically involved with Maria, what would you think could challenge their having a relationship?

H. Assume Jack is a supervisor in a private company and Luis and Alejandra report to him. If the company said it was trying to eliminate undocumented employees, what could be the problem for the supervisor?

I. If Larry and Jack had asked Dale to help them tutor their child in math and Dale showed up at their home wearing a "Make America Great Again" baseball cap, what could be the problem? Consider what if in the above scenario the family were undocumented persons? What if in the above scenario the child was sexually transitioning?

J. If Alejandra had been assaulted in a hate crime and Larry and Greg were the responding officers, what could be a problem? What if in the above scenario the victim was wearing an "Impeach Trump" T-shirt?

K. What if Alejandra was having a conversation with Ronnie and Lito and she said she was concerned her child would be picked on by a teacher at school for being a Latino, what do you think could happen next?

Debriefing the Vignettes

These scenes provide us an opportunity to examine our personal assumptions about intergroup arguments. It also allows us to consider our perceptions about persons who ascribe to beliefs contrary to our own. The proposed interactions shape the risk for intergroup animus we have come to anticipate in our social interactions with members of varying cultural and political out-groups.

As a heuristic process, review of these vignettes can be employed to generate questions for further inquiry. For example, in which of the scenes would you anticipate one or more of the individuals using avoidance tactics? In which would there be a civil discussion of differences and which scenes might result in emotionally volatile arguments? Would any of these vignettes result in the degradation of friendships or openness to ongoing association? Could any of these scenarios result in some form of discriminatory behavior? Do any of these scenes likely result in the cessation of the relationship? Finally, which of these scenes are closest to your own experience? How has that turned out for you?

If we look more closely at these exemplar situations, it is important to consider in what ways issues of bias, stereotyping, and ideology moderate the conflict in each vignette. Do these scenes present conflicts that are mutually experienced, meaning do the issues of power or identity found in a scenario impact all parties similarly? Do some of the interactions fundamentally create internal conflicts for the individual? For example, do attitude differences about undocumented persons appear all but unresolvable? Does religious faith similarly create de facto divisions in our relationships? From a cultural perspective, do group norms and values dictate how some of these individuals might be expected to behave in cross-cultural conflicts?

Let's consider scenario A, the proposition of a hard policy tactic of control of Muslims is proposed—monitoring and incarceration. The potential form of relational failure is how individuals may disagree about such a harsh form of immigration reform. Culturally, none of the three characters are Muslim, nor is there evidence of significant contact with Muslims. All three of the men are unemployed or in low-income jobs. One of them (Louis) has a history of being in warfare in the Middle East whereas another was a victim of a hate crime and has many connections with people who are undocumented. The amplifying agent in this scene is, of course, alcohol. Experimentally, alcohol is associated with the use of hate speech; as such there is greater risk of this escalating because of the disinhibitory effects of the characters being intoxicated (Reeves & Nagoshi, 1993). Possible "hard" argument topics would include invocation of terror threat—a coercive tactic—that can escalate hostility toward the target of bias (Muslims); a soft tactic might be Luis saying he knows many immigrants and he may encourage empathy from the other two men. What we don't know, of course, is the identity status of Luis. In this case how does his ethnic identity influence his readiness to discuss his own experience with the other two men? Risk factors for the escalation of conflict in this interaction besides the presence of alcohol, include the target of bias being a viable terror threat, and the life experience of one character being in life and death situations with the target of bias. The willingness to enter into contention may be anticipated for one individual based on the combat experience and for another their personal experience of hate victimization.

As with the other vignettes, this first scenario allows us to examine our personal reactions to intergroup contact and cultural and political differences. If we dispassionately consider these situations—and more importantly the actual situations we encounter—our sense of allegiance and opposition can be observed. Our personal biases need to be recognized in how we respond to these conflict situations. To complement this, let's consider how much we don't know in these scenarios as well as in our actual intergroup encounters. What we don't know are the countervailing experiences of the person holding an alternate cultural or political belief from our own. In context of the issue of hate and political differences, we do not know from a political choice if the other person is a virulent racist or simply disagrees with our preferred candidate. We do not know in more superficial interactions, for example, whether the other person has a significant capacity for empathy or holds to values of tolerance and respect for differences—or not. Arguably, empathy for an out-group individual can be acquired (Hein et al., 2016). Our abstinence from using stereotypes and reifying persons who express different political beliefs may transform contention into moments of intergroup collaboration or tolerance. Perhaps the choice is more our own rather than that of political strategists or hate organizers.

The scenarios presented above are not simply training exercises, but the sort of questions that many individuals are encountering in their relationships. As the evolution of policies under the Trump administration begins, some of the issues of diversity, terror risk, and social justice will become more meaningful as when they become federal policies and not simply campaign rhetoric. The recasting of the policies of our public institutions will inherently shape many of the presumptions about diversity in our post-11/8 society.

Consistent with the themes found in the vignettes, in the consultation room what I am hearing about is the breakdown in relationships predicated on the activation of intergroup animus. The emergence of alt-right rhetoric is particularly problematic in that it is exactly at this time that vulnerable persons need to find a sense of membership and identity. It is also worth noting that the either–or nature of political argumentation dramatically reduces an opportunity for societal consensus. By remaining divided the capacity of the general populace to establish a platform for government accountability is stifled. The ramping-up of social animus further facilitates a scapegoating of out-groups and misdirects the need for real social change away from the state and onto marginalized groups.

There are many challenges in combating hate violence in a society of radically divergent attitudes concerning the rights of women, immigrants, and visible ethnic minorities. As has been noted for many individuals the 11/8 election reminds them of a traumatic life event such as the

9/11 World Trade Center terror attacks or the death of a family member. Presently, we are also watching the impact of intolerance on our "little worlds." Importantly, our sense of social support is being compromised, and in some cases destroyed, as a consequence of the hate speech of the new (ab)normal.

Summary

The 2016 election and the fallout that has ensued have divided persons in their social relationships, jobs, schools, and families. From the survey study I conducted immediately after the 2016 election I found that women were more likely to be engaged in debate than men about the outcome of the election. Additionally, young adults under 30 were more likely to engage in conflict with other individuals about the election and its aftermath.

The frequency of interpersonal conflict related to 11/8 was largely unchanged from the period after the election when compared to survey responses gathered in the first month after the inauguration. Survey findings revealed minimal change in the reported frequencies of conflict related to the presidential election. The majority of individuals—roughly three out of four persons—in both the first few weeks after the election and during the first month of the Trump presidency reported a negative impact on their relationships. Conflicts with coworkers were more frequently reported than in close intimate relationships. Very few of these conflicts led to physical aggression, with avoidance and unfriending tactics being much more frequently used. In these periods after the election and the inauguration roughly 10% of the respondents noted being a target of hate speech.

Experiences of interpersonal conflict are characterized by four conditions—relational failure, the linking of the disagreement to collective identities, the presence of amplifying factors, and a willingness to enter into contention—which shift the center of discourse from political opinion to a winner and loser identity, one in which the individual becomes an exemplar of their social group. The dynamics of stereotype activation and between-person differences in managing conflict have been described in a series of vignettes. These exercises provide the interested reader an opportunity to consider the attributions and cultural assumptions concerning allies and opponents in the culture wars of the new political climate.

CHAPTER 8

Swimming against the Current: Coping in Politically Fluid Environments

Ieu sui Arnautz . . . E nadi contra suberna.
I am Arnaut . . . who swims against the current.

—Arnaut Daniel

I will make no bargains with monstrosity.

—Lesley Hazelton

The rapid political shift following the U.S. presidential election has impacted our assumptions about intolerance, civil liberties, and personal safety. The outcome of 11/8 additionally revealed deep divisions among the general public. At a personal level, a significant concern is how to cope while living through this cultural cataclysm. It is worth considering what we can learn from others of our own time and from prior generations who have endured living under political systems of oppression. What follows is an examination of how individuals cope in situations of acute and chronic intolerance. This discussion will examine individual strategies to maintain a social consciousness while enduring autocratic regimes and intergroup violence. Three themes will be addressed: discussion of the characteristics of persons who have endured political oppression, a review of coping with bias and hate victimization, and challenges for stakeholders in enforcing hate crime statutes in an ambiguous political environment.

The substantial body of historical (Snyder, 2005; Snyder, 2015) and political (Prilleltensky & Gonick, 1996) research on state-sponsored oppression dwarfs what is found in the mental health field. For clinical scholars such as Carlos Sluzki (2005) the problems of oppression are most immediately encountered in the consultation room. The eminent psychiatrist Chester Pierce (1995) has provided a clinically informed mnemonic to analyze individually experienced forms of oppression—"S-T-E-M"—that is, the control of the individual's space, time, energy, and motion. We also need to draw a distinction between finding a way to adjust to living in a society in which *tolerance* has been abandoned—in our discussion a shift away from a multicultural state toward that of a faux democracy—in contrast to surviving under regimes practicing *elimination* or *extermination* of out-groups. Totalitarian regimes do not marginalize dissent but seek to eradicate it. Where 11/8 will ultimately deliver us is at this point undetermined.

Personal Coping Strategies with Societal Cataclysm

The 9/11 terror attack provides a means for understanding how people cope in the face of national tragedy. A study conducted in the aftermath of the World Trade Center attack—the Behavioral Risk Factor Surveillance System (BRFSS)—conducted with New York City area respondents shortly after 9/11, found that many individuals sought some form of social support or consultation. Contact with immediate family members was most frequently mentioned (36%) as was engagement with friends and neighbors (31%). Nearly 50% of respondents participated in religious or community (memorial) services within two months of 9/11. Women were more likely than men to participate in religious services after the terror attacks. Nearly 12% of the survey sample reported difficulty accessing psychosocial help after the attacks.

An important distinction between 9/11 and 11/8 (which in the Wave One survey study was the primary association drawn by over one-quarter of the respondents) is that after 9/11, virtually everyone in the country came together in response to a common tragedy. People felt more connected through this collective trauma. In the aftermath of 11/8, however, the experiences of people were divided along stark political and cultural lines. This harkens back to our Civil War metaphor, in which families were spit in their allegiance to the North versus the South. So, as with the storyline of brothers fighting against one another in the 1860s, the post-11/8 period has witnessed families being separated and old friendships ended. For the losers, there is an absence of connection with friends and loved ones, in coping with the loss of the established social order. So in our post-11/8 world, some of us have experienced a retraumatization of first losing a sense of cultural stability and thereafter experiencing a loss of connection with our cohorts who fall on the other side of the battle lines of our cultural war.

Case Illustrations: Coping and Surviving under Oppression

What are the means of coping during periods of escalating hate victimization and of state-sponsored oppression? What follows are illustrations of the forms of coping that individuals have employed to survive during insufferable situations. I will then discuss the coping strategies from a conceptual standpoint in what I will call the basic adaptive strategy or "stance" that these individuals have utilized to survive hatred and oppression.

The Isolated Scholar

One of my teachers when I was an undergraduate at a college in New England was Benjamin. "Ben" looked as if he was from central casting for a 1930s movie, playing the part of the European professor, complete with the mustache, glasses, and tweed coat. He had been a professor of medieval Crimean history and was active since right before World War II in his profession. Ben made the point that some of the books he had translated on the history of the Russian revolution had been authored by people who had suddenly disappeared. Ben ultimately had his own life detoured by being placed in the Gulag by the state for having failed to teach a social realist perspective in his scholarship of the 13th century. He described to me how he spent nearly three years in solitary confinement, during which time he noted he learned to pray and to meditate to not go crazy. He noted how at some point during World War II he was deported from the Gulag and Soviet Union. His captors apparently came to realize that as a Polish Jew they had no use for him. After the war he returned to teaching and resumed his study of ancient Jewish language and culture. Through his own experiences he also became a resource for the Soviet dissidents of the 1970s and 1980s. Ben described how when he was released from the Soviet Union, he was able to practice his *mitzvah* in helping other intellectuals to speak out against oppression. Ben adopted a stance of self-regulation—via prayer and meditation—while being controlled in terms of his movement and space (to refer to Chester Pierce) and ultimately reconnecting with his intellectual community and faith.

Going into the Lower Circle of Hell

The White Rose movement—*die Weiße Rose*—is the name for a group of young University of Munich students who took on the Nazis from

1942 into 1943, at the height of World War II (Wittenstein, 1997). This children's crusade against the standing government had its basis in pacifism and classical German literature and philosophy. Principally active in the distribution of leaflets denouncing the government, crimes against the Jews, and the war effort, this group of young people included Alexander Schmorell and the siblings Hans and Sophie Schloss, whose father had been a liberal politician before the war. The leaders of the movement were unfortunately identified—Sophie and Hans were arrested distributing their leaflets—and executed by a Nazi-sponsored people's court.

The White Rose movement drew on the cultural anchors of literature and religious traditions of Germany in framing their argument against the Nazi regime. They pushed against the imposed silence and learned helplessness of their totalitarian society. The use of soft influence strategies of information and a relationship to the past became part of their argument against the state. The stance of these individuals was the use of cultural anchoring, sublimation, and active resistance.

The Case of Silence

Karl Hartmann, a Bavarian classical composer (1905–1963), has been called the greatest German symphonist of the 20th century. A lifelong pacifist, one of his most recognized compositions was his Concerto Funebre (1939) for violin and orchestra, commemorating the tragedy of the invasion of Czechoslovakia by Germany. His music was condemned before the war by the Nazis. Of note was his complete withdrawal during World War II from music performance—during the war he refused to perform his music in Germany—and his adopting a compositional silence during this time. His complete isolation from his country and the musical community was his form of endurance while living under Nazi rule in Munich. The practice of silence and the attainment of silence may offer a deeper form of emotional and spiritual sustenance to persons living in societies of oppression. As Sarah and Diat (2017) have noted, all that is great and creative is formed through silence. Silence can become a portal or port key to a place of consciousness that is not to be controlled by the oppressor.

After the war had ended, Hartmann resumed a fully active artistic life during the last 20 years that he lived in Germany. During this later period he composed, taught, and helped to rebuild a musical culture after the fall of Nazism. Hartmann adopted a stance of removal and silent resistance; I would speculate he relied on his art as a hermetic form of self-sustenance. As with Ben, he engaged in a renewal of his intellectual life when freed from the totalitarian regime.

Making Art from Victimization

The creative experience derived from being a victim is revealed in the story of Father James Whittaker, a first-generation American Shaker, who, according to the stories we have, was, along with another Shaker, tied to a tree by an angry mob in Harvard, Massachusetts, in 1783, and beaten. When he was cut free, abandoned and bloodied, he began to sing a song now known as "Father James' Song," a solemn wordless chant that is often performed today by traditional music performers, such as the Boston Camerata. As Mother Ann Lee—the founder of the Shakers—said when seeing his injuries, "without suffering there is no redemption." So, Father Whittaker took a step into his art as a victim of religious hatred instead of going into silence. His stance was that of community, sublimation, and devotional faith.

The "Mad Dog" Who Survived Mao

There was a man I knew years ago—who used the name "John" for Westerners—who had been a university professor of history in a career that spanned the 1960s into the 1980s. John relayed to me how he survived the experience of teaching at his university during the Cultural Revolution of the middle 1960s into the later 1970s. During this state-sanctioned uprising, it is estimated that up to 30 million people died (Scaruffi, 1999) under the riots, purges, and state-sanctioned terror events. A core theme of the revolution as proposed by Chairman Mao Zedong was the eradication of bourgeoisie elements of the Chinese society (Esherwick, Pickowicz, & Walder, 2006). Among others, this included university faculty. As was typical, a recent account by Zhang Lifan, a university researcher at the time, stated "There were no standards. I saw a university student being beaten by a female Red Guard, and the people around told her to stop. And then this Red Guard said self-righteously, 'Chairman Mao told me to beat him!'" (Gao, 2017). This is an example of the anti-intellectual attitudes and the culture of random acts of violence found in many AUX-type movements such as the Cultural Revolution.

John described how the way he survived in the university system was to be a "mad dog," that is, assume the most radical perspective on social and political issues as a means of removing suspicion from him. He recounted how many in the academy stayed working by adopting an archly reactionary political rhetoric consistent with that demanded by the Red Guards—the enforcers of the principles of the Cultural Revolution. I recall the regret he expressed in having to assume such a role to avoid the persecution he saw meted out to other intellectuals. He spoke of this with a sense of caution, almost as if the revolution might return and come for him. John's form of coping—his stance of resistance—involved adopting a public and private face and the use of an internalized sense of an ideology in opposition to the state.

Passive Resistance

An alternative form of disobedience is found in the stories of *Good Soldier Schweik*, which is characteristic of practiced resistance while inside the castle, that is, being a negligent participant of the state, in this case the tottering-on-the-edge Austro-Hungarian Empire. Based on the unfinished novel of Czech writer Jaroslav Hašek (1883–1923), the story of Schweik recounts the pointlessness of militarism and futility of authoritarianism, which Hašek experienced while a soldier in World War I. In this story, Schweik reveals his increasingly passive resistance to the authoritarian state, one marked by superficial compliance but driven by alienation and disengagement.

The "Ghost in the Machine"

Active resistance while part of the political powers that be is exemplified by Representative John Lewis. Representative Lewis became one of the first in the Washington, D.C., establishment to take on Donald Trump. Lewis, a highly regarded member of the 1960s civil rights movement, challenged the legitimacy of Trump given the mounting concerns about the role the Russian government played in undermining the campaign of Hillary Clinton. In a televised news program that aired prior to the January 20, 2017, inauguration, Lewis stated, "I don't see the president-elect as a legitimate president. I think the Russians participated in helping this man get elected," he added, also calling it a "conspiracy." "They helped destroy the candidacy of Hillary Clinton" (Memoli, 2017). For Lewis, his protest of the election outcome came at a time many in the liberal Democratic political camp were still in a state of shock. As he had done years before, his protest helped to define the struggle that is likely to follow concerning the influence of a foreign government in the U.S. election and the inertia of the standing government to respond to this challenge. As Lewis no doubt anticipated, Trump attacked him and his constituency; for Lewis, this probably only motivated him more. For Lewis, his stance has involved active resistance and engagement, as well as empathy and engagement in his community to fight oppression.

Victims Who Become Advocates

I have known people led by violence about diversity to become advocates for peace. The story of Erin McLaughlin, who was gay-bashed as a young woman, has been recounted elsewhere (McLaughlin, 2016). Erin has written, taught, and talked about her experiences of being severely assaulted for being a lesbian and having to endure indifference of law enforcement and in some cases her own friends as a hate crime victim. She has also discussed the dilemma of being involved with an undocumented person who suffered hate violence and the ever-present issue of the risk of deportation. She has described her evolution from crime victim to that of a community advocate for other victims as well as for the destitute mentally ill.

Another advocate I knew, Michael, was a young man in his late teens who had been raised in the Sotell-13 gang of Los Angeles. While still on probation, he chose to leave his violent past and became a peacemaker with the rival gangs. I met him through a program I was working with concerning violent youth diversion; "Mikie" was working on his high school equivalency certificate and said he wanted to be a Mercedes-Benz car mechanic and raise a family. Michael, his head always wrapped in a bandana, brokered on his own a cease-fire between Latino and black gangs in his community. He did this by talking about having been in gangs his entire life, having been incarcerated, and emphasizing the futility of perpetrating violence against young persons just like himself. He was a classic charismatic leader, spoke well, had the street credibility needed, and was smart. This was before there were the concerted efforts we see today of law enforcement agencies trying to engage in interdiction. I remember one day another member of his home gang saying to me "Mikie is dead." His compadre related how Michael had gone to a local park to try and resolve differences between two rival Latino gangs and was shot dead—apparently for calling out the leaders to "talk and not hate"—an expression he used often with me. A few days later a neighborhood paper ran a brief story headlined "Another Useless Death." Erin and Michael influenced their peers through their own experience, their ability to articulate what had happened to them and what to do about it (what we will call value expression), and their willingness to go into diverse communities to change attitudes.

Practicing *Orenda*

What these people did, in their own way, was to practice *Orenda*, a term from the Iroquois that connotes the power of the human will to change the world in the face of powerful forces. The vignettes of these individuals detail the range of strategies used for living in times of hatred and oppression. Contemporary mental health phraseology might call these *coping styles*. Susan Folkman and Richard Lazarus (1984) have discussed the varying ways of coping in terms of the use of logic, seeking social support, affect expression, planful problem solving, and emotion regulation. How people cope with political oppression is additionally representative of something that is, however, more than behavioral technique; it is emblematic of the character of the individual. Classical psychoanalytical theory would consider these coping styles as ego defenses, which are characteristic of mature—that is, more adaptive—forms of defense (Vaillant, 1977). These defenses are pervasive across time and situation and serve as a protective factor in responding to psychosocial stress. The use of empathy, sublimation, and suppression are found as part of the strategies used by these individuals. These people practiced patience, worked hard, pulled back from circumstances of coercion, and retained an alternate ideology to that of the ultranationalists. It is also worth considering that only one of the individuals I have described was a political leader. Individuals such as Gandhi, Mandela, or Eleanor Roosevelt, by comparison, give us examples of how healthy coping styles were employed to allow persons in positions of political power to inspire millions in the pursuit of human rights.

Two important characteristics of the individuals I described above are what I will call the practice of value expression and self–other orientation. These strategies were employed out of choice—or in some cases necessity—to maintain the individual's physical health and to retain an alternative means of comprehending the world intolerance found in their social environments.

Value expression is the conscious personal articulation of a liberal democratic and tolerant ideology. The practice of value expression can serve as a form of self-succorance or a form of social commentary. In the former, value expression works similarly to a mantra in yoga or an aphorism in Alcoholics Anonymous in which the recurring core belief serves to stabilize the individual—and allows them to stay sane by drawing on this belief for the individual's psychic and material survival. This was exemplified by Ben while in the Gulag. When practiced as a form of social commentary, value expression is revealed via advocacy and protest. John Lewis, Erin, and the White Rose movement all reflect this later quality.

Self–other orientation strategies reflect the process of self-regulation of the individuals' internal states that may be employed to interact with the external (social) environment. Behaviorally, this strategy serves to regulate adverse reactions to S-T-E-M forms of oppression and hatred. The practice of self-regulatory behaviors is important given the substantial evidence of how racism (Clark, Anderson, Clark, & Williams, 1999) and other forms of bias negatively impact the health status of the individual. Self–other regulation also involves the concepts of manageability (see Antonovsky [1979], below) and locus of control. Locus of control has been examined in a range of circumstances (Rotter & Mulry, 1965; Strickland, 1989) and is critical to our ideas of stress and health. In the vignettes we have seen how self–other regulation serves as being either personal or external. This self–other orientation allows for the healthy adaptation under contexts that control freedom of speech and expression. In some contexts this social control is institutional—such as in incarceration, forced psychiatric treatment for political outcasts, and corrective "treatment" of sexual minorities. For some individuals coping means living in the Gulag, or through conversion therapy treatment, or being made a psychiatric patient as a consequence of political dissent. As in the pathological family, the presentation of the self is accomplished by negotiating through periods of acute and chronic distress.

In a series of studies that I conducted in U.S. universities (Dunbar, Liu, & Horvath 1995; Dunbar & Svensson, 2016), I found that young adults generally felt better about themselves when they responded to experiences of (nonviolent) bias victimization via confrontation and active problem-oriented coping. Greater satisfaction was found for both men (consistently) and women (generally) in responding to an incident of bias by telling the offending party that their (the provocateurs') behavior was because of out-group hostility. People who engaged in seeking help—often from their peers and other informal social networks—reported less anxiety and symptoms of depression following the hate incident. Consistent with Folkman and Lazarus, forms of active coping, as compared to denial, avoidance, and isolation, were related to better postincident outcomes.

In looking at coping strategies, it is clear there are healthier and risker ways to respond to oppression. The bifurcation or splitting of the social self—or what we might call living as a converso—invariably requires significant psychic energy. Hiding and lying constitute a unique cognitive load for the individuals. It takes effort to practice healthy paranoia— that is the engagement of a cautious and vigilant way of living that does not expose the inner self to the toxicities of the outer malevolent world. At the same time, this learning to be careful in a world that does not protect you is not news for many persons of color in North America; as one colleague said about life following the 9/11 terrorist attacks, "Welcome to feeling black." What for some of us is a new sense of oppression is a variation on the same old song for others.

An arguably undesirable form of dealing with a cultural cataclysm such as 11/8 is to expatriate—that is to go abroad to "the safe house." This has been practiced for decades by intellectuals and minority artists who have left their country of origin to live in more tolerant societies. A recent example of this is that of a social scientist who moved his family to Central America after the November 2016 election. He noted he left the United States as a means of dealing with the concern he felt for their safety while living in urban America under the Trump administration.

One of the coping strategies I have heard often about from individuals since 11/8 was avoidance; this seemed to split between avoiding information about the Trump victory/administration via the media or avoidance of people of an opposing political belief. As one educator friend put it "I'm going to put one thousand acres between me and the next person, grow my food, maybe I'll even live in a cave."

Coping strategies that are yet again more inherently problematic include passive acceptance, repudiation of the norms of tolerance and equity, or the ascription to the political values of the ascendant alternative model of governance. Some individuals employ more absolute denial. I have spoken with persons who have described their effort to avoid media and news programming that raises awareness of the Trump administration; for these persons the effort is to become unaware of the aftershocks of the cataclysm of 11/8. Living in the world but not knowing how it is changing may prove untenable and again draws on psychological resources needed for daily functioning.

Challenges to Identity in Societies of Oppression

In my country today there are people who are wondering if the Resistance had a real military impact on the course of the war. For my generation this question is irrelevant: we immediately understood the moral and psychological meaning of the Resistance. For us it was a point of pride to know that we Europeans did not wait passively for liberation. And for the young Americans who were paying with their blood for our restored freedom it meant something to know that behind the firing lines there were Europeans paying their own debt in advance.

—Umberto Eco

As a clinician I was stressing shortly after the election to "be closer to those you are close to, become active in some cause you care deeply about." However, what many people in the field of hate studies realize is we do not know *where* this new regime will take us societally. What is happening, perhaps imperceptibly, is the reconsideration of who *we* are and who *we can get along with*.

One of the important issues I have found in dealing with hate victimization is how positive in-group identity, such as pride and involvement with one's Chinese heritage, and engagement with in-group social networks, help-seeking from a student gay/lesbian center, contribute to recovery from experiences of discrimination. For most of the losers of the U.S. presidential campaign, and particularly for at-risk visible ethnic and racial minorities, engagement with in-group social networks may prove essential. Along with a stronger sense of one's cultural and social identify, adjusting to a growingly xenophobic society may mean a strengthening of the in-group enclave.

What I have discussed elsewhere, recovering from, as well as living through, experiences of hate victimization require the establishment of a sense of coherence in one's life (Dunbar & Svensson, 2016). This concept of sense of coherence (SOC) as originally articulated by Antonovsky (1979; Antonovsky & Bernstein, 1986) identified the role of psychological states of comprehensibility, manageability, and meaningfulness of their circumstances in maintaining a state of well-being, which he referred to as salutogenesis—the state of human health and well-being. For Antonovsky, SOC involves the individual's orientation to view the world and themselves in terms of their ability to control their own lives in balance with their social and cultural environments. When living in a society that is governed by a xenophobic and ultranationalist ideology, this sense of coherence is found through the strengthening of bonds with people like ourselves. This strategy is not without its social costs. Any movement of people toward a more balkanized form of coexistence runs the risk of reducing positive intergroup contact and cooperation (Pettigrew & Tropp, 2006; Pettigrew, Tropp, Wagner, & Christ, 2011). In surviving in a societal order of oppression we become more inward looking, more isolated, and potentially less interculturally competent.

Building Our Cultural Immunocompetency

> It will end … Someday. The very idea of place. Not governed and governing, but people.
>
> —Philip K. Dick

To take the metaphor of cultural well-being and health a bit further, we can think of adjustment to intolerance as being analogous to our immunological health—our "collective immunocompetency"—in surviving a hate-based autocracy. In the Human Rights Campaign (HRC) study of postelection reactions of youths, it was noted that, in spite of the high frequency of harassment seen or experienced by their respondents, many of these adolescents (57%) expressed feeling more motivated to help people in their community. As one teenager wrote, "the best way for adults to reassure youth, especially minorities, is to get involved in the community and take action to make the world a better place, whether it is through volunteering at a homeless shelter, working on a campaign, or something else. Actions speak louder than words."

The process of coping with intolerance can test the resilience of our social groups to resist political and cultural toxins. So in essence we can speak about the hardiness or immunocompetency of an individual or a collective to survive culturally cataclysmic events. Immunological health involves detection of toxins, creating antibodies to protect from and eradicate the toxins, the mobilization and engagement of the killer cells with the toxins, and the creation of an immunological memory to ward of future attacks. Similarly being able to adjust to and work against intolerance is revealed through a range of personal and group ways of coping. Healthy coping reveals a staying power and capacity for looking forward to periods after the toxins are eradicated; we all need to develop our cultural antibodies.

Burnette and Figley (2015) have studied coping strategies of traditionally vulnerable out-groups in the United States, such as American Indian and Alaskan native people, groups that are vulnerable to trauma, given the high rates of violence in their communities and the noted health and mental health disparities also found in these same communities. For them, resilience to psychosocial stressors must incorporate cultural traditions and strengthening familial relationships to support the individual in periods of acute and chronic stress. For Burnette and Figley (2016) interventions with at-risk groups also means addressing the impact of historical oppression on communities and individuals. They propose that to transcend the tradition of oppression mental health intervention needs to be framed in terms of cultural traditions and informed by principles of social justice and human rights. Through this approach the authors suggest that such an engagement can help to explain, predict, and prevent violence. These principles of care, I would argue, are now applicable to all persons struggling in this time of incipient autocracy.

Stakeholders Coping with Societal Cataclysm

How we cope with hate violence in the aftermath of 11/8 without considering the issues facing our stakeholder professionals would be incomplete. Stakeholder groups include public safety personnel, law enforcement, the judiciary, the media, and policy makers. Reporting hate violence requires specialized skills and knowledge that, frankly, is extraneous to the core competencies of these stakeholders. Sheriffs are elected. Prosecuting attorneys have pay-for-performance ratings based substantially on their conviction rates. "Hate crimes," as one senior law enforcement spokesperson (not a trained officer) said, "are a pain in the ass." As such, many stakeholders find that hate crimes are aspects of their job where contention and confusion follow.

Responding to hate crimes in the pre-11/8 society was problematic in terms of investigation and documentation for law enforcement professionals. One of the earlier efforts to examine the effectiveness of hate crime documentation was conducted by Nolan and Akiyama (1999). Their work with police departments in various parts of the country identified factors that they felt were related to agency effectiveness in reporting hate crimes. These included organizational culture, department–community relationships, efficacy of officer and resource allocations, and supportive organizational policies and practices (which at the time of their study may have been influenced by the inclusiveness of the state laws in which the agencies were situated). In addition to these institutional resource and process factors, Nolan and Akiyama also identified how attitudes of responding officers and what they termed organizational commitment determined agency effectiveness in reporting hate crimes.

From the initial promulgation of hate crime policies in the early 1990s until 2016, there has been incremental changes and refinement in the laws, in investigation and documentation procedures, and research on hate crimes. In what is proposed under the new regime, these improvements most likely will be rolled back at a federal level. In an ultranationalist society working on hate crimes might put you out of work. Consider the implications of wanting to investigate a crime as bias-motivated in a community where there is strong opposition to voting equity, to same-sex marriage, to a woman's reproductive rights and where perceived immigrants are profiled and harassed. How would this line of inquiry go forward? How might this impact conducting field interviews? How would your fellow officers view you? How might a public prosecutor view a case that came his or her way with a hate-enhancement charge added to the report? Experienced prosecutors frankly already consider the community and the juror pool in determining whether to prosecute a case as bias motivated. In our post-11/8 world the prior problems of underreportage of hate crimes will most certainly increase. The old problems of stakeholders not wishing to comply with the federal laws will shift, as federal justice oversite will inevitably be drastically reduced. Over the coming four years there will be a clear challenge in documenting and enforcing hate crime laws at the federal level. The post-11/8 problems of documenting hate incidents will likely lead to a greater split between the more multiculturally sensitive states (read as "Clinton states") and the more conservative regions of the country. In spirit and in practice the important work will fall to those states ready to do the hard work.

Law enforcement also struggles under problems of what I have referred to as "the authoritarian conundrum" (Dunbar, 2016) in the recording and enforcement of hate crimes. As I have commented, "Law enforcement personnel are inherently authoritarian in their work roles and are classically asked to punish individuals who deviate from the prescribed social norms. This paradoxically mandates the protection of social minority groups—the very individuals most vulnerable to police harassment. The issue of value similarity of law enforcement personnel with many anti-government and bias-motivated offenders is a particular dilemma in the fight against hate crimes. Often the hate crime perpetrators reflect the social biases of substantial numbers of the dominant culture. The ascription to anti-immigration, anti-taxation, pro-gun ownership, and hostility to sexual minorities—which arguably reflect the worldview of many U.S.-based domestic terrorists—are commonly endorsed by many Americans in national opinion surveys" (Marsden, 2012). We may well see a more overtly authoritarian approach to not only police work but also personnel dealing with immigrants. The prospect of loosening administrative controls with the stakeholder groups such as border agents may prove problematic and invite abuse.

A critical theory perspective would argue a newly installed autocratic regime might (superficially) remain indifferent to the rule of law but then understaff the department as a means to minimize federal activity, all the while suggesting outwardly that the rights of vulnerable persons are still being protected. The shadow of the leadership in the White House could serve to minimize, abandon, and misinterpret data collection and enforcement of federal hate crime statutes. I also think that more sensational cases such as the Dylann Roof mass murder of members of a black church in South Carolina have value to an autocracy. By that I mean there is an advantage to having hate crimes depicted as being the work of alienated loners who appear marginalized and problematic. This helps to obscure the problem of hate violence committed by members of society such as college students, working adults, and law enforcement officers.

Beyond law enforcement, the challenge for community-based organizations (CBOs) to advocate for, and collaborate with, other stakeholder groups becomes more challenging with the current regime change. If there is a stance of indifference at a federal level, it is likely that at a state and community level there will be a greater cleavage than ever between regions of the country that remain committed to civil liberties and multiculturalism and those regions where local policy leaders will actively work to restrict support for diversity. In this later case, local and state policy makers might monitor public agencies that push for enforcement of hate crime laws. This author has seen one instance where a small city disbanded its police department because of the number of hate crimes that were documented—including several homicides—as a means of improving the public image of the community. The department had done too good a job of exposing interracial violence for the public officials to find tolerable. This may prove to be a harbinger of things to come. Serving vulnerable groups such as transgendered persons, immigrants, the homeless, or the disabled may prove to be politically untenable in many cities and states where there is a strong right-shifting political leadership.

To frame the issue of how stakeholders may respond to hate violence, let's return to the model of political and cultural attitudes. Under a multicultural political model, hate crime policies are generally supported and revised to reflect trends in intergroup problems. Law enforcement would put adequate resources into documentation and additionally CBOs and public agencies would be involved in coalitions that engage in prevention and early detection work to curb incipient hate conflict. The media would also seek to provide a clear portrayal of critical events and engage in more thorough analysis of the scope of the problem. Similarly the judiciary would uphold the rule of law in terms of civil rights and anti-bias laws. Policy makers would be responsive to changes in law and the role of government to safeguard vulnerable groups. In liberal democratic systems the practice of stakeholder groups is largely consistent with that of multicultural democracies. However, regional norms and biases, as well as diverse social attitudes held by policy makers and the media, would be expected to mitigate against full enforcement of the law.

By comparison, essentially antidemocratic systems will more readily fail to enforce laws or eliminate policies that are inconsistent with autocratic rule: law enforcement becomes inconsistent in protecting the rights of citizens, judges adhere to forms of bias consistent with the ruling government and majority culture, the media ignores incidents of minority group violence. In totalitarian regimes, the role of the stakeholder is simply that of carrying out the desires of the despot. Most typically this extends the use of violence and control to all members of society, not simply vulnerable out-groups. This model of change in the role of stakeholder groups is summarized in Table 8.1 below.

The preceding argument is that how stakeholders respond to hate violence is a direct consequence of the political ideology of the leadership. As such, legal precedent may be discarded under periods of cataclysmic change. This may be fueled by the circumstance of a terror threat. A recent illustration of this is the opinion put forth by Alberto Gonzales, who had served as the U.S. attorney general in the period after the World Trade Center terrorist attacks, that provisions of the Geneva Convention on Human Rights concerning rights of detainees were deemed "quaint," which he stated was because "the war against terrorism is a new kind of war."

Even in such volatile times like these, the academy is a weak link. The lack of collaboration—and arguably interest—of academics and researchers in responding to social change goes on unabated. Even one of the most simple of tasks, gathering information after 11/8, is mired in institutional balkanization. For example, in trying to conduct online surveys through a research institution to address 11/8, the institutional review board (IRB) process took months. If I had worked through this institution the very issue I was studying would have been a thing of the past. Likewise, colleagues of mine trying to teach the issue of dealing with autocracy have seen proposals also lost in review processes that inherently lose momentum.

The collaboration among researchers and practitioners about 11/8 and hate violence remains a major challenge. As one human relations expert commented to me, trying to work with some of the research groups that supposedly track hate crimes is frustrating. "They don't return our emails—our findings are very different than theirs. I would love to work with them and get all of our organizations collaborating but it seems they don't want to deal with the community." An issue worth examining prospectively is how people who adhere to a liberal democratic tradition will adjust to this period of great societal disruption. Will individuals who accurately anticipate the social and personal problems ahead prove capable of maintaining a sense of coherence and identification

Table 8.1   Cultural–Political Status: Stakeholder Role in Hate Violence

Multicultural Model

Law enforcement:	Protect out-groups from hate violence, create coalitions
Judiciary:	Adhere to or expand rule of law to protect out-groups
Public officials:	Advocate for social equity and inclusion
Media:	Incorporate out-groups into public discourse

Liberal Democratic Model

Law enforcement:	Enforce established human rights laws and policies
Judiciary:	Adhere to rule of law to protect out-groups
Public officials:	Respond to political influence of out-groups
Media:	Respond to marketplace trends that engage out-groups

Oligarchies and Theocracies

Law enforcement:	Indifference to violence against out-groups
Judiciary:	Engage in informal discrimination against out-groups
Public officials:	Adhere to state policies on out-group liberties
Media:	Tolerate fake news

Authoritarianism Autocracy

Law enforcement:	Informal persecution of out-groups
Judiciary:	Serve as a tool for the autocrat
Public officials:	Support the oppression of free speech and intellectual life
Media:	Tolerate and produce fake news

Totalitarian Xenophobia

Law enforcement:	Actively engage in violence against out-groups
Judiciary:	Use the law as a form of persecution and extermination
Public officials:	Support genocide and persecution of intellectuals
Media:	Produce fake news and brainwash the populace

with values of social justice? The challenges of our time require research-ers to move out of the laboratory and into their communities.

The Shape of Things to Come

Let us not be too optimistic; political psychology and history makes clear that some forms of coping as a political outsider are reducible to little more than overt capitulation. The history of the Spanish Inquisition in the 14th and 15th centuries, for example, details the trials of both Jews and Muslims to "pass" as Christians under the church-dominated state (Meno-cal, 2002). The Jewish and Islamic citizens, stripped of their religious free-doms, were at best deemed conversos—those who had become Christian under threat of economic privation, societal expulsion, or, worse, death. Also called Marranos, these individuals were de facto forced into conver-sion to Christianity. The suspicion at the time—with probably a good deal of accuracy—was that many conversos continued to practice Judaism in secret. Not unlike the more contemporary coping strategy employed by many sexual minorities, coping in monocultural society may necessitate "going underground" or living in the closet, as a form of survival.

Under periods of severe state oppression, then, it may be that the sur-vival of the individual and their in-group may require the bifurcation of the sense of self into the public-facing conforming individual, which is coupled with an internalized identity and social value system that is shared only with members of the individual's in-group. John's "mad dog" strategy under the Cultural Revolution in our recent past or the decades of functioning as a converso under the Spanish Inquisition for Jews and Muslims alike make this point.

The respondents to the Wave One survey (conducted in the first six weeks following the 2016 election) frequently expressed their concern about the perceived threat to friends and family of being punished for their nonconformance to social norms—a classic consequence of living under an authoritarian government. The punishment of the individual is a classic theme in the dystopian society literature of the 20th century. Be it Orwell's *1984* or *Animal Farm*, or the urban folk song "Mr. Blue" by Tom Paxton, our recent cultural references allow us to consider where the 2016 elections may take us. The George Lucas film *THX 1138* provides an almost contemporary illustration of how the state can control thought and monitor behavior closely. In spite of this, I find the film *Casablanca* to have greater relevance for us today. This classic film presents the viewer with clear options as to whether we decide to live in a society where civil liberties go to the highest bidder. *Casablanca* captures some of the ambiguity of what being a good citizen means (the film is set in Morocco under the authority of Vichy France). The story portrays the fluid notion of shifting identities and allegiances that people must negotiate in a multicultural society in which the state relies on authoritarianism to govern in a ham-handed manner. In this context individuals must make decisions as to what their behaviors are to be. I think the idealist wants to be the Paul Henreid character; I for one would like to be Humphrey Bogart but am afraid in reality I would end up being Claude Raines. If you don't know this film, it is worth watching in context of this book—except the dialogue far outstrips what you are getting from me.

Reasons to Be Cheerful or "Waiting Out the Authoritarians"

Perhaps we need to take solace in the fact UAX regimes tend to self-destruct. The French revolution has outlasted the Russian revolution. The governance of Franklin Delano Roosevelt outlasted that of Adolf Hitler. So what does psychological science tell us about systems that rely on authoritarian principles? According to the leading scholar on right-wing authoritarianism, Robert Altemeyer, authoritarians are ill-suited to manage complex organizations in part due to their rigidity and inability to negotiate or delegate. In his experimental studies on authoritarian decision making (Altemeyer, 2003), he observed "in general, authoritarians produced dismal futures, beset by unemployment, famine, and disease." So the good news is autocrats don't do such a wonderful job of governing. The bad news is they may run the place into the ground during our lifetime.

The argument goes that autocratic systems rarely are efficient. As William Shirer discusses in his classic *The Rise and Fall of the Third Reich* (1960), the Nazi regime in collaboration with Ferdinand Porsche promoted the sale of the Volkswagen in 1937 as a car for all Germans; it was subsequently sold to citizens on a subscription basis. However the rank and file German never got their automobile, as the Beetle was only mass produced in 1945, with production carried out by Hungarian Jewish slave laborers. This is an illustration—in part—of the intolerance of authoritarians to diversity of opinion. As Janis (1972) has pointed out the groupthink of highly homogeneous groups tends to produce less adaptive and less enduring strategies for survival. Oppression of free speech inherently suppresses innovation. As Tetlock (1979) observed, highly homogeneous groups that establish policy simplify their perception of problems and promulgate strategies that are consistent with the values of the dominant group. So when we discourage or remove doubt what is left is dogmatism. The power of autocracy therefore removes the opportunity for legitimate questioning of basic assumptions and innovation. Like fundamentalists or religious dogmatists, the agents of autocracy have no questions, only answers consistent with their ideology.

A related problem of autocratic social systems is the absence of a realistic opposition to assign blame to when things go wrong. The German National Socialists showed us this could be effective for a relatively brief period of time. As a reigning political and ideological state, the Nazis rose to power on a highly anti-Semitic worldview. But they only ruled Germany in a period of peace for less than six years. It is questionable if a ruling political system that was supported by the minority of the populace (Payne, 1996) could have continued to govern drawing mainly on a platform of xenophobia and ultranationalism. The problem with finding a viable cultural "other" to assign blame to, when the UAX state maintains hegemony over the society, is daunting. Intolerant regimes need a discernible out-group to attribute social and economic failures to; the antidemocratic system needs a scapegoat when it fails to deliver on the faux populism of its political rhetoric.

Civil Society and the Phoenix

Psychological science gives us reason to anticipate that a homogeneous worldview, when foisted on a culturally diverse community, will sooner or later fail. It also suggests that political leaders who seek simple answers to complex social problems will fall under the weight of their own hubris, cynicism, and cultural encapsulation. In the meantime, collective efforts to maintain the values of a democratic and civil society constitute the ideology of the powerless, or, even worse, go underground as the conversos did in Spain during the inquisition. The mythical bird the Phoenix serves as one viable metaphor. In the ancient Greek myth the Phoenix is a bird that lives a long life, dies, and experiences a rebirth from the ashes of its predecessor.

> We're going to meet a lot of lonely people in the next week and the next month and the next year. And when they ask us what we're doing, you can say, we're remembering.
> —Ray Bradbury, *Fahrenheit 451*

As referenced in Ray Bradbury's 1950s novel *Fahrenheit 451*, social and cultural outsiders may have to learn to hold a value system in which individuals carry a book inside themselves, that is, the complete narrative, as a means of maintaining a body of knowledge or experience. In Bradbury's story these outsiders have each memorized books for an upcoming time when society is ready to rediscover them. Likewise our culture will need to hold on to the principles of liberal democracy when there is the resumption of a more tolerant societal stasis. When this time comes there needs to be a true *conviviencia*, a coexistence that exceeds toleration, one that is something warmer and constructive in our investigation of differences, where disagreement is entered into with respect and civility. We need a bit of decorum, for once.

After the Third Reich fell, the composer Karl Hartmann resumed composing. The political exile Ben, released from the Gulag, went back to teaching history. The executed students of the White Rose were honored—and remembered—as patriots. As with the mythical bird the Phoenix, our political philosophy and our capacity for finding the good in one another may also rise from a period of hatred and xenophobia.

Timothy Snyder, a noted historian on Russia and Eastern Europe, commented after 11/8, "Americans are no wiser than the Europeans who saw democracy yield to fascism, Nazism or communism" (2016). He suggests what we might learn from the history of Europe and has provided his own summary of the issues facing us today. Snyder detailed some fairly pointed and clear warning signs of what our cataclysmic shift toward autocracy could bring to the United States and other democratic countries. Snyder (2017) has identified markers of a further shift into autocracy (and beyond). Notably, he describes the role of authoritarian systems to collapse the functions of government and the limitation of engagement between the state, its actors, and the citizenry. In turn I am laying out what I consider to be 10 critical social psychological warning signs of the risky shift of democracy into an authoritarian/autocratic state. This list is presented in Table 8.2. It might be a good thing to print this out and tape to you refrigerator door, just to serve as a reminder. We may need it.

Sweating Sickness of Our Age

Many individuals—as found in the studies conducted right after 11/8—are clearly concerned about the outcome of the 2016 election. The initial response, for many, of shock and derealization will—as with many traumatic events—find some new status over time of semiconsciousness. By analogy, an illness called "the sweating sickness" of the age of Henry VIII in England would begin with symptoms of apprehension, cold spells, motor dysregulation, and then heat and sweating. This would

Table 8.2   Warning Signs of a Risky Shift Away from Democracy

1. Popular Culture's Embrace of Ultranationalism
2. Suppression of Nongovernmental Civil Society Institutions
3. Elimination of Free Speech Protections
4. State Regulation of Media
5. Codification of Civil Dissent as Domestic Terrorism
6. Co-Opting Religion as a Government Institution
7. Nationwide de Jure Voter Suppression
8. Criminalizing Civil Dissent as Slander
9. Abandonment of Laws against Hate Violence
10. Faux-retaliatory Warfare against Straw Man Opponents

subsequently give way to lethargy and sleep and finally death. Many of the family of the English monarchy suffered from the sweating sickness; the artist Hans Holbein succumbed to the disease in 1543. Similarly, we may go from agitation to illness and then to a state of somnolence—slipping into a learned helplessness of disease. What we are all at risk of is forgetting the significant shift in our government and our civil rights with the 2016 election.

It is imperative to not let the rapid change to our political climate wash over us and leave us numb and indifferent. A lot has happened that individuals who wish to live as informed citizens need to remember. For now we need to swim against the current.

Summary

Americans, as a collective, have limited firsthand experience in living under an autocratic system that employs intolerance as a defining characteristic of national identity. How individuals cope with this cultural cataclysm will challenge many people to develop new resiliency skills in the months and years ahead. In speaking to the tradition of coping with racism, Pierce has proposed how recognizing challenges to personal use of space, time, energy, and movement serve as warning signs of oppression.

Our adjustment to living under an autocracy calls on individuals to employ varying forms of coping defenses to sustain a healthy means of surviving under periods of intolerance. The review of individual ideological—value expression—and self–other strategies in adjusting to environmental stresses has been presented via case illustrations. These internalizing–other-oriented and value expressive strategies also serve to maintain a cultural identity, not unlike what we practice to maintain immunological health to fight off biological toxins. Holding the line on the principles of civil society inherently challenges our stakeholder groups in their role of protecting the public good.

Resources to Address Hate Violence

It is my firm belief that no one raised in the United States can fully comprehend what it is like to live under an absolute dictatorship.
—George J. Wittenstein[1]

This resource list is organized into these categories of organizations: bias activities and hate crimes, and civil liberties. This is followed by a listing of useful Twitter sites. An updated listing is available at: http://www.h2hseries.com.

Bias Activities and Hate Crimes

- Anti-Defamation League. In 1913, the ADL was founded on Jewish values that inform our work, how we operate, and the changes we seek in the world. This has always meant stopping anti-Semitism and defending the Jewish people. Today, it also means fighting threats to our very democracy, including cyberhate, bullying, bias in schools and in the criminal justice system, terrorism, hate crimes, coercion of religious minorities, and contempt for anyone who is different.

  Web site: www.adl.org

- Southern Poverty Law Center. The SPLC is a nonprofit organization that combats hate, intolerance, and discrimination through education and litigation.

  Web site: www.splcenter.org/

---

1. George J. Wittenstein, http://www.historyplace.com/pointsofview/white-rose1.htm

- Simon Wiesenthal Center. The Simon Wiesenthal Center is a global human rights organization researching the Holocaust and hate in a historic and contemporary context. The center confronts anti-Semitism, hate, and terrorism, promotes human rights and dignity, stands with Israel, defends the safety of Jews worldwide, and teaches the lessons of the Holocaust for future generations. With a constituency of over 400,000 households in the United States, it is accredited as a NGO at international organizations, including the United Nations, UNESCO, OSCE, Organization of American States (OAS), the Latin American Parliament (PARLATINO), and the Council of Europe.

  Web site: http://www.wiesenthal.com

- RadicalisationResearch.org, a web-based resource on academic research on "radicalization."

  Web site: www.RadicalisationResearch.org

- Outright Vermont addresses bullying of gender-oppressed high school–age students in Vermont.

  Web site: http://www.outrightvt.org/

- Hope Not Hate. Hope Not Hate uses research, education, and public engagement to challenge mistrust and racism, and it helps to build communities that are inclusive, celebrate shared identities, and are resilient to hate.

  Web site: http://www.hopenothate.org.uk

- The Western New York Anti-Violence Project is here to support lesbian, gay, bisexual, transgendered, and queer, questioning, or gender nonconforming victims of violence and to work to lessen and prevent violent crimes against the LGBTQ community.

  Web site: http://www.wnyavp.org/

- National Center for Victims of Crime. The National Center for Victims of Crime is a resource center and advocacy organization for an array of crimes and engages with victims, elected officials, law enforcement, and policy makers. They sponsor programs on hate crimes.

  Web site: https://victimsofcrime.org/

- Anti-Violence Project. In 1993, the Date Rape and Dating Violence Education Project (DRDV) and the UVic Women's Centre submitted a proposal to the University to implement a full-time sexual assault officer. They were seeking space, funding, and administrative support for a campus-based sexual assault center.

  Web site: https://www.antiviolenceproject.org/

- California Association of Human Relations Organizations. CAHRO's three primary objectives are aimed at strengthening the infrastructure of human relations organizations in California: (1) To establish and support local and regional networks of human relations organizations, (2) To promote communication between local and regional networks of human relations organizations, and (3) To build the capacity of organizations addressing human relations issues through information sharing, training, and technical assistance.

  Web site: http://www.cahro.org/

Civil Liberties

- The mission of the National Association for the Advancement of Colored People (NAACP) is to ensure the political, educational, social, and economic equality of rights of all persons and to eliminate race-based discrimination.

  Web site: http://www.naacp.org/

- Council on American-Islamic Relations. The CAIR's vision is to be a leading advocate for justice and mutual understanding. CAIR's mission is to enhance understanding of Islam, encourage dialogue, protect civil liberties, empower American Muslims, and build coalitions that promote justice and mutual understanding.

  Web site: www.cair.com

- Mexican American Legal Defense and Educational Fund: Founded in 1968, MALDEF is the nation's leading Latino legal civil rights organization. Often described as the "law firm of the Latino community," MALDEF promotes social change through advocacy, communications, community education, and litigation in the areas of education, employment, immigrant rights, and political access.

  Web site: http://maldef.org/

- Indivisible: A Practical Guide for Resisting the Trump Agenda.

  Web site: www.indivisibleguide.com

- Vermont Workers' Center is a democratic, member-run organization dedicated to organizing for the human rights of the people in Vermont.

  Web site: www.workerscenter.org

- American Civil Liberties Union. For almost 100 years, the ACLU has worked to defend and preserve the individual rights and liberties guaranteed by the Constitution and laws of the United States.

  Web site: www.aclu.org

- HREA, the global human rights education and training centre. HREA is an international nongovernmental and nonprofit organization that supports human rights education, the training of human rights defenders and professional groups, and the development of educational materials and programming.

  Web site: www.hrea.org

- Political Research Associates: "Political Research Associates is a social justice think tank devoted to supporting movements that are building a more just and inclusive democratic society. We expose movements, institutions, and ideologies that undermine human rights."

  Web site: www.politicalresearch.org

- Lambda Legal, a 501(c)(3) nonprofit, is a national organization committed to achieving full recognition of the civil rights of lesbians, gay men, bisexuals, transgender people, and everyone living with HIV through impact litigation, education, and public policy work.

  Web site: http://www.lambdalegal.org/

Twitter Sites

Sites	Topic
https://twitter.com/MonroeWorkToday	Lynching/black sociology
https://twitter.com/PRAEyesRight	Social Justice Think Tank
https://twitter.com/ewdunbar	H2H Project: Psychology of Hate Crimes and Domestic Terrorism

Notes

Chapter 1

1. Differences in acute stress scores on ASDS for Clinton ($m = 52.05$) versus non-Clinton ($m = 30.34$) supporters, $t = 9.91, p < .03$.

2. Acute stress (ASDS scores) correlated with avoidance behaviors, $r = .45, p < .001$.

3. Zero-order correlation of ASDS scores with frequent thoughts about the election, $r = .46, p < .001$.

4. Acute stress (ASDS) correlated with Wave One (postelection) community risk for hate crimes, $r = .48, p < .001$, and terror activity, $r = .37, p < .001$; Wave Two (postinauguration) community risk for hate crimes, $r = .39, p < .001$, and terror activity, $r = .37, p < .001$.

5. Association between 9/11 and 2016 election, Wave One (postelection) 29.3%; Wave Two (postinauguration) 12.9%.

6. Correlation of ASDS scores with association to 9/11 terror attack, Wave One (postelection), $r = .17, p < .002$; Wave Two (postinauguration).

7. Wave Two (postinauguration) gender differences on acute stress symptoms (ASDS scores) for men ($m = 45.24$) and women ($m = 52.81$), $t = 7.41, p < .001$.

Chapter 3

1. Zero-order correlation of households below poverty level in 2010 U.S. Census at state level and percentage of voters supporting Trump candidacy, $r = .34 \ p < .015$.

2. Zero-order correlation of level of change in white residents at state level from 2000 to 2010 (U.S. Census) had lower voter support for the Trump candidacy, $r = -.35, p < .036$.

3. Zero-order correlation of white residents at state level in 2010 U.S. Census and percentage of voters supporting Trump candidacy, $r = .41, p < .003$.

4. Zero-order correlation of documented black lynching activity from 1880 to 1968 and percentage of voters supporting Trump candidacy, $r = .32, p < .03$; mean differences of black lynching activity 1880 to 1968 by state candidate support, $T = 3.61, p < .001$, for Trump ($m = 110.6$) and Clinton ($m = 6.4$).

5. Zero-order correlation of SPLC-identified hate groups and Trump popular vote, $r = -.04, p < $ n.s.; state candidate support, $T = 1.19, p < $ n.s., for Trump ($m = 19.93$) and Clinton ($m = 13.80$).

6. Zero-order correlation of percentage of voter support for Trump by state with ratio of law enforcement documentation of hate crimes 1992 to 2015, $r = -.31, p < .03$; mean differences ratio of law enforcement hate crime reportage 1992 to 2015 by state candidate support, $T = 4.63, p < .001$, Trump ($m = 0.34$) Clinton ($m = .71$).

7. Multiple regression models predicting Trump percentage of votes by state. Model one—economic privation ($R^2 = .55$, Adj. $R^2 = .53$), median family income 2015 ($B = -.28, t = -4.26, p = < .01$), 2010 to 2015 median family income change ($B = -1.18, t = -6.55, p = < .001$), families below poverty level 2015 ($B = -.71, t = -3.36, p = < .001$). Model two—hate indicators ($R^2 = .18$, Adj. $R^2 = .13$), history of black lynchings ($B = .35, t = 2.1, p = < .05$), ratio of hate crime reportage 1992–2015 ($B = -.19, t = -1.31, p = < .05$), SPLC identified hate groups ($B = -.24, t = -1.57, p = < .05$).

Chapter 5

1. Mean differences of SPLC reportage of post-11/8 hate incidents and state candidate support, $T = 2.16, p < .03$, for Trump ($m = 15.33$) and Clinton ($m = 30.55$); zero-order correlation of percentage of voter support for Trump by state with SPLC reportage of post-11/8 hate incidents, $r = -.44, p < .001$.

2. Relationship between SPLC reportage of post-11/8 hate incidents Union states, $m = 30.84$, confederate states, $m = 21.66$, unaligned, $m = 10.66$; $F = 2.31, p < $ n.s.

3. Zero-order correlation between SPLC reportage of post-11/8 incidents and ratio of law enforcement hate crime reportage 1992 to 2015 by state, $r = -.15, p < $ n.s.

4. Zero-order correlation between SPLC reportage of post-11/8 incidents and percentage of white residents by state in 2010 census, $r = -.32, p < .03$.

5. Terror risk perceptions: Increased significantly (40.5%), remained the same (56.7%), decreased somewhat (1.8%), significantly decreased (1.1%).

Chapter 7

1. Frequency of conflicts about the election by the age range: 18–30 years ($m = 1.75$), 30–40 years ($m = .71$), 40–50 years ($m = .61$), 50–60 years ($m = .58$), and 60-plus ($m = .56$), $F = 6.07, p = < .001$.

2. Frequency of avoidance tactics to deal with conflicts related to the election by age range: 18–30 years ($m = 1.0$), 30–40 years ($m = 1.25$), 40–50 years ($m = .99$), 50–60 years ($m = 1.12$), and 60-plus ($m = .90$), $F = 1.32, p = <$ n.s.

3. Age differences for use of interpersonal avoidance tactics 18–30 years ($m = 1.03$), 30–40 years ($m = 1.23$), 40–50 years ($m = 1.02$), 50–60 years ($m = 1.14$), and 60-plus ($m = .90$), $F = 1.97, p = < .09$. Frequency of interpersonal conflict 18–30 years ($m = 1.26$), 30–40 years ($m = .72$), 40–50 years ($m = .61$), 50–60 years ($m = .59$), and 60-plus ($m = .37$), $F = 8.61, p = < .001$.

4. Gender differences and use of avoidance tactics: men ($m = .71$) and women ($m = 1.42$), $t = 4.68, p = < .001$.

5. Zero-order correlation of ASDS with conflict with coworkers, $r = .22, p = < .001$, and intimate partners, $r = .19, p = < .001$.

6. Zero-order correlation of ASDS with avoidance tactics, $r = .44, p = < .001$, and unfriending cohorts, $r = .40, p = < .001$.

7. Zero-order correlation of ASDS with community terror risk, $r = .37, p = < .001$, and community hate risk, $r = .45, p = < .001$.

References

Adorno, T. W., Frenkel-Brunswik, E., Levinson, D. J., & Sanford, R. N. (1950). *The authoritarian personality*. New York, NY: Harper and Brothers.

Allport, G. (1954). *The nature of prejudice*. Reading, MA: Addison-Wesley.

Altemeyer, B. (1981). *Right-wing authoritarianism*. Winnipeg: University of Manitoba Press.

Altemeyer, B. (1996). *The authoritarian specter*. Cambridge, MA: Harvard University Press.

Altemeyer, B. (1998). The other "authoritarian personality." In M. Zanna (Series Ed.), *Advances in Experimental Social Psychology*: *Vol. 30* (pp. 47–92). San Diego, CA: Academic Press.

Altemeyer, B. (2003). What happens when authoritarians inherit the Earth? A simulation. *Analyses of Social Issues and Public Policy, 3*(1), 161–169.

Altemeyer, B. (2007). *The authoritarians*. Winnipeg: University of Manitoba Press.

Anti-Defamation League. (2006). *Confronting anti-Semitism myths . . . facts. . . .* New York, NY: Anti-Defamation League.

Antonovsky, A. (1979). *Health, stress, and coping*. San Francisco, CA: Jossey-Bass.

Antonovsky, A., & Bernstein, J. (1986). Pathogenesis and salutogenesis in war and other crises: Who studies the successful coper. In N. A. Milgram (Ed.), *Stress and coping in time of war: Generalizations from the Israeli experience*, 52–65. New York, NY: Brunner/Mazel.

Arendt, H. (1963). *Eichmann in Jerusalem: A report on the banality of evil*. New York, NY: Viking Press.

Asch, S. E. (1952). Group forces in the modification and distortion of judgments. In S. E. Asch, *Social psychology,* 450–473. New York, NY: Prentice-Hall.

Aytaç, S. E., Rau, E., & Stokes, S. (2016, November 2). Trump supporters vastly overestimate unemployment—and they blame politicians for it. *Washington Post.* Retrieved from https://www.washingtonpost.com /news/monkey-cage/wp/2016/11/02/trump-supporters-vastly-overes timate-unemployment-and-they-blame-politicians-for-it/utm_term =.a3497a484070

Bagley, R. O. (2011, September 11). 9/11: A personal story. Retrieved from www.forbes.com/sites/rebeccabagley/2011/09/11/911-a-personal -story/#bfc260077e27

Bail, C. (2016). *Terrified: How anti-Muslim fringe organizations became mainstream.* Princeton, NJ: Princeton University Press.

Bailey, Sarah Pulliam. (2016, November 9). White evangelicals voted overwhelmingly for Donald Trump, exit polls show. *Washington Post.* Retrieved from www.washingtonpost.com/news/acts-of-faith /wp/2016/11/09/exit-polls-show-white-evangelicals-voted-over whelmingly-for-donald-trump/?utm_term=.787d0dad7507

Banaji, M. R., & Greenwald, A. G. (1995). Implicit gender stereotyping in judgments of fame. *Journal of Personality and Social Psychology, 68,* 181–198.

Banaji, M. R., & Hardin, C. (1996). Automatic gender stereotyping. *Psychological Science, 7,* 136–141.

Banicki, J. S. (2015, December 14). The founder of a white nationalist website says Donald Trump is helping his cause. Retrieved from http://www .businessinsider.com/trump-helping-white-supremacist-website-2015-12

Bates, R. (1981). *Markets and states in tropical Africa.* Berkeley: University of California Press.

Baudrillard, J., & Foss, P. (1983). *Simulations.* New York, NY: Semiotext(e).

Beauchamp, Z. (2016, April 8). Watch: a ridiculous pro-Trump video starring Greek neo-Nazis. Retrieved from http://www.vox.com/2016 /4/8/11388844/trump-greek-neo-nazis

Beck, E. M., & Stewart E. (1990). The killing fields of the Deep South: The market for cotton and the lynching of blacks, 1882–1930. *American Sociological Review, 55*(4), 526–539.

Becker, E. (1973). *The denial of death.* New York, NY: Free Press.

Berkman, L. F. (1985). The relationship of social networks and social support to morbidity and mortality.

Berkman, L. F., & Glass, T. (2000). Social integration, social networks, social support, and health. *Social epidemiology, 1,* 137–173.

Berkman, L. F., & Syme, S. L. (1979). Social networks, host resistance, and mortality: A nine-year follow-up study of Alameda County residents. *American Journal of Epidemiology, 109*(2), 186–204.

Berkowitz, L. (1972). Frustrations, comparisons, and other sources of emotion aroused as contributors to social unrest. *Journal of Social Issues, 28,* 77–92.

Berry, J. W., Phinney, J. S., Vedder, P., & Sam, D. L. (Eds.). (2006). *Immigrant youth in cultural transition: Acculturation, identity, and adaptation across national contexts.* Mahwah, NJ: Lawrence Erlbaum Associates.

Bhawuk, D., & Brislin, R. (2000, January). Cross-cultural training: A review [Electronic version]. *Applied Psychology: An International Review, 49*(1), 162–192.

Binkowski, B. (2016, May 2). Klan leader endorses Trump for president. Retrieved from http://www.snopes.com/2016/05/02/klan-leader-endorses-trump

Black, M. C., Basile, K. C., Breiding, M. J., Smith, S. G., Walters, M. L., Merrick, M. T., . . . Stevens, M. R. (2011). The National Intimate Partner and Sexual Violence Survey (NISVS): 2010 summary report. Atlanta, GA: National Center for Injury Prevention and Control, Centers for Disease Control and Prevention.

Blair, Karen L. (2016). A "basket of deplorables"? A new study finds that Trump supporters are more likely to be Islamophobic, racist, transphobic and homophobic. USAPP. Retrieved from http://blogs.lse.ac.uk/usappblog/2016/10/10/a-basket-of-deplorables-a-new-study-finds-that-trump-supporters-are-more-likely-to-be-islamophobic-racist-transphobic-and-homophobic/

Blanco, A., & Dunbar, E. (2016). Social attitudes concerning hate crime and human rights laws. In E. Dunbar, A. Blanco, & D. A. Crèvecoeur-MacPhail (Eds.), *The psychology of hate crimes as domestic terrorism: U.S. and global issues.* Santa Barbara, CA: Praeger.

Blasberg, D. (2015, December 14). Paris attacks survivor Isobel Bowdery shares her story. Retrieved from http://www.vanityfair.com/culture/2015/12/paris-attacks-survivor-story-isobel-bowdery

Blomberg, B. (2000). Modeling political change with a regime-switching model. *European Journal of Political Economy 16*(14), 739–762.

Bond, P. (2016, December 29). Milo Yiannopoulos strikes $250K book deal. Retrieved from http://www.hollywoodreporter.com/news/milo-yiannopoulos-strikes-250k-book-deal-959745

Bradbury, R. (1953). *Fahrenheit 451.* New York, NY: Ballantine Books.

Brand, B. (2016, December 14). [Personal interview].

Brandt, M. J., & Crawford, J. T. (2016). Answering unresolved questions about the relationship between cognitive ability and prejudice. *Social Psychological and Personality Science, 7*(8), 884–892.

Brewer, M. (2000). Research design and issues of validity. In H. Reis and C. Judd (Eds.), *Handbook of research methods in social and personality psychology.* Cambridge, England: Cambridge University Press.

Bryant, R., Moulds, M., & Guthrie, R. (2000). Acute Stress Disorder Scale: A self-report measure of Acute Stress Disorder. *Psychological Assessment, 12*(1), 61–68.

Buchanan, Patrick (1992, August 17). *1992 Republican National Convention Speech* (Speech).

Buckley, C., Tatlow, D. K., Perlez, J., & Qin, A. (2016, May 16). Voices from China's cultural revolution. *New York Times.* Retrieved from https://www.nytimes.com/interactive/2016/05/16/world/asia/17china -culturalrevolution-voices.html

Burke, K. (1969). *A rhetoric of motives.* Berkeley: University of California Press.

Burnette, C. E., & Figley, C. R. (2015). Wellness of American Indian and Alaska Native youth. In B. D. Friedman & J. Merrick (Eds.), *Public health, social work and health inequalities,* 55–77. New York, NY: Nova Publishers.

Burnette, C. E., & Figley, C. R. (2016). Risk and protective factors related to the wellness of American Indian and Alaska Native youth: A systematic review. *International Public Health Journal, 8*(2), 137–154.

Bytwerk, R. (1998). The ceremony of the Hitler Youth at the 1936 Nuremberg Party rally. Retrieved from http://research.calvin.edu/german-propaganda-archive/pt36hj.htm

Canetti-Nisim, C., Halperin, D., Sharvit, K., & Hobfoll, S. E. (2009). A new stress-based model of political extremism personal exposure to terrorism, psychological distress, and exclusionist political attitudes. *Journal of Conflict Resolution, 53*(2), 363–389.

Canovan, M. (1981). *Populism.* New York, NY: Houghton Mifflin Harcourt.

Carter, R. T. (1990). The relationship between racism and racial identity among white Americans: An exploratory investigation. *Journal of Counseling & Development, 69*(1), 46–50.

Carvacho, H., Zick, A., Haye, A., González, R., Manzi, J., Kocik, C., & Bertl, M. (2013). On the relation between social class and prejudice: The roles of education, income, and ideological attitudes. *European Journal of Social Psychology, 45,* 272–285.

Celebrity Net Worth. (2015, November 4). Ann Coulter net worth. Retrieved from https://www.celebritynetworth.com/richest-politicians/republicans/ann-coulter-net-worth/

Centers for Disease Control and Prevention (CDC). (2002, September 6). Psychological and emotional effects of the September 11 attacks on the World Trade Center—Connecticut, New Jersey, and New York, 2001. Retrieved from https://www.cdc.gov/mmwr/preview/mmwrhtml/mm5135a2.htm

Cikara, M., Bruneau, E. G., & Saxe, R. R. (2011). Us and them: Intergroup failures of empathy. *Current Directions in Psychological Science, 20*(3), 149–153.

Clark, K. B., & Clark, M. P. (1947). Racial identification and preference among Negro children. In E. L. Hartley (Ed.), *Readings in social psychology*. New York, NY: Holt, Rinehart, and Winston.

Clark, R., Anderson, N. B., Clark, V. R., & Williams, D. R. (1999). Racism as a stressor for African Americans: A biopsychosocial model. *American Psychologist, 54*(10), 805–816.

Cobb, S. (1976). Social support as a moderator of life stress. *Psychosomatic Medicine, 38*(5), 300–314.

Coester, M. (2016). Right-wing extremism and right-wing hate crimes in Germany: Development, extent, influence and prevention of a social problem. In E. Dunbar, A. Blanco, & D. A. Crèvecoeur-MacPhail (Eds.), *The psychology of hate crimes as domestic terrorism: U.S. and global issues*. Santa Barbara, CA: Praeger.

Cohen, S., & Wills, T. A. (1985). Stress, social support, and the buffering hypothesis. *Psychological Bulletin, 98*(2), 310.

Comegys, R. S. (1982). Potter Stewart: An analysis of his views on the press as fourth estate. *Chicago-Kent Law Review, 59*, 157.

Committee to Protect Journalists (n.d.) 56 journalists killed in Russia since 1992/Motive confirmed. Retrieved from: https://cpj.org/killed/europe/russia/

Compton, M. T., Thompson, N. J., & Kaslow, N. J. (2005). Social environment factors associated with suicide attempt among low-income African Americans: The protective role of family relationships and social support. *Social Psychiatry and Psychiatric Epidemiology, 40*(3), 175–185.

Conger, J. A., & Kanungo, R. N. (1998). *Charismatic leadership in organizations*. Thousand Oaks, CA: Sage Publications.

Cook Political Staff. (2016, December 16). 56 Interesting facts about the 2016 election. Retrieved from http://cookpolitical.com/story/10201

Cornell, D. G., Warren, J., Hawk, G., Stafford, E., Oram, G., & Pine, D. (1996). Psychopathy of instrumental and reactive violent offenders. *Journal of Consulting and Clinical Psychology, 64*, 783–790.

Curthoys, A. (2013). *Identifying the effect of unemployment on hate crime.* Syracuse University. Retrieved from http://surface.syr.edu/cgi /viewcontent.cgi?article=1030&context=honors_capstone

Daniel, A., & Wilhelm, J. J. (1981). *The poetry of Arnaut Daniel* (Vol. 3). London, England: Taylor & Francis.

Danieli, Y. (1981). Differing adaptational styles in families of survivors of the Nazi holocaust. *Children Today, 10*(5).

Danieli, Y. (Ed.). (1998). *International handbook of multigenerational legacies of trauma.* Boston, MA: Springer Science & Business Media.

Danieli, Y. (2009). Massive trauma and the healing role of reparative justice. *Journal of Trauma Stress, 22*(5), 351–357.

Danieli, Y., Norris, F. H., & Engdahl, B. (2016). Multigenerational legacies of trauma: Modeling the what and how of transmission. *American Journal of Orthopsychiatry, 86*(6), 639–651.

David, E. J. R. (2013). *Internalized oppression: The psychology of marginalized groups.* New York, NY: Springer Publishing Company.

Davies, A., Blanco, A., & Miron, L. (2016). Hate and revenge in the life of a repented killer. In E. Dunbar, A. Blanco, & D. A. Crèvecoeur-MacPhail (Eds.), *The psychology of hate crimes as domestic terrorism*: *U.S. and global issues.* Santa Barbara, CA: Praeger.

Dollard, J., Doob, L. W., Miller, N. E., Mowrer, O. H., & Sears, R. R. (1939). *Frustration and aggression.* New Haven, CT: Yale University Press.

Donald Trump announces a presidential bid. (2015, June 16). *Washington Post.* Retrieved from https://www.washingtonpost.com/news /post-politics/wp/2015/06/16/full-text-donald-trump-announces-a -presidential-bid/?utm_term=.8825c4486697

Dong, A. (1997). *Licensed to Kill.* DeepFocus Productions.

Downs, A. (1957). *An economic theory of democracy.* New York, NY: Harper and Row.

Draper, S. (n.d.). Timeline of slavery in America 1501–1865. https://sha rondraper.com/timeline.pdf

Drop, K. A. (2015, December 21). *Why does Donald Trump perform better in online versus live telephone polling?* Retrieved from https:// morningconsult.com/wp-content/uploads/2015/12/Morning-Consult -Donald-Trump-online-versus-live-polling-methods-study1.pdf

Drury, J., & Reicher, S. (2009). Collective psychological empowerment as a model of social change: Researching crowds and power. *Journal of Social Issues, 65*(4), 707–725.

Dunbar, E. (1995). The assessment of the prejudiced personality: The Pr scale forty years later. *Journal of Personality Assessment, 65,* 270–277.

Dunbar, E. (2001). Counseling practices to ameliorate the effects of discrimination and hate events: Toward a systematic approach to assessment and intervention. *The Counseling Psychologist, 29*(2), 279–307.

Dunbar, E. (2003). Symbolic, relational, and ideological signifiers of bias-motivated offenders: Toward a strategy of assessment. *American Journal of Orthopsychiatry, 73,* 203–211.

Dunbar, E. (2016). Cultural and psychological characteristics in the evolution of hate crime initiatives. In E. Dunbar, A. Blanco, & D. A. Crèvecoeur-MacPhail (Eds.), *The psychology of hate crimes as domestic terrorism: U.S. and global issues.* Santa Barbara, CA: Praeger.

Dunbar, E. (In Press). *Hate, ideology, and intergroup violence: Bias motivation and membership in a multicultural world.* Santa Barbara, CA: Praeger.

Dunbar, E., & Blanco, A. (2013). Psychological perspectives on culture, violence, and intergroup animus: Evolving traditions in the bonds that tie and hate. In F. T. L. Leong (Ed.), *APA handbook of multicultural psychology, Vol. 2: Applications and training.* Washington, DC: American Psychological Association.

Dunbar, E., & Blanco, A. (2015). Social attitudes concerning hate crime and human rights laws. In E. Dunbar, A. Blanco, & D. A. Crèvecoeur-MacPhail (Eds.), *The psychology of hate crimes as domestic terrorism: U.S. and global issues.* Santa Barbara, CA: Praeger.

Dunbar, E., Blanco, A. & Crèvecoeur-MacPhail, D. A. (Eds.). (2017). *The psychology of hate crimes as domestic terrorism: U.S. and global issues.* Santa Barbara, CA: Praeger.

Dunbar, E., Blanco, A., Sullaway, M., & Horcajo, J. (2004). Human rights and ethnic attitudes in Spain: The role of cognitive, social status and individual difference factors. *International Journal of Psychology.* 39(2), 106–117.

Dunbar, E., Liu, J. F., & Horvath, A. M. (1995). Coping with culture-based conflict: Implications for counseling research and practice. *Cultural Diversity and Mental Health, 1*(2), 139–148.

Dunbar, E., & Molina, A (2004). Opposition to the legitimacy of hate crime laws: The role of argument acceptance, knowledge, individual differences, and peer influence. *Analyses of Social Issues and Public Policy, 4*(1), 91–113.

Dunbar, E., Saiz, J. L., Stela, K., & Saiz, R. (1999). Personality and social group value determinants of out-group bias: A cross-national comparison of Gough's Pr/To scale. *Journal of Cross-Cultural Psychology, 31*, 267–275.

Dunbar, E., & Simonova, L. (2003). Individual difference and social status predictors of anti-Semitism and racism: US and Czech findings with the prejudice/tolerance and right wing authoritarianism scales. *International Journal of Intercultural Relations, 27*(5), 507–523.

Dunbar, E., Sullaway, M., Blanco, A., Horcajo, J., & de la Corte, L. (2007). Human rights attitudes and peer influence: The role of explicit bias, gender, and salience. *International Journal of Intercultural Relations, 31*(1), 51–66.

Dunbar, E., & Svensson, A. (2016). Psychotherapeutic treatment with victims of bias aggression and hate violence: Identity, coping, and "dealing with the nonsense." In E. Dunbar, A. Blanco, & D. A. Crèvecoeur-MacPhail (Eds.), *The psychology of hate crimes as domestic terrorism: U.S. and global issues*. Santa Barbara, CA: Praeger.

Dunbar, E., Wild, M., & Toma, R. (2016). The tradition and practice of human relations work in responding to community-based hate violence. In E. Dunbar, A. Blanco, & D. A. Crèvecoeur-MacPhail (Eds.), *The psychology of hate crimes as domestic terrorism: U.S. and global issues*. Santa Barbara, CA: Praeger.

Earle, G. (2016, October 15). "Believe me, I wasn't impressed": Having trashed Clinton as a "criminal," now Trump goes after Hillary's appearance as campaign goes deeper into the gutter. Retrieved from http://www.dailymail.co.uk/news/article-3839058/Believe-wasn-t-impressed-Having-trashed-Clinton-criminal-Trump-goes-Hillary-s-physical-appearance-campaign-goes-deeper-gutter.html#ixzz4U46YxKns

Eco, U. (1995). Ur-Fascism. *New York Review of Books*. Retrieved from http://www.nybooks.com/articles/1995/06/22/ur-fascism

Edelman, A. (2016, February 25). Donald Trump supported by former KKK leader David Duke. Retrieved August 17, 2017, from http://www.nydailynews.com/news/national/trump-endorsed-kkk-neo-nazis-america-white-article-1.2543847

Edmunson, D., Chaudoir, S., Mills, M., Park, C., Holub, J., & Bartkowiak, J. (2011). From shattered assumptions to weakened worldviews: Trauma symptoms signal anxiety buffer disruption. *Journal of Loss and Trauma, 16*(4), 358–385.

Edsall, T. (2016, May 11). How many people support Trump but don't want to admit it? *New York Times*. Retrieved from https://www.nytimes.com/2016/05/11/opinion/campaign-stops/how-many-people-support-trump-but-dont-want-to-admit-it.html?_r=0

Eisenberg, N. (1992). *The caring child*. Cambridge, MA: Harvard University Press.

Elwert, G. (2003). The socio-anthropological interpretation of violence. In W. Heitmeyer & J. Hagan (Eds.), *International handbook of violence research* (pp. 261–290). Dordrecht, the Netherlands: Kluwer Academic Publishers.

Epstein, J. N., Saunders, B. E., Kilpatrick, D. G., & Resnick, H. S. (1998). PTSD as a mediator between childhood rape and alcohol use in adult women. *Child Abuse and Neglect, 22*, 223–234.

Esherwick, J. W., Pickowicz, P. G., & Walder, A. G. (2006). *The Chinese cultural revolution as history*. Palo Alto, CA: Stanford University Press.

Eversley, M. (2016, December 14). NYPD arrest Muslim woman who claimed attack by Trump supporters. Retrieved August 22, 2017, from   https://www.usatoday.com/story/news/2016/12/14/ny-woman-admits-trump-supporters-did-not-harass-her-grab-hijab/95450002/

Ezekiel, R. S. (1995). *The racist mind: Portraits of American neo-Nazis and Klansmen*. New York, NY: Penguin.

Ezikoglu, C. (2016, November 24). The triumph of anti-intellectualism. Retrieved from http://independentturkey.org/triumph-anti-intellectualism/

Falchi, F. (2016, April 16). La "grieta" argentina. Retrieved from http://front.losandes.com.ar/article/la-grieta-argentina

Federal Bureau of Investigation. (2011). Uniform crime report: Hate crime statistics, 2010. Retrieved from https://ucr.fbi.gov/hate-crime/2010/resources/hate-crime-2010-about-hate-crime.pdf

Feierabend, I. K., & Feierabend, R. L. (1966). Aggressive behaviors within polities, 1948–1962: A cross-national study 1. *Journal of Conflict Resolution, 10*(3), 249–271.

Fernholz, T. (2016, October 9). Donald Trump threatened to prosecute Hillary Clinton if he's elected president. Quartz. Retrieved from http://qz.com/805160/presidential-debate-donald-trump-threatened-to-prosecute-hillary-if-hes-elected-president

Field, J. (2017). Rush Limbaugh net worth. Retrieved from http://net-worths.org/rush-limbaugh-net-worth

Figley, C. R., & Burnette, C. E. (2016). Building bridges: Connecting systemic trauma and family resilience in the study and treatment of diverse traumatized families. *Traumatology. 23*(1): 95.

Filipovic, G. (2016, January 5). Balkan war-crimes suspect calls for Serbs in US to back Trump. Retrieved from https://www.bloomberg.com/news/articles/2016-01-05/balkan-war-crimes-suspect-calls-for-serbs-in-u-s-to-back-trump

Fingerhut, H. (2016, April 9). On abortion, persistent divides between—and within—the two parties. Pew Research Center. Retrieved from http://www.pewresearch.org/fact-tank/2016/04/08/on-abortion-persistent-divides-between-and-within-the-two-parties-2

Fiol, C. M., Harris, D., & House, R. (1999). Charismatic leadership: Strategies for effecting social change. *The Leadership Quarterly, 10*(3), 449–482.

Foa, E., Molnar, C., & Cashman, L. (1995). Change in rape narratives during exposure therapy for posttraumatic stress disorder. *Journal of Traumatic Stress, 8*(4), 675–690.

Foa, E. B., Rothbaum, B. O., Riggs, D. S., & Murdock, T. B. (1991). Treatment of post-traumatic stress disorder in rape victims: A comparison between cognitive-behavioral procedures and counseling. *Journal of Consulting and Clinical Psychology, 59*, 715–723.

Folkman, S., & Lazarus, R. S. (1984). *Stress, appraisal, and coping.* New York, NY: Springer Publishing.

Fowler, J. H., & Christakis, N. A. (2008). Dynamic spread of happiness in a large social network: Longitudinal analysis over 20 years in the Framingham Heart Study. *BMJ, 337*, a2338.

Freedom in the world 2016. (2016). Retrieved from https://freedomhouse.org/report/freedom-world/freedom-world-2016

French J. R., & Raven, B. H. (1959). The bases of social power. In Cartwright, D. (Ed.), *Studies in Social Power* (pp. 159–167). Ann Arbor: Michigan Institute for Social Research.

Gainous, J. (2011). The new "new racism" thesis: Limited government values and race-conscious policy attitudes. APSA 2011 Annual Meeting Paper. Retrieved from SSRN: https://ssrn.com/abstract=1901738

Gano, J., & Gano, D. (1996, December 4). Interview with Pearl Harbor eyewitnesses. Retrieved from http://teacher.scholastic.com/pearl/transcript.htm

Gao, H. (2017, January 18). Opinion: A scar on the Chinese soul. *New York Times*. Retrieved from http://www.nytimes. com/interactive/2016/05/16/world/asia/17china-cultural-revolution-voices.html?_r=0

Gentile, G. (2011). *Origins and doctrine of Fascism: With selections from other works.* Piscataway, NJ: Transaction Publishers.

Gessen, M. (2012). *The man without a face: The unlikely rise of Vladimir Putin.* New York, NY: Riverhead Books.

Gilbert, D. T. (1989). Thinking lightly about others: Automatic components of the social inference process. In J. S. Uleman & J. A. Bargh (Eds.), *Unintended thought* (pp. 189–211). New York, NY: Guilford Press.

Giroux, H. (2005). *Against the new authoritarianism: Politics after Abu Ghraib*. Winnipeg, AB, Canada: Arbeiter Ring Publishing.

Glick, P., & Fiske, S. T. (1997). Hostile and benevolent sexism: Measuring ambivalent sexist attitudes toward women. *Psychology of Women Quarterly, 21*, 119–135.

Glick, P., Fiske, S. T., Mladinic, A., Saiz, J. L., Abrams, D., Masser, B., & López López, W. (2000). Beyond prejudice as simple antipathy: Hostile and benevolent sexism across cultures. *Journal of Personality and Social Psychology, 79*, 763–775.

Goebbels, J. (1934). Erkenntnis und Propaganda. *Signale der neuen Zeit*, 29–30.

Goldsmith, A. H., Veum, J. R., & Darity, W. (1977). Unemployment, joblessness, psychological well-being and self-esteem: Theory and evidence. *Journal of Socio-Economics, 26*(2), 133–158.

Gotlib, I. A., & Joormann, J. (2010). Cognition and depression: Current status and future directions. *Annual Review of Clinical Psychology, 27*(6), 285–312.

Grab your wallet (n.d.). Retrieved from: https://grabyourwallet.org

Green, D. P., Glaser, J., & Rich A. (1998). From lynching to gay bashing: The elusive connection between economic conditions and hate crime. *Journal of Personality and Social Psychology, 75*, 82–92.

Greenberg, J., Pyszczynski, T., Solomon, S., Rosenblatt, A., Veeder, M., Kirkland, S., & Lyon, D. (1990). Evidence for terror management II: The effects of mortality salience on reactions to those who threaten or bolster the cultural worldview. *Journal of Personality and Social Psychology, 58*, 308–319.

Grieger, T. A., Cozza, S. J., Ursano, R. J., Hoge, C., Martinez, P. E., Engel, C. C., et al. (2006). Posttraumatic stress disorder and depression in battle-injured soldiers. *American Journal of Psychiatry, 163*, 1777–1783.

Guliyev, F. (2009). Oil wealth, patrimonialism, and the failure of democracy in Azerbaijan. *Caucasus Analytical Digest, 2*, 2–5.

Gurr, T. (1970). *Why men rebel*. Princeton, NJ: Princeton University Press.

Haas, I. J. (2016). Political neuroscience. In J. R. Absher & J. Cloutier (Eds.), *Neuroimaging personality, social cognition, and character: Traits and mental states in the brain*. Cambridge, MA: Elsevier. doi:10.1016/B978-0-12-800935-2.00019-1

Habermas, J. (2000). From Kant to Hegel: On Robert Brandom's pragmatic philosophy of language. *European Journal of Philosophy, 8*(3), 322–355.

Hainmueller, J., & Hopkins, D. J. (2014). Public attitudes toward immigration. *Annual Review of Political Science, 17,* 225–249.

Hamilton, D., Austin, A., & Darity W. (2011). Whiter jobs, higher wages: EPI briefing paper. Retrieved from www.epi.org/files/page/-/Briefing Paper288.pdf

Hamilton, J. D. (2005). What's real about the business cycle? *Federal Reserve Bank of St. Louis Review, 87,* 435–452.

Hamilton, J. D., & Lin, G. (1996). Stock market volatility and the business cycle. *Journal of Applied Econometrics, 11,* 573–593.

Harmon-Jones, E., Simon, L., Greenberg, J., Pyszczynski, T., Solomon, S., & McGregor, H. (1997). Terror management theory and self-esteem: Evidence that increased self-esteem reduces mortality salience effects. *Journal of Personality and Social Psychology, 72*(1), 24–36.

Harrison, T. (2002). *Greeks and Barbarians.* London, England: Taylor & Francis.

Hauptmann, E. (1996). *Putting choice before democracy: A critique of rational choice theory.* Albany: State University of New York Press.

Hayes, H. (2001). *U.S. immigration policy and the undocumented.* Westport, CT: Praeger Publishers.

Hazelton, L. (2016, November 10). Healing? No way. Retrieved from http://accidentaltheologist.com/

Healy, P., & Haberman, M. (2015, December 6). 95,000 words, many of them ominous, from Donald Trump's tongue. *New York Times.* Retrieved from https://www.nytimes.com/2015/12/06/us/politics/95000-words -many-of-them-ominous-from-donald-trumps-tongue.html?_r=0

Heikkinen, M., Aro, H., & Lönnqvist, J. (1994). Recent life events, social support and suicide. *Acta Psychiatrica Scandinavica, 89*(s377), 65–72.

Heilman, M. E. (2001). Description and prescription: How gender stereotypes prevent women's ascent up the organizational ladder. *Journal of Social Issues, 57*(4), 657–674.

Heilman, M. E. (2012). Gender stereotypes and workplace bias. *Research in Organizational Behavior, 32,* 113–135.

Hein, G., Engelmann, J. B., Vollberg, M. C., & Tobler, P. N. (2016). How learning shapes the empathic brain. *Proceedings of the National Academy of Sciences, 113*(1), 80–85.

Heintz, C. (2016). Does prospect theory explain Trump and Brexit votes? Retrieved from http://cognitionandculture.net/blog/christophe -heintzs-blog/does-prospect-theory-explain-trump-and-brexit -votes

Henderson, N. (2014, October 8). White men are 31 percent of the American population. They hold 65 percent of all elected offices.

Washington Post. Retrieved from https://www.washingtonpost.com /news/the-fix/wp/2014/10/08/65-percent-of-all-american-elected-offi cials-are-white-men/?utm_term=.78851452271c

Henley, J. (2016, November 9). White and wealthy voters gave victory to Donald Trump, exit polls show. *The Guardian*. Retrieved from https://www.theguardian.com/us-news/2016/nov/09/white-voters -victory-donald-trump-exit-polls

Hepworth, J. T., & West, S. G. (1988). Lynchings and the economy: A time-series reanalysis of Hovland and Sears (1940). *Journal of Personality and Social Psychology, 55*(2), 239–247.

Herek, G. M., Gillis, J. R., & Cogan, J. C. (1999). Psychological sequelae of hate-crime victimization among lesbian, gay, and bisexual adults. *Journal of Consulting and Clinical Psychology, 67*(6), 945–951.

Historian, Bureau of Medicine and Surgery. (n.d.). Ruth Erickson: Veteran story. Retrieved from http://www.military.com/history/ruth-erickson -veteran-story.html

Ho, D. Y. F. (1994). Filial piety, authoritarian moralism and cognitive conservatism in Chinese societies. *Genetic, Social & General Psychology Monographs, 120*(3), 349–359.

Hochschild, A. (2016). *Strangers in their own land: Anger and mourning on the American right.* New York, NY: The New Press.

Hodson, G., & Busseri, M. A. (2012). Bright minds and dark attitudes lower cognitive ability predicts greater prejudice through right-wing ideology and low intergroup contact. *Psychological Science, 23*(2), 187–195.

Hopkins, D. J. (2008). No more Wilder Effect, never a Whitman Effect: When and why polls mislead about black and female candidates (PDF). Department of Government, Harvard University.

Hopkins, D. J., Sides, J., & Citrin, J. (2016). The muted consequences of correct information about immigration (June 18, 2016). Retrieved from SSRN: https://ssrn.com/abstract=2798622.

Horowitz, M., Wilner, N., & Alvarez, A. (1979). Impact of events. *Psychosomatic Medicine, 41*(3), 209–218.

House, R. J., Spangler, W. D., & Woyke, J. (1991). Personality and charisma in the US presidency: A psychological theory of leader effectiveness. *Administrative Science Quarterly*, 364–396.

Hovland, C. I., & Sears, R. R. (1940). Minor studies of aggression: VI. Correlation of lynchings with economic indices. *Journal of Psychology, 9*(2), 301–310.

Hsu, F. L. (1981). *Americans and Chinese: Passage to differences.* Honolulu: University of Hawaii Press.

Huang, L. L., Liu, J. H., & Chang, M. (2004). "The double identity" of Taiwanese Chinese: A dilemma of politics and culture rooted in history. *Asian Journal of Social Psychology, 7*(2), 149–168.

Human Rights Campaign. (2017). Violence against the transgender community in 2016. Retrieved from http://www.hrc.org/resources /violence-against-the-transgender-community-in-2016

Hunter, J. D. (1991). *Culture wars: The struggle to define America.* New York, NY: Basic Books.

Huntington, S. P. (2004). *Who are we? The challenges to America's national identity.* New York, NY: Simon and Schuster.

Inskeep, S. (2016, December 11). A finder's guide to facts. Retrieved from http://www.npr.org/2016/12/11/505154631/a-finders-guide-to-facts

Intel Chief James Clapper: Russia behind "fake news" in 2016. (n.d.). The Daily Beast. Retrieved from http://www.thedailybeast.com /cheats/2017/01/05/clapper-russia-behind-fake-news.html?via=deskto p&source=copyurl

Jacobs, J. B., & Potter, K. A. (1998). Comprehensive handgun licensing & registration: An analysis & critique of Brady II, gun control's next (and last?) step. *Journal of Criminal Law and Criminology, 89*(1), 81–110.

James, M. (2015, November 18). Political ad spending estimated at $6 billion in 2016. *Los Angeles Times.* Retrieved from http://www .latimes.com/entertainment/envelope/cotown/la-et-ct-political-ad -spending-6-billion-dollars-in-2016-20151117-story.html

Janis, I. L. (1972). Victims of groupthink: A psychological study of foreign-policy decisions and fiascoes. Boston, MA: Houghton Mifflin.

Janoff-Bulman, R. (1989). Assumptive worlds and the stress of traumatic events: Applications of the schema construct. *Social Cognition, 7*(2), 113–136.

Janoff-Bulman, R. (1992). *Shattered assumptions.* New York, NY: Free Press.

Janoff-Bulman, R., & Frieze, I. H. (1992). A theoretical perspective for understanding reactions to victimization. *Journal of Social Issues, 39,* 1–17.

Johnson, J. V., & Hall, E. M. (1988). Job strain, work place social support, and cardiovascular disease: A cross-sectional study of a random sample of the Swedish working population. *American Journal of Public Health, 78*(10), 1336–1342.

Jonas, E., & Fischer, P. (2006). Terror management and religion: Evidence that intrinsic religiousness mitigates worldview defense following mortality salience. *Journal of Personality and Social Psychology, 91*(3), 553–567.

Jones, M. (2013, August 23). Witnesses recall the power of "I Have a Dream" 50 years later. Retrieved from http://archive.jsonline.com/%20news/milwaukee/witnesses-recall-the-power-of-i-have-a-dream-50-years-later-b9982113z1-220873691.html

Kazin, M. (1995). *The populist persuasion: An American history*. Ithaca, NY: Cornell University Press.

Kelman, H. C. (1958). Compliance, identification, and internalization: Three processes of attitude change. *Journal of Conflict Resolution, 2*(1), 51–60.

Kendzior, S. (2006). Inventing Akromiya: The role of Uzbek propagandists in the Andijon massacre. *Demokratizatsiya, 14*(4), 545.

Kendzior, S. (2011). Digital distrust: Uzbek cynicism and solidarity in the Internet Age. *American Ethnologist, 38*(3), 559–575.

Kessler, G. (2016, November 30). Trump's repeated claim that he won a "landslide" victory. *Washington Post*. Retrieved from https://www.washingtonpost.com/news/fact-checker/wp/2016/11/30/trumps-repeated-claim-that-he-won-a-landslide-victory/?utm_term=.6e9c40933be1

Kim, C. (2016, December 4). Muslim NYPD officer says man threatened her, her son. Retrieved from http://abc7ny.com/news/muslim-nypd-officer-says-man-threatened-her-her-son/1639503/

Kim, J. (2016, June 2). North Korea says Trump isn't screwy at all, a wise choice for president. Retrieved from https://www.reuters.com/article/us-northkorea-usa-trump-idUSKCN0YN35S

Kinder, D. R., & Sanders, L. M. (1996). *Divided by color: Racial politics and democratic ideals*. Chicago, IL: University of Chicago Press.

Klein, J. G., Smith, N. C., & John, A. (2002, June). Why we boycott: Consumer motivations for boycott participation and marketer responses. *London Business School*, 1–41. Retrieved from: http://facultyresearch.london.edu/docs/03-702.pdf

Klonoff, E., & Landrine, H. (1995). The schedule of sexist events. *Psychology of Women Quarterly, 19*(4), 439–470.

Kozinets, R. V., & Handelman, J. M. (1998). Ensouling consumption: A netnographic exploration of boycotting behavior. In J. Alba & W. Hutchinson (Eds.), *Advances in consumer research: Vol. 25* (pp. 475–480). Provo, UT: Association for Consumer Research.

Krefetz, G. (1982). *Jews and money: The myths and the reality*. New Haven, CT: Ticknor & Fields.

Krefetz, G. (1986). *Leverage: The key to multiplying money*. New York, NY: Wiley.

Kruse, M. (2017, January 18). He has this deep fear that he is not a legitimate president. Politico. Retrieved from http://www.politico.com/maga zine/story/2017/01/trump-biographers-presidency-legitimate-214655

Kuhn, T. S. (1962). *The structure of scientific revolution*. Chicago, IL: University of Chicago Press.

Kumar, K. (1993). Civil society: An inquiry into the usefulness of an historical term. *British Journal of Sociology, 44*(3), 375–395.

Kurtz, M. J. (2004). *Free market democracy and the Chile and Mexican countryside*. Cambridge, England: Cambridge University Press.

Kushner, M., Riggs, D. S., Foa, E. B, & Miller, S. M. (1993). Perceived controllability and the development of posttraumatic stress disorder (PTSD) in crime victims. *Behaviour Research and Therapy, 31*(1), 105–110.

Ladd, J. M. (2006). *Attitudes toward the news media and political competition in America* (Doctoral dissertation). Princeton, NJ: Princeton University.

Ladd, J. M. (2012). *Why Americans hate the media and why it matters*. Princeton, NJ: Princeton University Press.

Lantz, T. E. (1993). Urban-rural difference: The effect of place of residence on racial attitudes. Theses, Dissertations, Professional Papers. Paper 5395.

Lapierre, C. B., Schwegler, A. F., & LaBauve, B. J. (2007). Posttraumatic stress and depression symptoms in soldiers returning from combat operations in Iraq and Afghanistan. *Journal of Traumatic Stress, 20,* 933–943.

Lavender, P. (2016, October 7). These might be Donald Trump's most disgusting comments yet about women. The Huffington Post. Retrieved from http://www.huffingtonpost.com/entry/donald-trump -women-comments_us_57f8016de4b0e655eab4148d

Ledbetter, C. (2016, December 19). A&E is making a show about the Ku Klux Klan called "Generation KKK." The Huffington Post. Retrieved from http://www.huffingtonpost.com/entry/ae-is-making -a-show-about-the-ku-klux-klan-called-generation-kkk_us _58580460e4b08debb789f3f4

Lewandowsky, S., Ecker, U. K. H., Siefert, C., & Cook, J. (2012). Misinformation and its correction continued influence and successful debiasing. *Psychological Science in the Public Interest, 13*(3), 106–131.

Lewandowsky, S., Gignac, G. E., & Oberauer, K. (2013). The role of conspiracist ideation and worldviews in predicting rejection of science. *PloS One, 8*(10), e75637.

Lewandowsky, S., Gignac, G. E., & Vaughan S. (2012). The pivotal role of perceived scientific consensus in acceptance of science. *Nature Climate Change*. Advance online publication. doi:10.1038/nclimate1720

Lewandowsky, S., Oberauer, K., & Gignac, G. E. (2013). NASA faked the moon landing—therefore (climate) science is a hoax: An anatomy of the motivated rejection of science. *Psychological Science*, 24(5), 622–633.

Lewis, G., & Doyle, M. (2009). Risk formulation: What are we doing and why? *International Journal of Forensic Mental Health*, 8(4), 286–292.

Li, X., Liu, Y., Luo, S., Wu, B., Wu, X., & Han, S. (2015). Mortality salience enhances racial in-group bias in empathic neural responses to others' suffering. *NeuroImage*, 118, 376–385.

Lichtblau, E. (2016, September 16). Hate crimes against American Muslims most since post-9/11 era. *New York Times*. Retrieved from https://www.nytimes.com/2016/09/18/us/politics/hate-crimes-american-muslims-rise.html?_r=0

Liu, J. H., Sibley, C. G., & Huang L. L. (2013). History matters: Effects of culture-specific symbols on political attitudes and intergroup relations. *Political Psychology*, 35(1), 57–79.

Lukacs, J. (1994). *Budapest 1900: A historical portrait of a city and its culture*. New York, NY: Grove Press.

Madestam, A., Shoag, D., Veuger, S., & Yanagizawa-Drott, D. (2012). Do political protests matter? Evidence from the Tea Party movement. *American Enterprise Institute*. Retrieved from http://www.aei.org/wp-content/uploads/2012/12/-veuger-tea-party-working-paper_095614741243.pdf

Mak, T. (2016, April 19). China endorses Donald Trump. Retrieved from http://www.thedailybeast.com/china-endorses-donald-trump

Makow, H. (2017, January 24). Rothschilds used Dreyfus affair to divide & conquer. Retrieved from https://www.henrymakow.com/was_the_dreyfus_affair_another.html

Marsden, S. V. (2012). Successful terrorism: Framework and review. *Behavioral Sciences of Terrorism and Political Aggression*, 4(2), 134–150.

Maruyama, M. (1969). *Thought and behavior in modern Japanese politics*. (Vol. 291). London, England: Oxford University Press.

McCarthy, J. (2016,). Americans' support for gay marriage remains high, at 61%. Gallup. Retrieved from http://www.gallup.com/poll/191645/americans-support-gay-marriage-remains-high.aspx

McConahay, J. B., Hardee, B. B., & Batts, V. (1981). Has racism declined in America? It depends on who is asking and what is asked. *Journal of Conflict Resolution*, 25(4), 563–579.

McConahay, J. B., & Hough, J. C. (1976). Symbolic racism. *Journal of social issues*, 32(2), 23–45.

McLaughlin, E. (2016). A hate crime retrospect. In E. Dunbar, A. Blanco, & D. A. Crèvecoeur-MacPhail (Eds.), *The psychology of hate crimes as domestic terrorism*: *U.S. and global issues*. Santa Barbara, CA: Praeger.

McMath, R. C. (1993). *American populism: A social history 1877–1898*. New York, NY: Hill and Wang.

Memoli, M. A. (2017, January 13). Rep. John Lewis: Russia election "conspiracy" makes Donald Trump's presidency illegitimate. *Los Angeles Times*. Retrieved from http://www.latimes.com/nation/poli tics/trailguide/la-na-trailguide-updates-john-lewis-russia-election -1484341200-htmlstory.html

Menocal, R. M. (2002). *The ornament of the world: How Muslims, Jews, and Christians created a culture of tolerance in medieval Spain*. New York, NY: Back Bay Books.

Mercury News. (2013, November 19). Reader's letters: Recollections of JFK assassination. Retrieved from http://www.mercurynews.com /2013/11/19/readers-letters-recollections-of-jfk-assassination/

Milgram, S. (1963). Behavioral study of obedience. *Journal of Abnormal and Social Psychology*, *67*(4), 371–378.

Mookadam, F., & Arthur, H. M. (2004). Social support and its relationship to morbidity and mortality after acute myocardial infarction: Systematic overview. *Archives of Internal Medicine*, *164*(14), 1514–1518.

Moore, J. (2015, April 10). Are we losing the Civil War? Retrieved from http://www.ogd.com/blogs16/are-we-losing-the-civil-war-20150410? gallerydate=2017-02-02Z

Moreno, R., & Mayer, R. (1999). Cognitive principles of multimedia learning: The role of modality and contiguity. *Journal of Educational Psychology*, *91*(2), 358–368.

Morton, V. (2016, March 3). Trump says he'd force U.S. military to commit war crimes. *Washington Post*. Retrieved from http://www.wash ingtontimes.com/news/2016/mar/3/donald-trump-says-hed-force-us -military-commit-war/

Mouffe, C. (1993). *The return of the political*. New York, NY: Verso.

Musser, S. J. (1987). *The determination of positive and negative charismatic leadership*. Grantham, PA: Messiah College.

Newport, F., Moore, D. W., & Saad, L. (1999, December 6). The most important events of the century from the viewpoint of the people. Gallup. Retrieved from http://www.gallup.com/poll/3427/most-important -events-century-from-viewpoint-people.aspx

Niederland, W. G. (1961). *The problem of the survivor: Part I, some remarks on the psychiatric evaluation of emotional disorders in survivors of Nazi persecution*. N.p.: n.p.

Nolan, J. J., III, & Akiyama, Y. (1999). An analysis of factors that affect law enforcement participation in hate crime reporting. *Journal of Contemporary Criminal Justice, 15,* 11–127.

Orange County Human Relations Commission (OCHRC) (2016). 2015 hate crime report. Retrieved from: http://www.ochumanrelations.org /wp-content/uploads/2016/08/HateCrimeRpt_7-28-16.pdf

Orth, U., Trzesniewski, K. H., & Robins, R. W. (2010). Self-esteem development from young adulthood to old age: A cohort-sequential longitudinal study. *Journal of Personality and Social Psychology, 98*(4), 645.

Orwell, G. (1949). *Nineteen Eighty-Four.* London, England: Secker and Warburg.

Papenfuss, M. (2016, December 4). UNLV erupts after instructor threatens to turn in undocumented immigrant students. Huffington Post. Retrieved from http://www.huffingtonpost.com/entry/nevada -professor-immigrants_us_584237bde4b09e21702ed2f8

Papenfuss, M. (2016, December 11). Muslim NYPD officers ask for meeting with Trump over hate crime spike. Huffington Post. Retrieved from http://www.huffingtonpost.com/entry/ nypd-hate-crime-trump -meeting_us_584cf127e4b0bd9c3dfd2f86

Patchen, K. (1968). *Collected poems of Kenneth Patchen.* New York, NY: New Directions.

Paul, D., & Smith, J. L. (2008). Subtle sexism? Examining vote preferences when women run against men for the presidency. *Journal of Women, Politics & Policy, 29*(4), 451–476.

Paxton, T. *The compleat Tom Paxton* [CD]. (1971). Elektra.

Payne, S. G. (1996). *A history of fascism.* Madison: University of Wisconsin Press.

Pearce, K. E., Freelon, D., & Kendzior, S. (2014). The effect of the Internet on civic engagement under authoritarianism: The case of Azerbaijan. *First Monday, 19*(6).

Pearce, K. E., & Kendzior, S. (2012). Networked authoritarianism and social media in Azerbaijan. *Journal of Communication, 62*(2), 283–298.

Peppers, M. (2013, May 23). More than half of Americans have never traveled outside the country—and a third do not even own a passport. Retrieved from http://www.dailymail.co.uk/femail/article-2329298 /More-half-Americans-NEVER-traveled-outside-country--passport.html

Perr, J. (2016, August 28). Trump campaign hopes for reverse "Bradley Effect." Retrieved from http://www.dailykos.com/story /2016/8/28/1563638/-Trump-campaign-hopes-for-reverse-Bradley -Effect

Pettigrew, T. F., & Tropp, L. R. (2006). A meta-analytic test of intergroup contact theory. *Journal of Personality and Social Psychology, 90*(5), 751–783.

Pettigrew, T. F., Tropp, L. R., Wagner, U., & Christ, O. (2011). Recent advances in intergroup contact theory. *International Journal of Intercultural Relations, 35*(3), 271–280.

Pew Research Center. (2012, July 31). Two-thirds of Democrats now support gay marriage. Retrieved from http://www.pewforum.org/2012/07/31/2012-opinions-on-for-gay-marriage-unchanged-after-obamas-announcement/

Pew Research Center. (2015, May 13). From telephone to the web: The challenge of mode of interview effects in public opinion polls. Retrieved from http://www.pewresearch.org/2015/05/13/from-telephone-to-the-web-the-challenge-of-mode-of-interview-effects-in-public-opinion-polls

Philosophy 103: Introduction to logic argumentum ad baculum. (n.d.). Retrieved from http://philosophy.lander.edu/logic/force.html

Pierce, C. (1970). Offensive mechanisms. In F. Barbour (Ed.), *The black seventies* (pp. 265–282). Boston, MA: Porter Sargent.

Pierce, C. (1995). Stress analogs of racism and sexism: Terrorism, torture, and disaster. *Mental Health, Racism, and Sexism*, 277–293.

PolitiFact (n.d.). Donald Trump's file. Retrieved from: http://www.politifact.com/

Pound, E. (1910). *The Spirit of romance*. London, England: Dent.

Pratto, F., Sidanius, J., Stallworth, L. M., & Malle, B. F. (1994). Social dominance orientation: A personality variable predicting social and political attitudes. *Journal of Personality and Social Psychology, 67*(4), 741.

Prilleltensky, I., & Gonick, L. (1996). Polities change, oppression remains: On the psychology and politics of oppression. *Political Psychology, 17*(1), 127–148.

Pulliam, Bailey S. (2016, November 9). White evangelicals voted overwhelmingly for Donald Trump, exit polls show. *Washington Post.* Retrieved from https://www.washingtonpost.com/news/acts-of-faith/wp/2016/11/09/

Pyszczynski, T., Abdollahi, A., Solomon, S., Greenberg, J., Cohen, F., & Weise, D. (2006). Mortality salience, martyrdom, and military might: The great Satan versus the axis of evil. *Personality and Social Psychology Bulletin, 32*(4), 525–537.

Pyszczynski, T., Greenberg, J., & Solomon, S. (2003). *In the wake of 9/11: The psychology of terror*. Washington, DC: American Psychological Association.

Quattrone, G. A., & Tversky, A. (1988). Contrasting rational and psychological analyses of political choice. *The American Political Science Review, 82,* 719–736.

Raven, B. H. (1965). Power and leadership. *Current Studies in Social Psychology,* 371–382.

Raven, B. H. (1992). A power/interaction model of interpersonal influence: French and Raven thirty years later. *Journal of Social Behavior & Personality, 7*(2), 217.

Raven, B. H. (1999). Kurt Lewin address: Influence, power, religion, and the mechanisms of social control. *Journal of Social Issues, 55,* 161–186.

Raven, B. H., Schwarzwald, J., & Koslowsky, M. (1998). Conceptualizing and measuring a power/interaction model of interpersonal influence. *Journal of Applied Social Psychology, 28,* 307–332.

Reed, J. (2006). *Ten days that shook the world.* London, England: The Folio Society.

Reeves, S. B., & Nagoshi, C. T. (1993). Effects of alcohol administration on the disinhibition of racial prejudice. *Alcoholism: Clinical and Experimental Research, 17*(5), 1066–1071.

Restuccia, A. (2016, November 27). Trump's baseless assertions of voter fraud called "stunning." Politico. Retrieved from http://www.politico.com/story/2016/11/trump-illegal-voting-clinton-231860

Richeson, J. A., & Ambady, N. (2001). Who's in charge? Effects of situational roles on automatic gender bias. *Sex Roles, 44*(9), 493–512.

Richter, W. (2016, November 22). The Trump effect on Americans' perception of the economy. Retrieved from http://wolfstreet.com/2016/11/22/the-trump-effect-on-americans-perception-of-the-economy/

Rickert, E. J. (1998). Authoritarianism and economic threat: Implications for political behavior. *Political Psychology, 19,* 707–720.

Romero, A. (n.d.). Topic: Advertising industry in the U.S. Retrieved from https://www.statista.com/topics/979/advertising-in-the-us/

Rothman, L. (2015, April 4). 9 moving reactions to Martin Luther King Jr.'s 1968 assassination. Retrieved from http://time.com/3758959/mlk-assassination-letters/

Rotter, J. B., & Mulry, R. C. (1965). Internal versus external control of reinforcement and decision time. *Journal of Personality and Social Psychology, 2*(4), 598.

Rudman, L. A., & Fairchild, K. (2004). Reactions to counterstereotypic behavior: The role of backlash in cultural stereotype maintenance. *Journal of Personality and Social Psychology, 87*(2), 157–176.

Rudman L. A., & Mescher, K. (2012). Of animals and objects: Men's implicit dehumanization of women and likelihood of sexual aggression. *Personality and Social Psychology Bulletin, 38*(6), 734–746.

Ruiz-Grossman, S. (2017, February 23). Millennials are the foot soldiers of the resistance. Huffington Post. Retrieved from http://www.huffington post.com/entry/trump-protest-poll_us_58addc16e4b0d0a6ef47517e

Rupar, A. (2016, October 13). Trump suggests women speaking out are too ugly for him to sexually assault. Retrieved from https://thinkpro gress.org/trump-says-sexual-assault-accusers-are-too-ugly-for-him -d3be41c0a565#.tcl5bjwry

Sarah, R., & Diat, N. (2017). *The power of silence: Against the dictatorship of noise*. San Francisco, CA: Ignatius Press.

Sasaki, F. (2012). *Nationalism, political realism and democracy in Japan: The thought of Masao Maruyama*. London, England: Routledge.

Scaruffi, P. (1999). The worst genocides of the 20th and 21st centuries. Retrieved from http://www.scaruffi.com/politics/dictat.html

Schamis, H. E. (2006). Populism, socialism, and democratic institutions. *Journal of democracy*, *17*(4), 20–34.

Schnurr, P. P., Friedman, M. J., Engel, C. C., Foa, E. B., Shea, M. T., Chow, B. K., … Bernardy, N. (2007). Cognitive behavioral therapy for posttraumatic stress disorder in women: A randomized controlled trial. *Journal of the American Medical Association 297*(8), 820–830.

Schwartz, S. (2015). Cultural values influence and constrain economic and social change. In L. Harrison & Y. Yasin (Eds.), *Culture matters: In Russia and everywhere* (pp. 287–302). Lanham, MD: Lexington Books.

Seligman, A. B. (1998). Between public and private. *Society*, *35*(3), 28–36.

Shafer, J. (2016, August 13). Donald Trump talks like a third-grader. Politico. Retrieved from http://www.politico.com/magazine/story/2015/08 /donald-trump-talks-like-a-third-grader-121340

Shirer, W. L. (1960). *The rise and fall of the Third Reich*. New York, NY: Simon and Schuster.

Sibley, C., & Duckitt, J. (2008). Personality and prejudice: A meta-analysis and theoretical review. *Personality and Social Psychology Review, 12*, 248–279.

Sidanius, J., Liu, J., Shaw, J. & Pratto, F. (1994) Social dominance orientation, hierarchy-attenuators and hierarchy-enhancers: Social dominance theory and the criminal justice system. *Journal of Applied Social Psychology, 24*, 338–366.

Sidanius, J., & Pratto, F. (1993). The dynamics of social dominance and the inevitability of oppression. In P. Sniderman & P. Tetlock (Eds.), *Prejudice, politics, and race in America today* (pp. 173–211). Stanford, CA: Stanford University Press.

Sidanius, J., & Pratto, F. (1999). *Social dominance: An intergroup theory of social hierarchy and oppression.* Cambridge, UK: Cambridge University Press.

Silman, A. (2016, November 23). For the alt-right, dapper suits are a propaganda tool. *New York Magazine.* Retrieved from http://nymag.com/thecut/2016/11/how-the-alt-right-uses-style-as-a-propaganda-tool.html

Sinclair, H. (2016, April 30). Donald Trump finds an unlikely supporter in Vladimir Putin. Retrieved from http://www.independent.co.uk/news/world/americas/donald-trump-finds-unlikely-support-from-vladimir-putin-a7008601.html

Sluzki, C. E. (1993): Toward a general model of family and political victimization. *Psychiatry, 56,* 178–187.

Sluzki, C. E. (2005). Deception and fear in politically oppressive contexts: Its trickle-down effect on families. *Review of Policy Research, 22,* 5.

Smith, J. L., Paul, D., & Paul, R. (2007). No place for a woman: Evidence for gender bias in evaluations of presidential candidates. *Basic and Applied Social Psychology, 29*(3), 225–233.

Snyder, T. D. (2005). *Sketches from a secret war: A Polish artist's mission to liberate Soviet Ukraine.* New Haven, CT: Yale University Press, .

Snyder, T. D. (2015). *Black Earth: The Holocaust as history and warning.* New York, NY: Tim Duggan Books.

Snyder, T. (2016, November 21). 20 lessons from the 20th century on how to survive in Trump's America. Retrieved from http://inthesetimes.com/article/19658/20-lessons-from-the-20th-century-on-how-to-survive-in-trumps-america

Snyder, T.D. (2017). *On tyranny.* New York, NY: Tim Duggan Books.

Sottek, T. C. (2016, July 3). Who at Trump's campaign copied, modified, and tweeted neo-Nazi propaganda? The Verge. Retrieved from http://www.theverge.com/2016/7/3/12090338/trump-tweet-incompetent

Southern Poverty Law Center (SPLC) (2016, November 29). Ten days after: Harassment and intimidation in the aftermath of the election. Retrieved from https://www.splcenter.org/20161129/ten-days-after-harassment-and-intimidation-aftermath-election

Southern Poverty Law Center (SPLC). (2016, December 16). Update: 1,094 bias-related incidents in the month following the election. Retrieved from https://www.splcenter.org/hatewatch/2016/12/16/update-1094-bias-related-incidents-month-following-election

Southern Poverty Law Center (SPLC). (2017, February 15). Hate groups increase for second consecutive year as Trump electrifies radical right.

Retrieved from https://www.splcenter.org/news/2017/02/15/hate-groups
-increase-second-consecutive-year-trump-electrifies-radical-right

Staff, T. H. (2016, June 13). Orlando shooter's imam is pro-Trump. Retrieved from http://thehill.com/blogs/blog-briefing-room/news/283218 -orlando-shooters-imam-is-pro-trump

Statistic Brain. (2016, August 22). Illiteracy statistics. Retrieved from http:// www.statisticbrain.com/number-of-american-adults-who-cant-read

Stephan, W. G., Stephan, C. W., & Gudykunst, W. B. (1999). Anxiety in intergroup relations: A comparison of anxiety/uncertainty management theory and integrated threat theory. *International Journal of Intercultural Relations, 23*(4), 613–628.

Sterling, J., Jost, J. T., & Shrout, P. E. (2016). Mortality salience, system justification, and candidate evaluations in the 2012 US presidential election. *PloS One, 11*(3), e0150556.

Strickland, B. R. (1989). Internal external control expectancies: From contingency to creativity. *American Psychologist, 44*(1), 1.

Strochlic, N. (2015, June 30). The dumbest stuff Donald Trump has ever said. Retrieved from http://www.thedailybeast.com/articles/2015 /06/30/

Sue, D. W. (2010). *Microaggressions in everyday life: Race, gender, and sexual orientation.* Hoboken, NJ: John Wiley& Sons.

Sullaway, M. (2004). Psychological perspectives on hate crime laws. *Psychology, Public Policy, and Law, 10*(3), 250.

Sullaway, M. (2016). Hate Crime, Violent Extremism, Domestic Terrorism—Distinctions without Difference?. In E. Dunbar, A. Blanco, & D. A. Crèvecoeur-MacPhail (Eds.), *The psychology of hate crimes as domestic terrorism: U.S. and global issues.* Santa Barbara, CA: Praeger.

Tajfel, H. (1981). *Human groups and social categories: Studies in social psychology.* Cambridge, England: Cambridge University Press.

Tajfel, H., Billig, M. G., Bundy, R. P., & Flament, C. (1971). Social categorization and intergroup behaviour. *European Journal of Social Psychology, 1*(2), 149–178.

Tangney, J. P., & Dearing, R. L. (2003). *Shame and guilt.* New York, NY: Guilford Press.

Tetlock, P. E. (1979). Identifying victims of groupthink from public statements of decision makers. *Journal of Personality and Social Psychology, 37*, 1314–1324.

Tharoor, I. (2015, July 14). Donald Trump tweets image of Nazi soldiers inside the U.S. flag, then deletes tweet. *Washington Post.* Retrieved from https://www.washingtonpost.com/news/worldviews/wp/2015/07/14

/donald-trump-tweets-image-of-nazi-soldiers-inside-the-u-s-flag-then
-deletes-tweet/?utm_term=.52e55481450b

Tilly, C. (2003). *The politics of collective violence*. Cambridge, England: Cambridge University Press.

Tilly, C. (2005). *Identities, boundaries, and social ties*. London, England: Paradigm Publishers.

Tilly, C., Tilly, L., & Tilly, R. (1975). *The rebellious century, 1830–1930*. Cambridge, MA: Harvard University Press.

The Triumph of Hitler. (2001). Retrieved from http://www.historyplace .com/worldwar2/triumph/tr-will.htm

Trump: Bush is "poor, pathetic, low-energy guy." (2016, January 21). *Washington Post*. Retrieved from https://www.washingtonpost.com /video/politics/trump-bush-is-poor-pathetic-low-energy-guy/2016 /01/21/efd1347c-c090-11e5-98c8-7fab78677d51_video.html

Trump: Cruz is "sick," "something wrong with this guy." (2016, February 23). Retrieved from https://www.bloomberg.com/politics /videos/2016-02-23/donald-trump-cruz-is-sick-something-wrong -with-this-guy

Turner, A. (2017, January 18). New survey of 50,000+ young people reveals troubling post-election spike in bullying & harassment. Retrieved from http://www.hrc.org/blog/new-survey-of-50000-young -people-reveals-troubling-post-election-spike-in-b

Tuskegee University. About the USPHS Syphilis Study. http://tuskegee bioethics.org/about-the-usphs-syphilis-study/

Tversky, A., & Kahneman, D. (1991). Loss aversion in riskless choice: A reference-dependent model. *Quarterly Journal of Economics, 106*(4), 1039–1061.

Twain, M. (1859). *The innocents abroad*. New York, NY: Hippocrene Books.

U.S. Census Bureau. (2004). *Income, poverty, and health insurance coverage in the United States: 2004 (PDF)*. Census.gov. Retrieved from http://www.census.gov/prod/2005pubs/p60-229.pdf

U.S. Census Bureau. (2005). *Current population reports, P60-229, income, poverty, and health insurance coverage in the United States: 2004*. Washington, DC: U.S. Government Printing Office.

U.S. Census Bureau. (2015). *Current population reports, P60-252, income and poverty in the United States: 2014*. Washington, DC: U.S. Government Printing Office.

Vaillant, G. E. (1977). *Adaptation to life*. Cambridge, MA: Harvard University Press.

Valentino, N. A., Brader, T., Groenendyk, W., & Hutchings, V. L. (2011). Election night's alright for fighting: The role of emotions in political participation. *Journal of Politics, 73*(1), 156–170.

Van Knippenberg, A., Dijksterhuis, A., & Vermeulen, D. (1999). Judgement and memory of a criminal act: The effects of stereotypes and cognitive load. *European Journal of Social Psychology, 29*(2–3), 191–201.

Van Zomeren, M., Postmes, T., & Spears, R. (2008). Toward an integrative social identity model of collective action: A quantitative research synthesis of three socio-psychological perspectives. *Psychological Bulletin, 134*, 504–535.

Walton, D. (2000). *Scare tactics: Arguments that appeal to fear and threats.* New York, NY: Springer Science and Business Media.

Walzer, M. (1997). *On toleration.* New Haven, CT: Yale University Press.

Wang, A. (2016, November 16). "Post-truth" named 2016 word of the year by Oxford dictionaries. *Washington Post.* Retrieved from https://www.washingtonpost.com/news/the-fix/wp/2016/11/16/post-truth-named-2016-word-of-the-year-by-oxford-dictionaries/?utm_term=.fcb7ff7656a5

Wang, S. (2008, September 27). The disappearing Bradley effect. Retrieved from http://election.princeton.edu/2008/09/27/the-disappearing-bradley-effect

Wayne, C., Valentino, N., & Oceno, M. (2016, October 23). How sexism drives support for Donald Trump. *Washington Post.* Retrieved from https://www.washingtonpost.com/news/monkey-cage/wp/2016/10/23/how-sexism-drives-support-for-donald-trump/?utm_%20term=.dc7f2fd98365&utm_term=.394b05ad0cbc

Weber, M. (1946). The sociology of charismatic authority. In H. H. Gerth & C. W. Mills (Eds.), *Max Weber: 714 essays in sociology.* New York, NY: Oxford University Press.

Widdig, B. (2001). *Culture and inflation in Weimar Germany* (Vol. 26). Berkeley and Los Angeles: University of California Press.

Winning in the States. (2016). Retrieved from http://www.freedomtomarry.org/pages/winning-in-the-states

Wittenstein, G. (1997). Memories of the White Rose. Retrieved from http://www.historyplace.com/pointsofview/white-rose1.htm

Wodtke, G. T. (2016). Are smart people less racist? Verbal ability, anti-black prejudice, and the principle-policy paradox. *Social Problems, 63*(1), 21–45.

Wood, R. L. (2002). *Faith in action: Religion, race, and democratic organizing in America.* Chicago, IL: University of Chicago Press.

The world's smartest speakers revealed. (n.d.). Retrieved from https://quote.com/blog/smartest-speeches-analyzing-the-grade-level-of-leaders-public-comments-the-dumbest-stuff-donald-trump-has-ever-said.html.

Yanay, N. (2012). *The ideology of hatred: The psychic power of discourse.* New York, NY: Fordham University Press.

Zablotsky, Peter A. (2012). Considering the libel trial of Émile Zola in light of contemporary defamation doctrine. *Touro Law Review, 29,* 1.

Zimmerman, N. (2015, September 9). Trump mocks Fiorina's physical appearance: "Look at that face!" Retrieved from http://www.thehill.com/blogs/blog-briefing-room/253178-trump-insults-fiorinas-physical-appearance-look-at-that-face

Zola, E. (1898). J'accuse!. *L'Aurore,* 1.

Index

About the Author

EDWARD DUNBAR, PHD, is a psychologist based in metropolitan Los Angeles. He is a clinical professor in the Department of Psychology at UCLA. He has been on staff at the UCLA Center for Study and Resolution of Interracial and Interethnic Conflict and the National Research Center on Asian-American Mental Health.

His mental health consultation activities have been in the areas of workplace harassment, crime victimization, psychological trauma, and violence risk assessment. He has also served as an assessment psychologist for fitness for duty of environmental disaster and NRC personnel, law enforcement agents, and government security personnel. Dunbar has consulted with the Los Angeles Police Department, the Los Angeles Unified School District, and the Los Angeles Gay and Lesbian Center in the areas of hate crime offender evaluation and violence prevention in the schools. Dunbar has developed and implemented training programs for intervention with victims of bias crimes and hate incidents.

Dunbar received his doctorate in counseling psychology from Columbia University. He holds professional certificates from Georgetown University in cross-cultural training and Harvard University in adult education. He completed his undergraduate study at Chaminade University of Honolulu, where he graduated with honors in education and behavioral sciences. He is the recipient of the 2001 American Psychological Association Distinguished Professional Contribution to Public Service Award and the California State Psychological Association Distinguished Humanitarian Contribution Award.

His publications have been in the areas of the clinical evaluation of racism, victimology, and intergroup relations. He has been involved in the analysis of hate crime activity with the Los Angeles Police Department and conducted cross-cultural studies of attitudes concerning human rights laws.

www.ingramcontent.com/pod-product-compliance
Lightning Source LLC
Chambersburg PA
CBHW050415280326
41932CB00013BA/1871